JERUSALEM'S TRAITOR

*"I will bring evil from the north
and a great destruction"*

JEREMIAH, IV, 6

Jerusalem's Traitor

Josephus, Masada,

AND THE

Fall of Judea

DESMOND SEWARD

DA CAPO PRESS
A MEMBER OF THE PERSEUS BOOKS GROUP

Designed by Brent Wilcox
Set in 11.25 point Garamond by The Perseus Books Group

Library of Congress Cataloging-in-Publication Data
Seward, Desmond, 1935–
   Jerusalem's traitor : Josephus, Masada, and the fall of Judea / Desmond
Seward.
      p.   cm.
   Includes bibliographical references and index.
   ISBN 978-0-306-81807-3 (alk. paper)
   1. Josephus, Flavius.   2. Jews—History—168 B.C.–135 A.D.   3. Jews—
History—Rebellion, 66–73   4. Rome—History, Military—30 B.C.–476 A.D.
5. Palestine—History, Military.   I. Title.
   DS115.9.J6S42 2009
   933'.05—dc22

                                                                 2009005716

Published by Da Capo Press
A Member of the Perseus Books Group
www.dacapopress.com

Da Capo Press books are available at special discounts for bulk purchases in
the U.S. by corporations, institutions, and other organizations. For more
information, please contact the Special Markets Department at the Perseus
Books Group, 2300 Chestnut Street, Suite 200, Philadelphia, PA 19103, or
call (800) 810-4145, ext. 5000, or e-mail special.markets@perseusbooks.com.

10 9 8 7 6 5 4 3 2 1

For James and Claire Heagerty

CONTENTS

LIST OF MAPS

ACKNOWLEDGMENTS

My interest in Josephus is a legacy from my father, who served in Palestine during the First World War. He always believed that he had been the first man to fly over Masada, having lost his way while returning from an attempt to intercept two German aircraft in 1916. During his time in the Sinai Desert, William Whiston's translation of *The Jewish War* became one of his favorite books, and he developed a respect for the fighting qualities of the Jews in both ancient and modern times, which he shared with me. He also instilled an admiration for Josephus's history of the Jewish struggle against Rome, together with a keen interest in its author's personality. My interest became fascination after reading the novels of Lion Feuchtwanger, based on Josephus's life.

As I hope will become clear, this book is intended to be an introduction to Josephus for general readers, not for academics. However, I must record a great debt to the scholars whose work made it possible for me to understand him and whose names are listed in the bibliography.

In addition, I owe a special debt to Edgar Feuchtwanger, Lion's nephew, for much encouragement and for drawing my attention to Andra Bunzel's recent study of his uncle's novels. I would particularly like to thank those who found the time to read the manuscript or part of it or who gave me helpful criticism or encouragement: André Ciechanowiecki, Annabel Hervey-Bathurst, Stella Lesser (who read the proofs), Margot Lovell, Jaqueline Mitchell, Aidan Nichols, Charles Sebag-Montefiore, John Sterling (who explained to me the meaning of the word *Khittim*), and Damian Thompson. I am also indebted to Sarah Ayed and to David Price-Hughes of AKG, who helped me to find the illustrations.

As so often before, I am grateful to the staffs of the British Library, the Cambridge University Library, and the London Library for all their patient assistance.

PREFACE

"Masada Shall Not Fall Again"

On a tall hill flanked by deep ravines, the fortress of Masada, commanding a promontory near the western shore of the Dead Sea, was one of the strongest in all Judea. It had been a refuge of King Herod, who had added a palace, a synagogue, and an arsenal. Cisterns in the rock caught an ample supply of rain water. After Jerusalem fell to the Romans in 70 CE, Masada held out for three years, defended by several hundred Jewish revolutionaries known as Zealots under the command of Eleazar ben Yair, who was convinced that it could never be captured. However, not only did the Roman legionaries come and besiege Masada, but within a few months they built a ramp 400 feet high, from which they were finally able to breach the previously impenetrable walls with their siege engines.

On the night before the Romans' final assault, Eleazar, in an impassioned speech, ordered his troops to kill themselves and their families. When the enemy broke in the next morning, they found nearly a thousand bodies lying in neat rows. Only two women and some children, who had hidden in a cistern, were left alive to explain what had happened. Instead of feeling jubilant, the legionaries were awestricken.

One of the mottoes of the modern Israeli army is "Masada shall not fall again!" and recruits spend their last night of training trekking through the desert to see dawn break over the great fortress.

⌀

Our sole source for the story is Flavius Josephus—Yossef ben Mattityahu ha-Kohen, to give him his true name—who was not present at the siege and who despised Zealots as lowborn fanatics. Even so, he was deeply moved by what the legionaries told him of Masada. As a Jewish general, and then as a Roman prisoner, he had already witnessed the campaign of 66–70 CE, which turned out to be the worst disaster suffered by his people between the Babylonian captivity in the sixth century BCE and the Nazi Holocaust in the twentieth century CE. In *The Jewish War* and in his *Life*, written at Rome, he gives us an eyewitness account of the First Jewish-Roman War. The story of Masada restored Josephus's pride in his nation, inspiring him to write two more books—one a historical study of Jewish religion and civilization, the other a defense of Judaism.

Often the narrative of *The Jewish War* reads like an adventure story, and it has the immediacy of a first-person historical novel (such as Robert Graves's *I, Claudius*). Besides being related by a member of the old aristocracy who somehow escaped the twofold menace of foreign invasion and revolution, it paints an astonishingly vivid, if not always entirely frank, self-portrait of the author. It is easy to understand why over the centuries his *Jewish War* has been the most widely read book by an ancient Jewish author other than those of the Bible. It is the only surviving contemporary history of Palestine in the days of Herod, the Dead Sea Scrolls, and Jesus of Nazareth.

"The war between the Romans and the Jews was the greatest of our time, in its own way greater than any war in history," he claims. "For the sake of everybody governed by Rome I decided to translate into Greek a book that I had written about it in my native tongue for the benefit of distant barbarians." He adds proudly, "I am a Hebrew myself, a priest from Jerusalem."

The Jewish War recreates the war as he experienced it, seen through his eyes, the Jews' fight against an overwhelmingly superior enemy—a war that ended in genocide. It describes the destruction of a nation driven into rebellion by Roman brutality. The climax of the Jews' struggle against the Roman legions was not Masada, however magnificent, but the siege of Jerusalem, during which the defenders' rival factions slaughtered each other between Roman assaults. When the end came, Jerusalem lay in smoking ruins—a million people had died, the survivors being crucified or sent to the arena or to the slave market. Yet Josephus believed that the war might have been avoided, while he also insisted that it was possible to be both Jewish and Roman. Coupled with nostalgia for a beloved Jerusalem that had vanished forever, this gives his account great poignancy.

No other ancient writer reveals so much about himself, and we know more about him as a human being than about any Jew of his time, however much he boasts or tries to portray himself in a favorable light. By any standards, he seems to have had a difficult personality, yet critics too easily forget the pride he took in his nation—he could not bear his readers to think that Jews could ever be cowards. *The Jewish War*, his most famous book, is supplemented by the short *Vita*, his so-called autobiography, which is largely a piece of special pleading in defense of his behavior when he was military governor of Galilee. There is also some information about both himself and the war in his lengthy *Antiquities of the Jews*, while a few further details are given in the *Contra Apionem*, his passionate defense of Jewish religion and culture. All of them provide glimpses into his mind.

Since Josephus's description of the siege is the only one to survive, apart from a few pages in Tacitus and Dio Cassius, it is impossible to check what he says. Occasionally, however, we can identify distortions that are obviously due to prejudice. This applies particularly to his enemies, the Zealots, whom he constantly denigrates and slanders, although sometimes he cannot deny their bravery. We know about them solely from his hostile account—which is rather as if we knew about the Russian revolutionaries of 1917 only from the memoirs of some White Russian general. He plays down the fact that a substantial number came from his own class. At the end of *The Jewish War*, however, when pride in his faith and his nation overcomes his dislike of the Zealots, he gives us a fairer picture in describing their refusal to surrender at Masada and admits that they included more than a few heroes.

Similarly, his figures for casualties are all too often unconvincing and usually must be questioned. Almost invariably, he seems to exaggerate when stating the number of those who were killed or wounded, died of starvation, or were sent to the slave market. His motive appears to have been a desire to impress his readers.

Those who have written about Josephus over the centuries have had vastly differing perceptions of him. Some imply that he was a quisling, in the twentieth-century sense of the term, although such a view does not stand up to examination. Others suggest that in his own way he was very much a patriot. The problem is that while one may question his account, there is nothing to put in its place. All we can say is that when he is talking about himself or about the Zealots, he is not always to be trusted, but that when writing about the war, he usually, if not invariably, seems to be telling the truth.

To produce as rounded a portrait as possible, I have used not only what he says about himself in *The Jewish War* and in the *Vita* but also what he reveals, sometimes inadvertently, in his other books. I have tried to set him in context during the second half of his life, as scholar, writer, and Roman citizen. Yet what tells us most about him is his behavior during the war with Rome, which needs careful investigation and constant questioning.

In recent years, the texts of Josephus's books, especially those of *The Jewish War* and of his so-called autobiography, have been examined and re-examined by distinguished scholars, who have produced subtle new interpretations of what he must have really meant, in volumes intended for a purely academic readership. What has been lacking is a straightforward narrative account of the man for ordinary readers who would like to learn more about him. Here is a modest and, I hope, readable attempt to fill the gap and to introduce to a wider public a remarkable figure, together with the war that he made so much his own.

THE HOLY LAND IN THE TIME OF JOSEPHUS

GALILEE

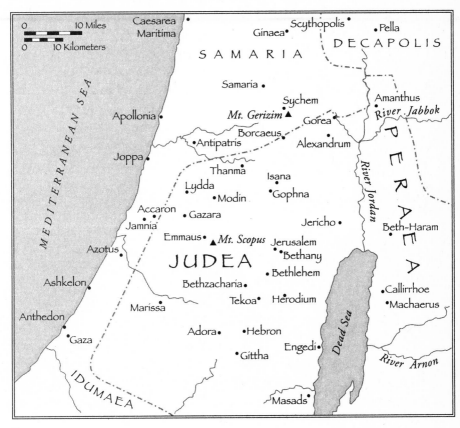

JUDEA

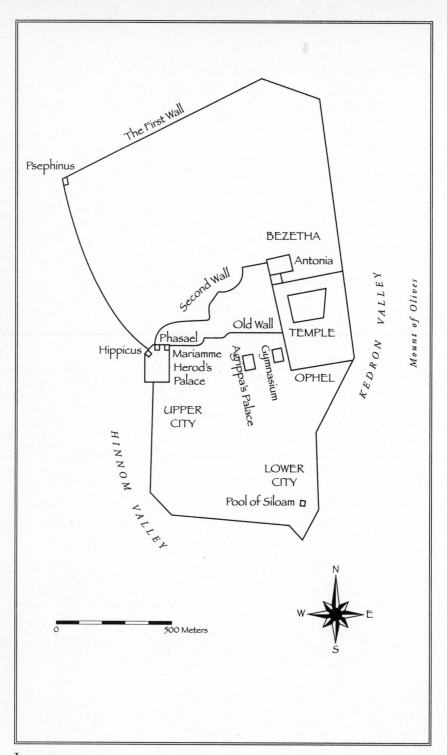

The First Wall

Psephinus

BEZETHA

Antonia

Second Wall

Old Wall

TEMPLE

Phasael

Hippicus

Mariamme

Herod's
Palace

Agrippa's Palace

Gymnasium

OPHEL

UPPER
CITY

KEDRON VALLEY

Mount of Olives

LOWER
CITY

Pool of Siloam

HINNOM VALLEY

0   500 Meters

N
W   E
S

JERUSALEM

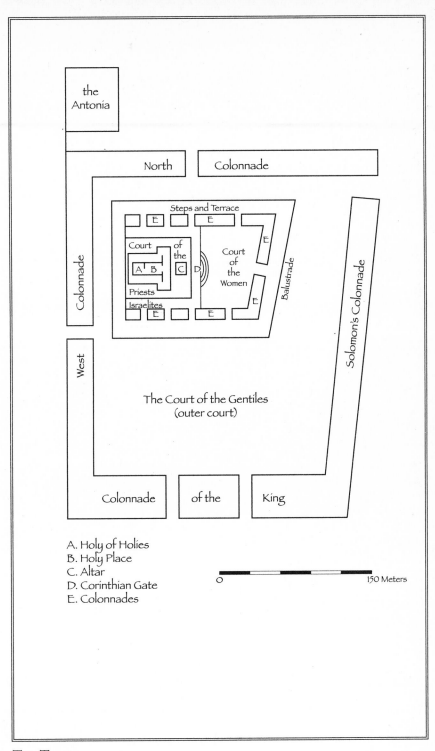

the
Antonia

North Colonnade

Colonnade

Steps and Terrace

E E

Court of the Court of the Women

A B C D

Priests

Israelites

E E

Balustrade

Solomon's Colonnade

West

The Court of the Gentiles
(outer court)

Colonnade of the King

A. Holy of Holies
B. Holy Place
C. Altar
D. Corinthian Gate
E. Colonnades

0   150 Meters

THE TEMPLE

Introduction

The Land Where Josephus Was Born

"Eastward their land is hemmed in by Arabia which forms the frontier, Egypt is on their southern border, Phoenicia and the sea lie to the west, while on the Syrian border to the north is a long range of mountains."

TACITUS, THE HISTORIES, V

WHAT TACITUS FORGETS to mention to his readers is that a Roman visitor would have been astonished at finding it was such a small country.[1] In modern terms, it was no bigger than Wales and about an eighth the size of Illinois, but its importance was always out of all proportion to its size. During Josephus's time it had long ceased to be Israel while it was not yet Palestine. However, even if many of the inhabitants were "Greeks"—Greek-speaking Syrians—the Romans still thought of it as the land of the Jews. Although the name was also that of one of its provinces, they called it "Judea."

The astonishingly varied landscape of Judea "from Dan to Beersheba"— the traditional boundaries—was an awe-inspiring mixture of fertile plains and arid desert, of stony hills and green forest. The population was equally varied. The coast was largely "Greek," while the south was Idumean (Arab). The actual province of Judea was wholly Jewish, but neighboring Samaria was peopled by a mixed race who had adopted a heretical form of Judaism. The inhabitants of Galilee were also of indeterminate origin, although they professed genuine Judaism.

What complicated matters was the presence of so many "Greeks" in the inland cities as well as in those on the coast, especially in Galilee, where Tiberias and even Sepphoris, the capital, were almost entirely Greek-speaking. In addition, there was the "Decapolis," the league of the ten Greek cities, most of which lay on the far side of the Jordan River, although Scythopolis was on the west, between Galilee and Samaria.

The provinces that Josephus came to know best were Galilee and Judea. "There are two Galilees, called upper and lower, bounded by Phoenicia and Syria," he writes. "On the west is the border of Ptolemais and Mount Carmel, once belonging to the Galileans but now belonging to Tyre, and nearby is Gaba, 'the horsemen's city,' which takes its name from being founded as a colony of cavalrymen paid off [with farms] by King Herod. On the south are Samaria and Scythopolis, reaching as far as the river Jordan. On the east are Hippene, Gadaris, Gaulonitis and the frontiers of Agrippa's realm. On the north is Tyre and the Tyrians' country. Lengthwise, lower Galilee extends from Tiberias to Zabulon (which adjoins Ptolemais on the coast), in breadth from the village of Xaloth in the Great Plain to Bersabe. Upper Galilee begins here, stretching across to the village of Baca on the Tyrian frontier—lengthwise, it runs from Melloth to Thella, a village near the Jordan."

"Despite their small size and the threat from powerful nations on their borders, the two Galilees have always survived any attempt at conquest by neighbors, since Galileans are warriors from the cradle and there are plenty of them, while they have never lacked courage or gallant leaders. Everywhere the soil is rich, providing excellent pasture and good for planting all kinds of trees, so that even the laziest peasants are keen to work hard. As a result, the land is very carefully farmed by the inhabitants—not a single bit has been left uncultivated. There are many towns here and because of the region's fertility its countless villages contain such large populations that the smallest holds at least 15,000 inhabitants."[2]

Josephus is wrong about the number of people in the villages, however, because the entire population of the province—seventy miles from north to south and less than forty across—has been reliably estimated at no more than 300,000. He does not mention that there was not a single truly large city, nor does he note the contrast between mountainous upper Galilee and the gentler landscape of lower Galilee, with its hills and its lake. But he is right about the province's fertility and the energy of its peasantry. Good farmers and fishermen, they were, by all accounts, a tough, hard-working race. He might have added, too, that the landscape of the province was often breathtakingly beautiful, the loveliest in all Judea, especially in spring when it was carpeted with flowers, full of orchards and vineyards that produced excellent fruit and wine.

He does not refer to the unfortunate reputation of the Galileans, whom other Jews looked down on. In addition to big concentrations of Syrians and Arabs, the majority of those in the province who called themselves Jews were largely of foreign immigrant stock, very mixed in origin, easily identifiable by their uncouth accent, and belonging to a despised group, the 'am ha-arez—"people of the land." Most were the lowest type of laborer, men whose ignorance resulted in a lax observance of the religious law and ritual uncleanliness. Some of them even kept large herds of pigs, like that encountered at Gadara by Jesus of Nazarus. Pharisees, Sadducees, and Essenes saw the 'am ha-arez as brutish semi-pagans; even the gentle Rabban Hillel, the leading Jewish teacher in the years before Josephus was born, regarded them as criminals who were little better than animals. The class war was at its strongest here, the inhabitants well aware of their superiors' contempt, which they bitterly resented. Galilee was always a hotbed of social and political unrest.[3]

Although Perea—ancient Gilead—to the east of Galilee on the other side of the Jordan, was larger, much of it was mountainous, a stony, desert land where no crops would grow, although there were plenty of sheep. A few areas were extremely fertile, however, and good for growing olives, vines, or palms. In addition, there were numerous springs flowing down from the hills that never failed, not even in the dog days. "The land of Moab is its southern frontier, Arabia, Silbonitis, Philadelphia and Gerasa its eastern."[4]

"In character Samaria is just like Judea," Josephus explains. "Both regions have hills and plains, with fine soil that richly repays farming. There are large numbers of trees, wild and cultivated, which bear an abundance of fruit. Although rivers are lacking, the rainfall is sufficient while what streams they have provide sweet water. Good grass ensures that the cows yield better milk than anywhere else. The best proof of the two regions' fertility is their teeming population."

For Jews, a "good Samaritan" was an impossibility. Descended from foreign settlers who had come during the Babylonian captivity, the Samaritans had evolved a heretical form of Judaism, accepting only the Pentateuch (the first five books of the Bible) and building a rival temple on Mount Gerizim. They were disliked even more than the Galileans. "When the Jews are in trouble, they deny any connection with them, in which they are quite right," says Josephus.[5] "But if they see the Jews prospering, then they immediately say that they are Jews too." A vicious feud existed between the two communities. Earlier in the century, the Samaritans had dragged corpses (or dead men's bones) into the Temple at Jerusalem, so as to pollute it and prevent the celebration of the Passover, and in 52 CE they ambushed Jews who were going on pilgrimage up to the Holy City. Sometimes they kidnapped their Hebrew neighbors and sold them into slavery.[6]

Josephus's native province was the one called Judea, a land that in parts could be made extremely fertile, despite a shortage of water and some arid areas. Every scrap of decent soil was farmed; hillsides held terraces of tiny vineyards and olive groves and small patches of grain. Sheep and goats, needed for sacrificial purposes, grazed where they could. Here is Josephus's terse account: "On the border of Samaria, the village of Anuath Borceos is the northern boundary of Judea. Measuring lengthwise, Judea's southern region ends at a village near the Arabian frontier, which local Jews call Jardan. Across, it stretches from the river Jordan to Joppa. At its centre lies the city of Jerusalem, a city to which some people, not without reason, have given the name of 'the country's navel.' Nor is Judea cut off from the sea, since it has a coastal area reaching as far as Ptolemais. It is divided into eleven districts, Jerusalem—the royal city—being the chief. . . . "[7]

In Pliny's view, Jerusalem was the most splendid city of the East. Its population was regularly increased by pilgrims, the majority bringing prosperity. It stood on three hills, which was one reason why people spoke of "going up to Jerusalem." (Even today, Jews still say they will "go up to Israel"—in modern Hebrew, *aliyah*—when they intend to settle there.) Amid arid country, stony and waterless, skirted by deep ravines, this was a site that made her almost inaccessible to enemies. The Upper City occupied the highest of the hills, separated from the others by a valley. Three walls of huge stone blocks surrounded the entire area, reinforced by a bastion every hundred yards. There were seven major gates, all fortified. Outside the walls were gardens and allotments, orchards and olive groves and, not very far away, beautiful woodland.

Herod's Palace stood on the summit of the northwestern hill at the west of the city, near the wall, marked out by three tall towers of white marble, which were named Hippicus, Phasael, and Mariamne. Its apartments were of dazzling luxury, with mosaic floors and jeweled furniture, most of the tables being of silver and gold; more than one of the dining rooms held couches for a hundred guests. It contained arcaded courtyards with lawns, groves and avenues of trees, ponds and canals flanked by rows of statues together with dovecotes, forming the only big gardens in Jerusalem. All this beauty would be burned and destroyed at the start of the war, a loss that Josephus acknowledged tormented him.

There were several other royal palaces as well, not quite so spacious but furnished with no less opulence. The most important was that of the client king, Agrippa II, in the center of Jerusalem. It enjoyed particular prestige among the inhabitants because, even if his kingdom lay outside Judea, Agrippa was the son of the last Herodian ruler.

The city's equivalent of the Tower of London was the mighty fortress-barracks known as the Antonia Fortress, which had a massive square tower at each corner. This stood on the northeast, overlooking Bezetha, the New City that lay still further to the north. Inside, with courtyards, baths, and squares, "it was just like a town," according to Josephus.[8] Permanently occupied by a Roman garrison, the Antonia was the key to Jerusalem, because it guarded the Temple.

"The Temple was the fortress protecting the city," says Josephus, from whose description alone we know how it appeared to contemporaries. Begun by Herod the Great in 19 BCE on the site where Solomon's Temple had once stood, this second Temple of Jerusalem would not be completed until 64 CE. The area it covered was larger than that of the Acropolis at Athens.[9] Constructed of white stone, its halls (such as the Grand Sanhedrin's Chamber) were paneled in marble or cypress and roofed with cedar. The Royal Portico, three aisles of Corinthian columns, was longer and higher than any cathedral. "It was clothed in plates of massy gold and at sunrise shone with such a fiery splendor that anyone who tried to look at it had to turn his eyes away, as if he had been trying to look into the sun itself," notes Josephus.[10]

To prevent the polluting of this holy place, no one suffering from diseases such as leprosy or gonorrhea, wearing dusty shoes, bearing a staff, or carrying parcels was allowed into the Temple complex by the guards. Beyond the massive fortified gateways, which held double gates plated in gold and silver, were four great courtyards laid out in succession: the Court of the Gentiles, the Court of the Women, the Court of the Israelites, and the Court of the Priests, each set slightly higher than the previous one and reached by steps. The enormous Court of the Goyim (gentiles), flanked by covered porticos with columns thirty-six feet high, was the meeting place for all Jerusalem. Another favorite area was the Portico of Solomon, which was entered by the Sushan gate and supported by a double row of columns; its two galleries overlooked the tombs of the Kedron Valley. The women's court was fenced off with timber palisades. Inscriptions in Greek and Latin forbade gentiles and women from penetrating any further than the courts that bore their names.

In the Court of Priests stood the altar of burnt offering, a pile of unhewn rocks thirteen feet high and nearly fifty feet square, with stone horns at all four corners and channels for the blood of the offerings. Lowing and bellowing, oxen, calves, rams, lambs, and goats were tethered next to the altar, to eight cedar pillars. Starting with two lambs at dawn and ending with two more lambs at sunset, hundreds were sacrificed each day, between three ritual pauses that were marked by readings from scripture and a ritual drinking of wine, together with chanting accompanied by a harp, a pipe, a lyre, and bronze cymbals as well as by blasts from a ram's horn (shofar) and a silver trumpet.

After the animals' throats had been cut with special knives by the officiating priests, they were gutted, skinned, and dismembered before being carried to marble tables, where they were ritually burned, clouds of priceless incense (prepared according to a secret recipe) mingling with the smoke. No less than seven hundred priests were always at work here, in silence. The blood was drained away by an elaborate cleaning system, water being supplied from thirty-four cisterns, filled by the winter rain from the nearby Pool of Siloam. Near the altar stood a great laver for ablutions whose water enabled the Levites, the priests' assistants, to cleanse everything for the next offering.

Above the courtyards stood the Sanctuary, which resembled a gigantic, freestanding, long gallery. Its great cedarwood door, studded with gold and surmounted by a golden vine with a cluster of grapes as tall as a man, was veiled by a Babylonian tapestry of blue, scarlet, and purple whose embroidery symbolized the heavens. In the first part of the "Holy House" stood the gold seven-branched candlestick—actually a lamp stand with seven lamps burning olive oil, representing seven planets—the gold altar for the incense of thirteen spices, and the gold table for the shewbread, which consisted of twelve consecrated, unleavened loaves that were renewed on every Sabbath. Its other, innermost part, veiled by a curtain, was the *qadosh haqedoshim* (Holy of Holies), which had once contained the Ark of the Covenant but was now entirely empty and in darkness, never entered except by the high priest on Yom Kippur (the Day of Atonement).

Many people liked to come to the Temple every day, so that they could face the Sanctuary when they prayed the Shema Yisrael ("Hear, O Israel: the Lord our God is one Lord . . .") or made the eighteen prostrations for the Shemone Esreh (the Eighteen Benedictions), as was required of every Jew. A staff of 25,000 manned the Temple, not just priests and Levites, but treasurers and janitors, musicians and cantors. At their head was the anointed high priest, living embodiment of the Law, who on Yom Kippur donned a miter encircled by a gold crown and a gold-embroidered breastplate to enter the Sanctuary to beg God's forgiveness for the sins of his nation, the only human being allowed to enter. He also officiated on every Sabbath and every new moon, and on festivals, in less dramatic robes.

Deeply respected, the high priest was a species of Jewish pope or caliph. He alone could summon the Sanhedrin. However, because Judea was a theocracy administered by an infidel colonial power, the high priest often faced political challenges, and it was not uncommon for him to be deposed after only a brief period by the Roman procurator. As a result, there were always several former holders of the office, each treated with honor, who were known collectively as "the high priests." In his *Vie de Jésus*, Ernest Renan compares them to "a miniature college of cardinals grouped around the Temple, living for politics, not too impressed by excessive religious zeal and even a bit suspicious of it, turning very deaf ears indeed to the various demands made by holy men or would-be reformers, since they did very well out of things as they were."[11]

Four times a day, seven silver trumpets sounded three times from the Temple to proclaim the sacrifice and the ritual pauses. In the evening, the trumpets summoned men and women to prayer. On the evening before Passover they sounded six times, preceded by the haunting wail of the shofar, the ram's horn. Intended to praise God (and not to bewilder Satan, as some non-Jewish sources have suggested, since the concept of Satan did not exist in Judaism), the blowing of the shofar was also used to announce the Sabbath and the holy days of Israel, as on the evening in September before Rosh Hashanah, the first day of the Jewish new year.

The Temple dominated Jerusalem. When a breeze blew on a hot day, her steep, narrow streets and stairways were filled with the odor of burnt flesh and incense wafting down from the Court of Priests, a smell known in other ancient cities but not on such an all-pervading scale. Thoroughfares were blocked by herds of animals being driven up for sacrifice. During such religious holidays as Passover, the city must have been so densely packed by pilgrims as to resemble modern Mecca. What Romans and other foreigners must have found odd was the absence of the statues that filled their own streets. The Jewish religion forbade any physical likeness of their god. For every Jew, the Temple of Jerusalem was the center of the universe and the gateway to heaven. Only here might sacrifices be offered to the one true God. For Josephus, who belonged to a priestly family, the Temple was the focus of all power and influence until he was in his mid-thirties. It also appealed to the poet in him. "When strangers first saw it from a distance, it looked like a mountain covered in snow," he recalled wistfully, "since it was so wonderfully white where it was not clad in gold."[12]

Clearly, the young Josephus was very much a man of Jerusalem and of the Temple.

1

A Young Nobleman

"With a pedigree like mine, of which I give details taken from the public archives, I can well afford to ignore anyone who tries to say something derogatory about my family."

JOSEPHUS, *VITA*, 6

JOSEPHUS WAS BORN in 37 or 38 CE, most probably at Jerusalem, during the first year of the reign of Gaius Caligula. (As the emperor of the Roman Empire, Caligula was supreme ruler of Judea, which had been acquired for Rome by Pompey during his conquest of the Near East a hundred years earlier.) "Beyond all question, my family is an aristocratic one, since it traces its descent from a very long line of priests," he writes. "Every race has different requirements for men to prove that noble blood flows in their veins, but with us [Jews] membership of the priesthood is the evidence which is required for proof of an illustrious ancestry."[1]

He often reminds his readers that he is a priest. Yet 18,000 priests were available to offer sacrifice at the Temple, every one of whom could claim unbroken male-line descent from Aaron, the brother of Moses and the first high priest, although the majority might never be called on to officiate. There was a big gap, however, between the upper priesthood, into which he was born, and the lower—between influential magnates and obscure peasant farmers who tilled the land with their own hands.

From the time of his great-great-great-grandfather Simon the Stammerer, Josephus's male forebears had belonged to the first of the twenty-
four courses or lines of priestly descent from Aaron that are listed in the
book of Deuteronomy. Records of their descent, originally oral but by now
written down, were kept at a kind of genealogical office at Jerusalem. The
males in this line married only the daughters of other priests. The first
course (*mishmeret*) was that of Jehoiarib, "most eminent of their clans." Although by ancient convention Judea's great nobles were the heads of a few
priestly families who had the symbolical right of providing wood for the
Temple's burnt offerings, in Josephus's time they needed to be rich in addition. Yet as religious leaders they were losing ground to the new class of
scribes, by now the real defenders of the Law, whose emphasis on spiritu-
ality and study of the scriptures had begun to play no less important a part
in Jewish life than the hallowed ritual at the Temple.

Josephus had another claim to be regarded as a patrician. "I am of royal
blood on the female side," he informs us.[2] He was descended from the
Maccabee kings through his great-great-great-grandmother, the Stammerer
having married a sister of Jonathan, who had been the first Maccabee high
priest. The later Maccabees were cruel and impious and had outraged the
more devout Jews. Even so, Josephus took an obvious pride in his illustrious ancestry.

Although the Torah stipulated that priests should not be landowners,
his family had a large estate outside Jerusalem. From childhood he was accustomed to luxury, as a member of Judea's small land-owning class, who
enjoyed "having their hands kissed in the market place," who went "clad
in purple and lawn," whose women dressed in silk. They lived in big mansions at Jerusalem, built with blocks of fine stone, decorated with frescoes
and mosaics—one excavated during the 1970s covered 600 square meters—and they were fond of throwing spectacular parties. They never
resided in the countryside, which they avoided.[3] Besides employing stew-
ards to administer their estates, they hired bands of armed servants to en-
force their wishes and were brutal in dealing with inferiors.

The Judean aristocracy had emerged only during the past century,
under the Herods or still more recently. In a country where the harvest was
dependent on an uncertain rainfall, their wealth had been acquired by
lending money to peasants in bad years and seizing their holdings when

they defaulted. In addition, just as the prophet Amos had written long ago, they manipulated the price of wheat so that "we may buy the poor for silver, and the needy for a pair of shoes" (Amos, viii, 6). Understandably, they were unloved by the tenants they gained in this way and hated by even the peacefully minded among the poor because of their greed, corruption, and ostentation. Throughout Judea there was deep hostility between the classes.

Even if the Romans' land tax and poll tax were no greater than anywhere else in the empire outside Italy, the added burden of tithes and the Temple tax reduced most Judeans to a state of misery. When drought, locusts, or cattle disease brought plague and famine, tax gatherers and landowners showed no mercy, so that after every bad harvest many people despaired. Some joined the ubiquitous bandit gangs who lived in caves; some relied on their kindred for food and shelter. Others migrated to the cities and begged for assistance from the charities run by devout Jews. In Greek cities, especially those on the coast, there was an increasingly savage animosity toward Jewish beggars from the countryside, which would soon find expression in pogroms.

Josephus informs us that his father, Mattathias, was highly thought of in Jerusalem because of his "upright character," although his popularity may have been restricted to members of his own class. Almost certainly a Pharisee, Mattathias was deeply religious and a close friend of a particularly distinguished high priest, Joshua ben Gamala, which shows that he was accustomed to moving in the capital's most influential circles. In later years Joshua would become an ally of Josephus who—as will be seen—referred to him with obvious admiration.

As high priest, Joshua dominated the Sanhedrin during his short term. A species of senate, the Sanhedrin was an assembly of seventy that was made up of the "princes of the priests" (the heads of the twenty-four courses), together with the most reputable scribes and other leading men. Its function was to supervise religious practice and maintain standards, so that it controlled every aspect of day-to-day life—it even had its own police force. The most powerful institution in Judea, the Sanhedrin was answerable only to the procurator, with whom it always did its best to cooperate, often in the face of gross provocation. Although Josephus does not say so, it is possible that his father was a member of this august body.

Joshua ben Gamala was genuinely benevolent. He set up a system for providing education in every district and town of Judea, under legislation that made it obligatory for parents to send their children to school at the age of five and proscribed punishments for lazy or truant pupils. He also encouraged the foundation of schools that made secondary education available to boys of outstanding intelligence.[4]

Clearly, Mattathias and his wife took pains to educate Josephus and his elder brother, also named Mattathias. Josephus specifically says "both parents," which is surprising since Jewish women had no right to education and no religious function.[5] Some rabbis were keen that girls should be taught the Torah by their fathers, but other rabbis thought that to do so was blasphemy. The fact that his mother had some scriptural knowledge and joined in educating her sons indicates that Josephus belonged to an unusually imaginative family. If one can believe Josephus, both parents had a gift for teaching.

Even so, it is not impossible that he attended a school of the sort advocated by Rabbi Joshua. Attached to a local synagogue, such a school was called a *beth hasefer* (house of the book) where, under the direction of the *hassan* or master of the synagogue, pupils learned the Torah by heart and were taught how to interpret the Holy Law that it enshrined. The Torah, which consisted of the first five books of the Old Testament, contained the meaning of life, explaining to Jewish men and women why they were the Chosen People of God and telling them how they should live. (The process of understanding the Torah was aided by Aramaic translations of key texts, known as Targums.) They also learned the Psalms by heart. In addition, they studied less seminal writings, notably commentaries on the Torah—in particular the *pesherim*, explanations of scriptural texts. Among other books studied were a collection of unofficial psalms and the uncanonical scriptural writings—the Apocalypse of Baruch and the Book of Jonah being the best known. Finally, there were such Jewish apocrypha as the Life of Adam and Eve, the Assumption of Isaiah, and the Assumption of Moses. In an otherwise exclusively religious syllabus, pupils were taught how to read and write Hebrew, as well as some history and geography.

It is worth stressing that at this period Jews differed to a bewildering extent in their understanding of the Hebrew Bible. Even if all accepted that the Law should govern every one of their actions, they did not follow it to the letter—each man or woman worked out what God wanted him or her to do. Not until the emergence of Reform and Liberal Judaism in Europe in the nineteenth century would Jews vary so widely in their interpretation of scripture.[6]

"I made remarkable progress with my education, acquiring a name for my unusually good memory and intellect," Josephus remembers. "When I was still only a boy of fourteen my enthusiasm for learning was so much admired that chief priests and important citizens began to ask my opinion." (This claim may well be true, since rabbis frequently consulted precocious children, on the chance they might have stumbled on insights denied to mature minds.) "When I was about sixteen, I made up my mind to find out about the various [religious] sects into which our nation is divided," he recalls. "There are three of these . . . The first are the Pharisees, the second the Sadducees and the third the Essenes. My object was to get to know them all and discover which was the best."[7]

The Essenes were Jewish monks, who are best known from the Dead Sea Scrolls and their monastery at Qumran on the Dead Sea. Living in the desert, they shared possessions, shunned women, gave up meat and wine, engaged in ritual baths, and practiced meditation. Josephus thought highly of them. "They deserve to be admired for leading better lives than any other men," he comments.[8] "Some can foretell the future, by careful reading of the scriptures, special forms of purification, and constantly reflecting on what the Prophets say," he tells us. "They are seldom wrong."[9] Throughout his life he believed that it was possible to see into the future if one knew the scriptures well enough and that to some extent he himself possessed this gift.

Another Essene tenet he always retained was a belief in fate. According to his way of thinking, no prophecy could ever have been accurate if the world were governed by chance. "The sect of the Essenes affirms that fate governs all things, and that nothing can befall men that is not decided by it," he was to write later.[10] "There is no way of avoiding it, even when we know what it is," he comments. He regarded it as almost sinister, even malevolent. "It creeps up on human souls and flatters them with pleasing hopes until it leads them into a situation from where there is no escape."[11] Nevertheless, it has been suggested that he regarded Essene theology as unsound, distorted by an apocalyptic outlook, that he had little interest in giving God any more than the minimum of worship due to him, and that he did not have much taste for prayer. Nor did he share the Essenes' fascination with angels and demons.[12]

"I put up with starvation and discomfort to investigate these three sects, obeying all the various disciplines they demanded," he informs us in his autobiography.[13] "Then I heard of a man called Bannus who lived in the desert, dressing only in what grew on trees and eating only what grew without being planted, who day and night took constant ablutions of cold water in order to check the lusts of the flesh. In order to purify myself too, I became his enthusiastic disciple, spending [most of] the three years with him."

"Having done what I had set out to do, I went back to living in the city. At nineteen I started to follow the way of life laid down by the Pharisees, a sect with certain resemblances to the people whom the Greek call Stoics."[14] Josephus states that "the Pharisees are considered the most accurate interpreters of our laws. They attribute everything to fate and to God's providence, although they accept it is in men's power to act rightly or wrongly provided fate co-operates."[15] One reason that he was attracted to them was that his father was probably a Pharisee. However, he never claimed to have been entirely committed to the sect, let alone to its leaders.

"Pharisee" (perushim) means those set apart, but their own name for themselves was "companions" (haberim), and Josephus admired their friendliness toward each other. Their fundamental tenet was that the Jewish faith must dictate every action performed by men and women, one consequence being that they considered Roman ways and contact with Romans impure, which was why they refused to enter Roman buildings. They claimed to be the only true interpreters of the Law, always seeking fresh meanings. There cannot have been more than 6,000 at any one time, many from the lower classes, but they wielded remarkable influence. They were more concerned with teaching in the synagogues than making sacrifices at the Temple—though several high priests were Pharisees—and they concentrated on explaining the Torah. At the same time, they tried to help the poor.

Like all puritans, they included a fair number of self-seekers and professional hypocrites of the sort attacked by Jesus of Nazareth, and they were frequently accused of insincerity. What has so often been overlooked is that Jesus was attacking only unworthy Pharisees, men who were denounced even in the Talmud, not the Pharisees as a whole, and that he was on friendly terms with more than a few of them. Even the uncompromisingly Catholic historian Henri Daniel-Rops admits that the great Pharisaic doctors of the Law were "virtuous, profoundly religious men and formed an elite without whom the Chosen People could never have been what it was in the years that were to come."[16]

Despite its formalism and hairsplitting, theirs was an optimistic creed, hopeful and consoling. They were convinced that religion should provide the true believer with reassurance and happiness, fear or gloom being alien to their outlook. Nor did they believe in a Last Day or a Last Judgment. "They rejoice at the prospect of being freed from the bonds of the flesh almost as if they were going to be released from a long spell in prison," is how Josephus describes the Pharisee belief in the survival of souls after death. "Like the Greeks, they teach that virtuous souls eventually find a dwelling beyond the ocean, in a land that suffers neither rain, snow or heat but is refreshed by gentle sea breezes. On the other hand, the wicked are imprisoned in a dark and terrifying cave, to undergo everlasting punishment." By "loving God with all your heart, all your soul and all your might, and your neighbor as yourself," those precepts from the Shema that he recognized as the bedrock of the Law, every Pharisee expected to end up soothed by the breezes. In another passage, however, he implies that they believed in reincarnation into another body.[17]

Like the Essenes, some Pharisees were attracted by neo-Pythagorism, a belief that each soul was a fragment of the one great, divine soul with which it would eventually be rejoined. Philo of Alexandria, a Pharisee, was a neo-Platonist influenced by neo-Pythagorism, who taught that this was why human souls could hope for union with God and transcend the body through the raptures of prayer. No doubt, Philo held unusual opinions, yet nothing in them was objectionable to Pharisees.

Pharisees regarded Sadducees as men lacking in true faith, traitors who welcomed the Roman invaders. Josephus could not avoid meeting these "Sons of Zadok," rich patricians who were often members of the Temple establishment, but he rejected their approach. Concentrating on an arid observance of the Law, Sadducees had little time for fatalism or an afterlife; there was no heaven, no hell. "They think God cannot be interested in whether we do evil or not," he tells us.[18] Nor did Josephus care for the way the Sadducees squabbled among themselves, unlike the Pharisees. The thought of a messiah arriving to upset their comfortable world made the Sadducees queasy; they viewed the Pharisees as religious maniacs and saw the Romans as a bulwark against social upheaval. With its built-in aversion to speculation or enthusiasm, the Sadducee creed held small appeal for an idealistic young man.

In practice, the distinction between Sadducees and Pharisees was blurred, even if their members sometimes quarreled about doctrine, to the extent of coming to blows. On the whole, most Jews seem to have been inconsistent, taking what they wanted from either approach, and it looks as if this was Josephus's position. Nor did the Sadducees monopolize the high priesthood; Rabban Joshua ben Gamala, for example, seems to have been a Pharisee. It is also likely that some of the *Perushim* were influenced by certain Essene practices, such as celebrating the Passover without roast meat.

Josephus's attitude toward Pharisees who were involved in politics was often antagonistic; we know that some leading members of the sect became his enemies. Even so, he continued to profess their creed in later life, perhaps partly because their self-discipline and fatalism had superficial resemblances to the stoicism fashionable among Roman patricians. To what extent he really was a Pharisee has been hotly debated by historians.[19] As for the Sadducees, he may have agreed with their approach to politics while rejecting their religious views. According to their way of thinking, Judaism was a world religion so there could be nothing wrong in collaborating with the Roman occupiers—provided the basics of the faith revealed by Moses were retained. Ultimately, they were universalists, an attitude that would attract the mature Josephus.

In addition, there were the followers of what Josephus calls the "Fourth Philosophy," founded by Judas the Galilean, whom Josephus describes as "a very clever teacher."[20] Their creed seems to have been a fundamentalist form of Phariseeism, with the difference that Judas and his Zealots (in Hebrew, *Kannaim*) refused to accept any ruler but God or call any man "lord," however great he might be. Fervent believers in an afterlife, they preached contempt for death, never mourning when their family or friends died, and were unshaken by torture.

Their movement had begun early in the century when, during the disorder after Herod the Great's death, Judas, a charismatic figure from the

Golan, together with a Pharisee named Zaddok (in no way a Sadducee), led a revolt over taxes and the census, the most resented features of Roman occupation. Although he lost his life, his sons spread his message, and for three decades before Josephus was born, Zealot knifemen (*sicarii*) terrorized Jerusalem, slipping into the city disguised as pilgrims and killing collaborators. Their message appealed to those who regarded Roman imperial rule as a national humiliation and yearned for an upheaval that would drive out the hated *Khittim*—the Romans. With its largely "have-not" membership, fanaticism, readiness for holy war, and suicidal assassins, it was tailor-made for a popular revolution.[21]

Predictably, the Fourth Philosophy was detested by Josephus. Temperamentally averse to extremism, he found no difficulty in getting along with Romans. "All sorts of misfortunes came from these men, the nation being infected by their doctrine to an incredible extent," he says of the Zealots in his *Jewish Antiquities*. "Judas and Zaddok spread a fourth sect of philosophy among us that attracted a great many followers, first plaguing the government with affrays and laying the foundations of all our future miseries."[22] Yet, judging from the appeal of the Zealot message, there must have been much more than he admits to Judas and his ideas.

Josephus's everyday language was Aramaic, the tongue in which he thought until early middle age. (A Semitic language closely related to Hebrew and used throughout the Middle East, Aramaic had been adopted by the Jews in place of Hebrew after their return from Babylon.) He also spoke Hebrew, which was enjoying a revival among learned men as a spoken tongue. And he knew a third language.

This was the "koine," the Roman Empire's lingua franca, which was spoken and written by most prosperous Jews, however devout, and not merely by the large "Greek" population of Judea. East of what is now the Balkan peninsula, it served as an official language, for dealing with Roman officials or foreigners. Scarcely the language of Thucydides, the koine's grammar had become less complicated and its vocabulary smaller than those of Attic Greek, despite incorporating loan words from other tongues, while its pronunciation seems to have been noticeably un-Hellenic. Nevertheless, a working knowledge of the koine enabled one to read classical Greek, though with some difficulty. It is reasonable to assume that as an ambitious young man, Josephus worked hard at polishing his command of the language, and there are indications that by his mid-twenties he spoke it quite well. An ability to speak fluent Greek, however inelegantly, would provide the opportunity that began his career.

On the other hand, it is unlikely that he had any acquaintance with Hellenist learning at this stage. "The Jewish scholar, proud of the pedantic knowledge which cost him so much grinding toil, had the same contempt for Greek culture that the learned Moslem of the present day has for European civilization," was Renan's not inaccurate comment in the nineteenth century.[23] Almost certainly, the young Josephus, being a devout Pharisee, had never read the Greek classics before he traveled outside Palestine. Yet it appears that there were a handful of Jews in the capital who studied Greek literature and that he knew men who did read the classics, though he probably thought they risked betraying Judaism. These books possessed the allure of the forbidden for someone with such a powerful and inquiring mind.

2

An Occupied Country

"And every day the flames were blown higher and higher, until finally they turned into full-scale war."

JOSEPHUS, *THE JEWISH WAR*, 2, 265

CALLED THE "PROVINCE OF JUDEA" by its Roman masters, the Jewish homeland was governed by a procurator appointed by the emperor, but it was not a colony in the twentieth-century sense of the word, for there were few, if any, Roman settlers. A better description is a protectorate, even if the land and people were under the rapacious heel of Rome. Procurators had absolute judicial powers, including those of life and death, their decisions being subject only to the emperor on the far side of the Mediterranean.

After returning from Babylon in the sixth century BCE, the Jews had been under Persian suzerainty, and then part of Alexander the Great's empire and its successors, until the Maccabees led a revolt in the second century BCE against a Seleucid attempt to force the Jews to adopt Greek culture and subsequently reestablished the kingdom of Judea. But during a civil war a century before Josephus was born, the Jews invited Pompey to restore order, and he had turned Judea into a Roman client state, minus its coastline and the Greek cities inland. It enjoyed a brief period of semi-independence under the Idumean Herod the Great, an Arab Jew. The last

Idumean king of Judea, Agrippa I, died when Josephus was about seven—although his son, Agrippa II, ruled a little foreign kingdom across the northeastern border—and was regarded by the Romans in much the same way that the nineteenth-century British would see an Anglophile rajah.

Most of the procurators in Josephus's time were mediocrities, second-rate men of obscure background, who lacked any sort of imagination or flexibility. All they knew was that it was Rome's mission to rule the world. Incapable of appreciating the grandeur of the Israelite religion, they regarded Jews as an inferior race of oriental barbarians who stupidly refused to worship those pillars of civilization, the gods and goddesses of Rome.

Rome was very far away, and the imperial courier took several weeks to reach the port of Caesarea Maritima on Judea's Mediterranean coast. This pleasant, newly built city was the residence of the procurator. Founded by King Herod for his Greek-speaking Syrian subjects, it was noticeably un-Jewish, with an amphitheater and pagan temples, including the one that Herod had erected in honor of his great patron, Emperor Augustus, who had, of course, been officially deified and ranked as a god. There were pagan statues throughout the city—of Pan, of the Nymphs, of the Echo of the Grotto. Yet while predominantly Greek, the city was also home to a thriving Jewish minority.

The procurator spent most of his time at Caesarea, preferring it to the royal palace in dangerous, up-country Jerusalem. The old capital was magnificent, but it was the center of the natives' strange religion, and its inhabitants were prone to riot if they thought the procurator was trying to interfere with their customs or when they were quarrelling among themselves—which was far from infrequent. Nor was it unknown for a mob from Jerusalem to arrive at Caesarea and demonstrate outside the palace. Whenever the procurator visited Jerusalem, which he did as little as possible, he took a strong bodyguard and, if he had any sense, used the utmost tact.

The Roman garrison in Judea was tiny, three cohorts and an *ala* (cavalry force) that together numbered no more than 3,000 men, which, as Tacitus comments, was altogether inadequate. About a thousand were stationed permanently at Jerusalem in the Antonia Fortress. These soldiers were not legionaries but local auxiliaries or "native troops" (Syrians, Samaritans, Idumeans, or Nubians, but never Jews), although their senior officers were Romans. Often badly equipped and poorly disciplined, always on the lookout for loot, and savage in dealing with the Hebrews whom they regarded as hereditary enemies, they were unreliable—resentful of discipline, bad in a crisis, and prone to panic. They also operated a kind of protection racket. "Don't ill-treat anybody, don't denounce anyone falsely," John the Baptist is recorded as telling troops of this type. "Be content with your pay."[1] Nevertheless, led with a mixture of brutality and bribery, these Judean recruits kept the peace, enforced taxation, and chased the bandits who plagued the countryside.

Undoubtedly, the occupation brought benefits for the Jews, though these were more apparent to society's richer members. It brought roads that enabled commerce, it brought justice of a sort, however corrupt, and it brought what Pliny proudly called the "immense majesty of Roman peace." For a long time, brigands and troublemakers, such as the itinerant prophets who stirred up the peasantry, were kept in check, although it was impossible to exterminate them. Merchants could sail across the Mediterranean without too much fear of piracy and travel the roads without too much fear of robbery.

The Roman government had no bureaucracy or district commissioners. Instead it relied on the ruling class to prevent any organized resistance from breaking out and used native officials to collect taxes.[2] For a time, the system worked well enough. Jews from the same background as Josephus realized that, for people like them, the advantages of Roman rule outweighed the drawbacks. Rich enough to pay their taxes without discomfort, they welcomed the presence of troops who kept the lower orders in place. They knew there was no alternative; recent history showed that Rome won every war, invariably defeating her opponents.

The procurator realized that his job was to maintain law and order so that the Jews would pay the taxes. It was complicated by every senior Roman official's determination to screw as much money out of a subject country as possible. "Naturally, governors want to get as much as they can, particularly the ones feeling insecure who expect to stay for only a short time," writes Josephus, quoting the Emperor Tiberius.[3] "Uncertain about when they will lose their post, they work all the harder at fleecing people." If allowed to stay in office, they eventually became gorged with plunder after extracting such vast amounts and grew less harsh, so that their successor's rule seemed almost intolerable in contrast.

The one thing that stopped a procurator from bleeding Judea dry was a fear that some Jewish delegation might make a successful complaint about his illegal exactions to the emperor or the legate of Syria. Yet at the same time, he knew that Rome would ignore most maladministration or corruption so long as it did not provoke rebellion. In order to ensure that the natives remained docile, he needed to avoid being caught up in the unending local quarrels (though not all procurators behaved so sensibly). Above all, he must be careful not to upset the Jews' religious sensibilities.

Many aspects of "Romanitas" did not accord with the faith of Israel, and procurators were aware that they were sitting on the brink of a volcano. A dangerous rebellion might break out at any moment. They remembered how when Herod the Great died in 4 CE, the bandit Judas, son of Hezekiah, had proclaimed himself king, as had the giant slave, Simon, who burned down the royal palace at Jericho. They recalled, too, how in Judea the shepherd Athronges and his brothers had raised an army, which ambushed a Roman century, killing the centurion and forty men before taking to the hills. Varus, legate of Syria, had found it necessary to crucify 2,000 Jews before he was able to restore order.

This explains Pontius Pilate's suspicion of Jesus of Nazareth. "At this time there lived Jesus, a wise man, if indeed one ought to call him a man, for he did amazing things—a teacher for men who listen joyfully to truth," says Josephus in a famous passage in his *Jewish Antiquities*, and one whose authenticity has been hotly debated. "He found many followers among both Jews and Greeks. He was the Messiah. When Pilate, after hearing him accused by men of the highest standing among us, condemned him to be crucified, those who had loved him from the start did not stop doing so. On the third day he appeared to them restored to life, God's prophets having prophesied this as well as other wonderful things about him. Even now, the tribe of Christians, named after him, has not yet disappeared."[4]

The references in this passage (known by scholars as the Testimonium Flavianum) to the resurrection and "the tribe of Christians" may be a second-century interpolation by a Christian copyist.[5] Otherwise, however, it is accepted as genuine by many authorities, including Geza Vermes. Even if the sentence about Christians was added later, it certainly looks as if Josephus mentioned Jesus, placing him among the wise to prove his point that Pilate was unjust. A Christian writer would never have been content with saying that Jesus was merely a wise man who did amazing things.[6]

Just before Josephus was born, Pilate caused outrage by bringing into Jerusalem his soldiers' eagles, the Roman symbol of victory that bears Caesar's image, although he took them out after a rioting crowd refused to be cowed by his troops' drawn swords. He also backed down after complaints that golden shields bearing Tiberius's name, which he had displayed at his residence, the former royal palace, were idolatrous. However, when he robbed the Temple treasury to pay for an aqueduct and the Jews gathered in the amphitheater at Caesarea to yell their disapproval, he let his men loose on them with clubs, and many died in the ensuing stampede. Finally, he went too far, ordering his men to butcher a group of Samaritans who had met on Mount Gerizim to pray. The Samaritans complained to Vitellius, the legate of Syria. Realizing that Pilate had become a liability, Vitellius sent him back to Rome in disgrace to answer their charges, and then he disappears from history.

Some Romans behaved more sensibly. When in 41 Caligula sent Publius Petronius, legate of Syria, to set up an image in the Temple of the deified emperor as a god, with orders to exterminate any protesters and enslave their countrymen, the legate wrote to the emperor, saying that a vast number of Jews had implored him not to do it and that the emperor must cancel his order unless he wanted to lose the country. Luckily, Caligula died before he could carry out his intention. The brief reign of Agrippa I, Herod the Great's grandson, who became the client king of Judea the same year, was a welcome respite from the procurators.

However, when he died in 44, his son, Agrippa II, was fobbed off with a border kingdom. The procurators returned, and over the next few years Rome usually appointed the wrong man. Over the next twenty years, law and order gradually broke down, as we can see from what Josephus tells us in *The Jewish War*.[7] In 45 CE, for example, a magician called Theudas persuaded a large crowd to follow him to the river Jordan, which he promised to divide with his staff, like Moses, but the new procurator, Cuspius Fadus, sent cavalry to disperse them, and the "prophet" was caught and beheaded—his head being taken back to Jerusalem.[8] Josephus also records that shortly afterward James and Simon, who were sons of Judas the

Galilean, were arrested and crucified by Tiberius Alexander, Fadus's successor, presumably for planning some sort of Zealot revolt.

The use of native troops, men recruited from places like Caesarea, who for racial reasons could be relied on to insult and mistreat Jews, was bound to cause trouble. During the Passover of 51 CE, when thousands of pilgrims had come to Jerusalem, a soldier who was on duty at the Portico of Solomon and guarding the outer precincts of the Temple, pulled up his kilt, displayed his bare backside to the worshippers and made a noise "in tune with his posture."[9] A mob of infuriated Jews stoned the troops until the procurator, Ventidius Cumanus, brought in reinforcements and threw them out of the Temple, many being killed. A more serious incident took place during the pursuit of some brigands when a soldier tore a copy of the Torah in pieces and threw it on a fire. The only way Cumanus was able to calm the uproar was to have the man beheaded in front of the Jews.

Meanwhile, a Galilean going up to Jerusalem for the Passover was murdered on his way through Samaria. Led by a bandit called Eleazar, Jews rushed down from the city to avenge him, attacking Samaritan villages and killing the inhabitants. After accepting a bribe from the Samaritans, Cumanus arrived in their country from Caesarea with mounted troops and slaughtered many of Eleazar's followers, dragging others back in chains to Caesarea. When the Jews appealed to the legate of Syria, Numidius Quadratus, he went to Caesarea and crucified Cumanus's prisoners, besides beheading a further eighteen who had been involved. He then sent the chief priest, Jonathan, to Rome with other important Jews and the Samaritan leaders to argue their case before the Emperor Claudius. He also ordered Cumanus and his second-in-command, the tribune Celer, to return to Rome and explain themselves. The smooth-tongued King Agrippa was the Jews' advocate, and Claudius decided in their favor. He had the three Samaritan leaders beheaded, banished Cumanus, and sent Celer back to Jerusalem in chains to be tortured and dragged through the city before being beheaded. Even the emperor realized that the country might easily erupt in revolt.

Antonius Felix, who replaced Cumanus as procurator—and is familiar to readers of the Bible as the man who imprisoned St. Paul[10]—was a former slave described by Tacitus as "ripe for any sort of villainy."[11] He got the job because his brother was Emperor Claudius's favorite adviser and because he had married King Agrippa's beautiful sister. Corrupt and cruel, he was always trying to feather his nest, and so the Jews were constantly complaining to Rome about his criminal activities. However, he managed to give the impression that he was restoring order, at least in the country-side. He captured the veteran bandit Eleazar, along with his whole gang, promised him a pardon, and then sent him in chains to Rome. Besides hunting down brigands and the villagers who sheltered them, he executed any "prophets" he could catch, crucifying large numbers of them.

While the countryside was being pacified—or at least cowed into sub-mission—trouble of another sort was breaking out in Jerusalem. The Zealot knifemen, the *sicarii*, were growing more active. (Their name came from their knives or small swords, which were curved like Roman sickles, or *sicae*.) Their first victim was the high priest, Jonathan, who had been grumbling that the procurator was not doing his job properly and threat-ening to complain to Rome. Felix bribed one of the high priest's friends to arrange for the *sicarii* to eliminate him.[12] After his murder, there were daily assassinations, and soon all Jerusalem was living in terror—"everybody ex-pected death at any moment, just as men do in wartime."[13] The assassins mingled with the crowds who packed the city's narrow streets during festi-vals and then, knives hidden in their clothes, stalked a victim, struck him down, and escaped by pretending to lead the pursuit. They even attacked in the Temple. According to Josephus, they were more than fanatics of the Fourth Philosophy; they were professional hit men who carried out con-tract killings.[14] Among the more obscure folk they tried to knife was an ex-Pharisee called Saul of Tarsus.[15]

In addition, a group of "magicians" pretended to be divinely inspired and persuaded a crowd to follow them into the desert, promising that once they were in the wilderness, God would show them how to win their lib-erty. Felix sent a force of infantry and cavalry in pursuit and killed most of them. He dealt in the same way with an Egyptian "prophet" who deluded a mob of 4,000 men—described as "murderers" in the New Testament—into believing that they could take over the city.[16] His troops slaughtered a large number of them, although they failed to catch the Egyptian, who fled into the desert. Later, a certain Saul of Tarsus was mistaken for him and arrested by the Roman authorities.

Meanwhile, because their leading men were richer than the Greeks, and because their numbers were swollen by starving peasants, the Jews of

Caesarea claimed that the city belonged to them exclusively, on the grounds that it had been built by King Herod, who was a Jew. This was a dangerous thing to do since the majority of the population were Greeks. When stones were thrown, several people were hurt, and some of the garrison joined in on the side of the Greeks. However, the Jews began to get the upper hand despite their inferior numbers, so Felix went into the main square and told them to go home. When they refused, he ordered his soldiers to chase them off the streets. Although his men inflicted severe casualties and looted Jewish houses, the rioting continued. Finally, he sent the leaders of both sides to Rome to argue their case before Nero.

Despite Felix's reasonable response to the upheaval in Caesarea, on the whole his behavior in Judea was deplorable. Tacitus says that "he liked to pretend he was a king although he had the mind of a slave, and enjoyed indulging a taste for cruelty and vice."[17] Serious trouble was looming by the time Nero recalled him in disgrace in 60 CE. He had relaxed his campaign against the brigands, who combined with the "prophets" in inciting country people to revolt, fight for their freedom, and kill anyone obedient to the government. Their message was so attractive that bands of thugs, welcomed by the peasants, roamed the countryside, plundering the houses of rich men, murdering well-to-do folk, and setting villages on fire—"until all Judea was filled with the consequences of their madness."[18]

Josephus implies that the next procurator, Porcius Festus (who sent Paul of Tarsus to Rome), was more capable. He says that Festus made the restoration of law and order in the countryside his priority, capturing most of the bandits who were causing all the trouble and putting many of them to death. He, too, had trouble with a "prophet," sending soldiers to exterminate the man's followers when they assembled in the desert. He seems to have been tactful in his dealing with the Jewish ruling class, and there is no record of his upsetting religious sensibilities. Unfortunately, he died after a mere two years in office. Had Festus lived longer, he might have averted the looming tragedy.

Before his replacement reached Judea, the high priest Ananus summoned the Sanhedrin and "brought before them James the brother of Jesus who was called Christ and others, charged with breaking the law, and had these men stoned."[19] Eusebius, writing in the fourth century, but quoting the lost writings of Heggesipus, who wrote in the second, adds that James,

Bishop of Jerusalem, was made to climb the topmost pinnacle of the Temple and ordered to abjure Jesus. After refusing, he was hurled down but survived the fall—to be stoned before being finished off with a grindstone. James had led the Judeo-Christians, who kept many Jewish observances, praying at the Temple at the prescribed hours.[20] The incident shows the increasing lawlessness of the upper class, since only a procurator had the power to condemn men to death.

This reference to James is generally accepted.[21] Josephus refers only twice to Jesus of Nazareth and the Christians in his books. His silence has been interpreted in different ways, the most likely explanation being that as a loyal Jew writing for a pagan readership, he tried to make men of his faith seem as admirable as possible. He probably saw little point in writing about Jesus, who, in his eyes, was no more than an obscure fanatic who had died disgracefully on a cross. (Even so, his eighteenth-century translator, William Whiston, reached the bizarre conclusion that Josephus had secretly been an Ebionite—a Jew partly converted to Christianity.)

In 62 CE, Nero, whose judgment was growing increasingly erratic, appointed Lucceius Albinus to succeed Festus. When the new procurator arrived, he made feeble attempts to hunt down the *sicarii*, but he proved to be an unmitigated disaster, weak and venal. "He did not do his job as the other [Festus] had done it while there was no species of graft in which he did not have a hand," says Josephus.[22] Besides using his position to rob and plunder everybody, he imposed new taxes that crushed the entire nation and allowed the relatives of anyone who had been imprisoned by the municipal authorities or former procurators to buy their freedom in return for cash. The only people left in jail were those who could not pay. The criminal element in Jerusalem grew more dangerous all the time. Its leaders bribed Albinus to turn a blind eye to their activities so that their thugs could rob law-abiding citizens with impunity. Nobody dared to complain.

What was peculiarly shocking was the behavior of men at the top of society, such as the former high priest Ananias ben Nedebaeus, who cultivated the friendship of the procurator and the current high priest Yeshua with lavish presents. A notorious "hoarder of money," he wanted a free hand to do as he liked. He sent his servants, armed with clubs, to the threshing floors, reinforced by professional criminals, to seize tithes from the poorer priests, who were beaten up if they tried to resist. In consequence, some of the

older clergy died from starvation during these years of bad harvests—
another reason for the breakdown of society.

Ananias "increased in glory every day." However, he met his match
when the *sicarii* kidnapped his son, Eleazar, the Temple captain, along
with his secretary and held them ransom until Ananias released ten *sicarii*
whom he had taken prisoner. After he let them go, the *sicarii* went on kid-
napping his officials whenever he arrested their fellow knifemen.

Other high priests besides Ananias employed armed bands, who fought
each other, as well as "plundering the goods of people weaker than themselves."[23] Just how much magnates of this sort were hated by ordinary folk
in Judea is conveyed by the Talmud: "House of Boethus? Woe upon us,
watch out for their whip! House of Kanthera? Woe upon us, watch out for
their pen! House of Annias? Woe upon us, watch out for their viper's hiss!
House of Ishmael ben Phiabi? Woe upon us, watch out for their blows!
They themselves are high priests while their sons are treasurers and so are
their fathers-in-law, all great men at the Temple. As for their servants, they
are always thrashing us with cudgels."[24]

By this time, Josephus was beginning to take an interest in public affairs. Looking back, he comments, "these were the days when seeds were
sown that would bring the city to destruction."[25] The richer magnates
began to exploit the dissatisfaction of the poor, recruiting them as strong-
men to use in the faction fighting that raged throughout the city streets. At
the same time, they recruited Zealot knifemen. But the priests and nobles
were starting to lose control. Class war had broken out, "men of power op-
pressing the masses and the masses doing their best to pull down the men
of power—one side bent on tyranny, the other on violence and stealing the
property of the rich."[26] The province was sliding into anarchy.

Yet the man whom Nero appointed as Albinus's successor in 64 CE,
Gessius Florus, made Albinus seem virtuous in comparison. Nevertheless,
full-scale revolution and war with Rome must have seemed inconceivable
when Josephus left Judea shortly before the recall of Albinus and the arrival of Florus. He must have had no inkling of the disastrous situation he
was going to find on his return to Jerusalem.

3

Rome and Poppaea

"Poppaea, Nero's wife, who was a worshipper of God . . ."

JOSEPHUS, *JEWISH ANTIQUITIES*, 20, 195

"WHILE FELIX WAS procurator of Judea some priests whom I happened to know, [both] thoroughly decent men, were sent by him to Rome in chains on the flimsiest of charges, supposedly to explain themselves to Caesar," Josephus tells us. "I wanted to find a way of freeing them, one reason being that I had heard how even in prison they never for a moment stopped practicing their religion, surviving on figs and nuts [in the absence of properly prepared, kosher food]." Despite Felix's recall in disgrace in the year 60 CE, they were left to rot in jail, with their case still unheard. Finally, Josephus decided to go and plead for their release. He says that he set out shortly after his twenty-sixth birthday—possibly in 63, certainly before March 64.[1]

We do not know what the original incident was that had led to the men's imprisonment. Felix may perhaps have sent them to be tried by the emperor for taking part in the fighting between factions that was by now making life in Jerusalem so unpleasant, but it is just as likely to have been a brazen attempt by the venal procurator to get the pair out of the way because they were key witnesses to one of his shabby crimes.

Josephus's motive was not just compassion, however. He always had too much of an eye for the main chance. If successful, he would make a name for himself and impress the Sanhedrin, who may have sent him on the mission because of his fluent koine Greek, although he does not make any mention of this—perhaps to claim more credit for himself. Certainly, there could be no better way of advancing his career. His visit to imperial Rome was going to be one of the most formative experiences of his entire life.

He knew exactly whom to approach when he got there. During the brief procuratorship of Felix's successor, Porcius Festus, from 60 to 62, King Agrippa II had a new dining room constructed on the east side of the royal palace, from where he could watch in comfort all that was going on inside the Temple. Outraged, the priests responded by building a high wall to block his view. Festus thought it wise to maintain good relations with Agrippa, who had important contacts at Rome, so he immediately demolished the wall, not realizing that it was within the Temple precincts. The Jews then asked the procurator for permission to send an embassy of ten leading citizens to Rome and seek justice from the emperor, although they were far from sure that they would get it. Festus made no objection. The ten were led by the current high priest, Ishmael ben Phiabi. Somewhat to their surprise they obtained everything they wanted after the Empress Poppaea intervened—either the wall was rebuilt or the dining room pulled down—although Ishmael and the Temple treasurer were made to stay in Rome as hostages for their people's behavior. This gave Agrippa the chance to depose Ishmael and appoint a more pliable high priest. Reports of the empress's friendly attitude must have circulated all over Jerusalem.[2]

Big ships sailed regularly to Rome from the great port of Caesarea, with its long mole and seawall, and carried a large complement of passengers. After going up the coast they would steer for Crete, then for Greece, and finally for Italy, putting in almost daily at harbors en route to take on fresh food and water and new passengers.

"I reached Rome only after an exceptionally dangerous sea voyage during which our vessel foundered in the Adriatic, leaving six hundred of us to swim throughout the entire night," he recalls. "Towards daybreak, however, by the mercy of God we spotted a ship from Cyrene, and I and about eighty others succeeded in outswimming the rest and were allowed to come on board." There was no room on the boat for the remainder of the passengers and crew, who were presumably left to drown, but Josephus was always philosophical about other people's misfortunes. Eventually he landed at Puteoli (modern Pozzuoli) near Naples and made his way to Rome.[3]

However beautiful and imposing Jerusalem may have been, it cannot have compared with the glittering megalopolis that Josephus found when he arrived. In today's terms it was a combination of Washington, New York, Los Angeles, and Chicago with London, Paris, and every other European capital thrown in, since it was not just the center of the Roman Empire but the political, economic, and cultural center of the civilized world. There was something monstrous about the scale of this vast urban conglomeration, which a Jew might be forgiven for comparing to Babylon of unhappy memory. Undeniably, it was magnificent, full of huge and wonderful buildings—the Capitol, the Forum, the Pantheon, and the Temple of Mars being only the best known. Their walls were covered in marble, their roofs in gilded tiles, while everywhere there were statues of marble, bronze, or even gold. Yet at the same time, the city was overcrowded and dirty, a rabbit warren of filthy lanes lying behind these marvels.

There were open air theaters for the miming companies whose spectacles and dancing, frequently obscene, drew audiences of thousands, together with amphitheaters for gladiatorial "games." There were also "circuses," long circuits for the hugely popular chariot races. However, it is unlikely that many Jews went to entertainments of this sort, which they considered impious. On the other hand, they must have enjoyed the numerous public gardens.

Josephus found plenty of his own people in Rome. Fifty years before, the geographer Strabo had complained that Jews were taking over every city in the world. In Josephus's own words, "there is not a single city, whether Greek or barbarian, not a single nation, which our custom of doing no work on the seventh day has not reached, where our fasts, lamp lighting and food rituals go unobserved."[4] Rome had become a center of the "Diaspora," the Jewish expatriate communities, with a Hebrew population numbering tens of thousands, who inhabited districts all over the city, each group living near a synagogue and with their own extensive cemeteries. Mainly merchants, many specialized in luxuries from the eastern parts of the Roman Empire— slaves and exotic animals, jewels and precious metals, silks and furs, ivory and perfume.

Roman traditionalists, who despised all foreigners except a few Greeks, looked down on them. Cicero had sneered at their "superstitions that deny all that Rome stands for,"[5] and Seneca condemned "this evil race's customs." The Emperor Tiberius had even started to banish them from Italy, although he changed his mind, and the Emperor Claudius had threatened them with expulsion as troublemakers—most likely due to the uproar caused in the synagogues by Christian missionaries.[6]

Today, it is hard for us to understand just how much the monotheism of Jews and Christians, interlopers from the alien East, affronted the innate polytheism of the ancient Romans. There were also those who found Jewish taboos not so much austere as ridiculous. Philo of Alexandria records that when he led an embassy to the Emperor Caligula, the entire court burst out laughing when Caligula asked him why Hebrews never touched pork.[7]

Hostility toward Jews during this time should not be exaggerated, however. Julius Caesar had introduced legislation to guarantee their religious liberty, a law that had been confirmed by Augustus, who exempted them from military service. Racial antipathy was far from widespread in a city whose population was so mixed, with a never ending flood of immigrants, and on the whole they found no trouble in fitting into Roman life. Although they did not make sacrifices to the gods of Rome, they had no objection to praying for the well-being of her government in their synagogues. It was a privilege granted to no other group.

Moreover, as in every other city where the Diaspora had settled, the Roman Jews, while retaining their faith, were strongly influenced by Philhellenism. At their services, they used the Septuagint, a translation of the Jewish scriptures into Greek, and the better educated read the classics of Greek literature, from Homer to the great philosophers and fashionable poets. The widely respected Philo of Alexandria, who died in about 50 CE, was himself a distinguished philosopher who employed Platonism to prove the existence of the Jewish God.

As a young man with a very good mind, Josephus could not have been uninfluenced by the Diaspora's intellectual climate. His stay at Rome was a period of intense intellectual development, the equivalent of a university education. Surely it was now that he began to read Greek authors, acquiring the foundations of the learning that would make him a great scholar.

We know from his writings that by the time he was middle-aged he had read not only Homer but Herodotus, Thucydides, and Xenophon, together with Sophocles, Euripides, Demosthenes, and Epicurus.

On the other hand, he would have noticed approvingly how Roman Jews never for a moment forgot that Jerusalem was their true home, scrupulously observing the Law. Although they read the Torah in Greek (the Pentateuch) and spoke the koine instead of Aramaic, very few apostatized to further their careers. (No practicing Jew could become an imperial official as it meant worshipping pagan gods.) Their staunch monotheism impressed their neighbors, making converts. To some extent they proselytized, activities the poet Horace laughed at good-naturedly in the Satires.[8] Many Romans who were interested but did not convert—to the extent of undergoing circumcision or taking ritual baths—remained fascinated by these extraordinary people.

It is likely that during his stay in Rome Josephus lived in one of the ramshackle tenements that housed most citizens; six, seven, or even ten stories high, jerry-built of rubble and the cheapest timber, these were apt to collapse without warning. Only the very rich could afford their own dwellings. The endless streets, many of which were soon to be demolished by the great fire of 64 CE, appear to have been as filthy as they were narrow. Belonging to a race noted for its cleanliness, he would have made a point of avoiding such amenities as the communal baths or the public lavatories, since Jews had their own, more fastidious arrangements.

He was able to go anywhere because there were Jews everywhere. His mission and background ensured a welcome, while among Romans as well as Jews he was helped by his fluent koine Greek. Educated by Greek tutors, upper-class Romans were bilingual, and instead of speaking Latin to each other, they spoke a polished version of the koine, in much the same way that eighteenth-century Europeans preferred to speak French. It was not only the language of intellectuals but the polite language. (Pace Shakespeare, when Julius Caesar was stabbed, he had cried, "Kai su, teknon!" not "Et tu, Brute!") Most useful of all, it was used in court circles.

It is quite likely that he went at least once to the games; although they were considered impious by Jews, the games were unquestionably the most popular entertainment in Rome. In the arena, watched by thousands, gladiators recruited from the large numbers of jailed prisoners of war and criminals fought each other to the death or were pitted against bears, wolves, and lions crazed with hunger; others were burned alive or fed to ravenous animals. These ghastly spectacles appealed to all classes. Even Cicero praised them as an admirable means of teaching young men to fear neither death nor physical suffering, although he felt sorry for the animals. Writing four centuries later, Augustine of Hippo describes in his *Confessions* how a gentle philosopher friend who had been dragged along against his will to see the same sort of games (they must have changed very little since Nero's time) succumbed to their dreadful fascination, despite having tried to keep his eyes shut:

> A sudden shouting made him open them . . . and as soon as he saw all the blood running it was as though he had swallowed some fiercely intoxicating magic potion. Instead of looking away, he now watched greedily, drinking in every detail of the scene. He reveled in the sheer horror, suddenly overwhelmed by a murderous thirst for killing. No longer the same person who had come to the arena, he was just the same as everybody else in that baying crowd . . . He gazed besottedly, cheering and cheering, feverish with savage excitement. When at last he left the arena, his mind had become so hopelessly diseased that he could think of nothing but the next games.[9]

If Josephus did go, he never could have guessed that before too long thousands of his fellow countrymen were going to be slaughtered methodically in games just like these, all over the empire. It is possible, however, that he made a point of staying away. The inspiration behind such spectacles was paganism at its most evil, utterly repugnant to a devout Jew. Yet he knew at least one coreligionist who had adopted a profession still more pagan than that of a gladiator—even if it was not quite as short-lived.

"I made friends with Alliturus who, besides being a Jew, was in favor with Nero because he was an actor," he tells us.[10] It has been suggested that the word he uses for actor, *mimologos*, implies that Alliturus was a mime actor of the sort who entertained the guests at court banquets, which would explain why Alliturus was in the emperor's good books. If so, it was a curious profession for a Jew, since the mimes that were staged must have included a considerable amount of bawdiness and pornographic tableaux, especially when celebrating pagan festivals: gods and goddesses copulated, satyrs raped nymphs.

Alliturus took the young Pharisee to the imperial court, in the hope of securing the priests' release. Some idea of what he saw can be obtained from the *Satyricon* of Petronius, which was probably written in 65—during Josephus's stay at Rome. If anyone knew Nero's court, it was the author whom the emperor made his "arbiter of elegance." He relied on Petronius's advice on sensual enjoyment taken to the extreme, on the ultimate refinements of debauchery, though later he forced him to commit suicide. Sardonic and pornographic, in exquisite prose the novel depicts a world in which money's only rival is sexual pleasure, whether heterosexual or homosexual. (At one point the narrator says he feels the entire population of Rome has been swallowing aphrodisiacs.) The most memorable section is the banquet given by the multimillionaire ex-slave Trimalchio—to some extent modeled on Nero—where the food includes dormice dipped in honey, sows' udders, and peahens' eggs, accompanied by acrobatic displays in which the acrobats know that a bad performance will be punished by death. That is what meals must have been like at court. No doubt Josephus had encountered luxury in the great houses of Jerusalem, but never on so obscene a scale.

The two people who presided over the court and set what might be called its tone were, of course, Nero and his wife, Poppaea. A practitioner of almost every known vice, horribly cruel, and responsible for many murders, the emperor was a neurotic hedonist who, not content with absolute power, wanted to be regarded as a great artist. Nonetheless, in his own way he did not lack intelligence. The empress was even more of an enigma.

"Through [Alliturus] I got an introduction to Poppaea, Caesar's consort," he explains. The loveliest woman of her time, whose legendary beauty is confirmed by one or two portrait busts, according to Tacitus, Poppaea Sabina "had every gift save an unpolluted mind," inspiring lasting devotion among the men who were her lovers.[11] Rich, high born, intelligent, and amusing, she was at the same time a byword for promiscuity and ruthlessness. Largely responsible for Nero's murder of his wife and of his mother, she had married him as her third husband after a carefully planned seduction. She also played a part in destroying his minister and former tutor, the disapproving Seneca.

Yet, surprisingly, this sinister termagant may have been a believer in the Jewish faith—despite her taste for astrology. Significantly, she took ritual baths and enrolled a large number of Jews among her entourage. Describing how Poppaea had helped Rabbi Ishmael's delegation, Josephus comments mysteriously and without elaboration that she was "a worshipper of God."[12]

On being presented to her—if we can accept Tacitus's description of Poppaea—Josephus found himself confronted by not a ferocious slut but a dignified, surprisingly prudish-looking young lady who, as far as he could make out, was staggeringly beautiful, although it was difficult to be sure because in public she hid her face behind a veil. She gave him a gracious welcome. "As soon as I could, I begged her to help me in getting the priests released from prison," he writes in his autobiography.[13] Poppaea took a strong liking to this eloquent, intelligent, and no doubt charming young Jewish nobleman. Not only did she obtain the priests' release, but she loaded him with expensive gifts.

If a fine first-century portrait bust really is that of Josephus, then it may well have been commissioned by Poppaea, which indicates a certain affection on her part. Handsome, sensitive, and a little melancholy, this is the face of someone who in time could have developed considerable force of character. The fact that it is indistinguishable from that of a young Roman patrician shows how quickly he had adapted to life at Nero's court.

However, if he developed any hopes of a career as one of the empress's courtiers, they came to an abrupt end at some date in 65 CE when her bad-tempered husband killed her with a kick when she was pregnant—"for scolding him for coming home late from the races."[14] There were rumors of poison, but in reality Nero was heartbroken. He had Poppaea embalmed instead of cremated and gave her a state funeral at which he praised her beauty and good qualities.[15]

Josephus spent from two to two and a half years at Rome. He must have been there during the firestorm that broke out on 18 July 64 and raged for ten days, destroying most of the city. The emperor himself was widely believed to have ordered his secret agents to start the fire, prompted by the whim that he could rebuild it more beautifully. "To get rid of the rumours, he falsely blamed the people popularly known as Christians, who were hated for their crimes, and punished them with exquisite tortures," says Tacitus, explaining that anybody who admitted to being one was wrapped in animal skins and fed to savage dogs, nailed to a cross or "set alight at dusk to illuminate the night."[16] Even the Roman mob felt sorry for them. Nero placed these human torches in his own gardens, which he opened to the public, so it is possible that Josephus saw them burning.

Although Josephus does not mention it—he was writing for the later Flavian emperors at the time—he may have actually met Nero, aside from simply seeing him on one of his frequent public appearances. "Of about average height, his body was pockmarked and smelly, while he had light yellow hair, good but not handsome features, blue, rather weak eyes, too thick a neck, a big belly and spindly legs," is Suetonius's feline description of the last of the Julian dynasty. "He was ridiculously fussy about his person and his clothes, having his hair done in rows of curls."[17] However, suggestions that the emperor personally recruited Josephus as a secret agent and gave him specific orders for undercover activities in Judea can be dismissed as melodramatic speculation.[18]

From talking to people in the street, he learned that the Romans were never going to forgive Nero for his murders, let alone for the fire. Jewish friends must have been worried by the regime's growing instability. Yet he may have received other favors from the emperor besides the release of the priests. His account of him, written years after, is remarkable for what it leaves out. While describing how Nero poisoned his brother, had his own mother murdered, and killed his wife Octavia, he condemns other historians for what they write about Nero: "they rave against him impertinently, telling all sorts of lies . . . with no respect for truth."[19] Perhaps such uncharacteristic restraint conceals some sort of gratitude.

He must have been received by Poppaea at Nero's colossal new palace, built after the fire, which reached from the Palatine Hill to the Esquiline and had a triple colonnade in front that was a mile wide. The entrance hall contained a statue of the Emperor Nero calculated to overawe the most hard-boiled; Suetonius says it stood one hundred and twenty feet tall. The palace's interior was covered in gold, inlaid with gems and mother-of-pearl. The ceilings in its dining rooms were made of carved ivory, with panels that opened to shower the guests with flower petals as pipes sprinkled them with perfume. The main banquet hall was circular and revolved. The baths were constantly filled with seawater or sulfur water.[20] But the "Golden House" was just one among the innumerable marvels of this amazing city.

Friends would point out the leading courtiers. Among them were three future rulers of Rome. The most distinguished was a bald, grim-faced septuagenarian, Servius Sulpicius Galba, an old-fashioned Roman aristocrat of whom Tacitus observed in a famous epigram, "had he never become Emperor, no one would have doubted his ability to reign."[21] Short and bandy-legged, Salvius Otho, who wore a wig, was more dangerous than he looked; the former husband of Poppaea, he had been forced to divorce her although he was wildly in love with her. The third, the perpetually drunken Aulus Vitellius, with his huge stomach and obsequious manner, was altogether lacking in dignity. Every courtier took care to flatter Nero, but Vitellius literally groveled in his presence. He was the cheerleader of the claque that shamelessly applauded whenever the emperor gave one of his stage performances.

Someone else who fawned on Nero was King Agrippa II. Born in 27 CE, the last of the Herodian dynasty, he was king of only a scrappy domain that included Gaulonitis, Batanea, and Trachonitis—east of the Sea of Tiberias—together with the Galilean cities of Tiberias and Taricheae. Constantly commuting between Caesarea and Italy, Agrippa frequented Nero's court in the vain hope of being created King of Judea. Despite his ancestors' Idumean blood, and although he had been brought up in Rome where he felt thoroughly at home, he regarded himself as totally Jewish and sometimes occupied his family palace at Jerusalem.

We know from what he wrote how much Josephus admired the soldiers of Rome. He must have watched the crack legionaries who regularly paraded on the Campus Martius with highly polished weapons and armor, led by eagle-bearers in lion skins, performing meticulous drill movements at the order of red-cloaked centurions—each in command of a century of eighty men. He would also have encountered the superb Praetorian guards at the gates of the imperial palaces. Here is a summary of his impressions after he had seen the legions in action.

What they undergo when training is in no way different from fighting, since each soldier is trained every day as if on campaign, with the utmost thoroughness, which is why they always stand up so well to the rigors of war. No setback affects their discipline, they are incapable of panic and cannot be frightened, while nothing tires them, with the result that they invariably defeat untrained opponents. It is no exaggeration to say that their drilling is a bloodless battle and their battles are blood-stained drilling. The enemy never has a chance of catching them off guard because as soon as they march into his territory they refuse to go into action until they have fortified their camp . . . Nothing is done without a command. At first light, the legionaries report to their centurions and the centurions go to salute their tribunes, every senior officer then going to their general, who gives them the watchword for the day together with his orders. . . .

Foot-soldiers wear breastplate and helmet, with a sword on each side, the longer on the left while that on the right is only nine inches long. The picked troops around the general are armed with a half-pike and small shield, but most of the infantry are equipped with a javelin and a long shield, a saw, a [hod-like] basket and a pick, together with an axe, a strap and a sickle, besides enough provisions for three days—so there is not much difference between an infantry man and a packhorse. A caval-ryman has a long sword at his right side and carries a lance, protected by a shield slanted to cover his horse's flank, while he also has a quiver hold-ing three broad-bladed javelins that are not much smaller than spears. Like the foot-soldiers, he wears breastplate and helmet.[22]

This account needs qualification. Although they had metal helmets, le-gionaries wore armor made from hardened leather straps and metal studs and carried oblong leather shields that were strengthened with iron. Offi-cers (including centurions) were distinguished by cuirasses of scale, chain, or plate armor, red horsehair crests, and colored cloaks. The sword—worn on the right side and not on the left, as Josephus says—was the gladius, a short, straight weapon with a blade two feet long and two inches wide. The javelin was the pilum, with a slender wooden shaft four and half feet long with a barbed iron head of the same length—its neck made of soft metal, which bent and hung down after piercing an enemy's shield, so as to hamper him. The stirrup had not yet been invented, and a charge by mounted troops did not have the impact it would have in later centuries. Nor does Josephus appreciate that the tools carried by the legionaries made them sappers as well as frontline troops. Disciplined until teamwork be-came second nature, trained not only to fight but as skilled siege engineers, they were capable of building or demolishing elaborate fortifications.

What he did not see on parade on the Campus Martius was the auxiliary cavalry recruited locally wherever the army was operating, light horse who were armed with bows, lances, and javelins. In addition there were swarms of auxiliary foot soldiers, such as archers and slingers.

"Because they always agree on a carefully thought out plan before going into action, and since the plan is implemented by such a formidable army, it is scarcely surprising that in the east the Euphrates, in the west the ocean, in the south the rich part of Africa, and in the north the Danube and the Rhine have become the frontiers of their empire," he tells us. He adds that "my reason for giving this description is not to praise the Romans, but simply to console all the people they have conquered, besides warning anybody who has any foolish ideas about trying to resist them."[23]

Most soldiers seen by Josephus in Judea had been recruited locally and were of poor quality, if good enough for tracking down bandits.[24] Even regular troops ran to seed in the East. "Legionaries brought in from Syria had been demoralized by not being on active service for a long time, and as a result the majority proved incapable of doing the job of a Roman soldier properly," says Tacitus, writing of a campaign against the Parthians about 60 CE. "There were veterans in their ranks who had never mounted guard or done sentry duty, and found any fortification totally impregnable, men who refused to wear helmets or body armour, a useless bunch of swaggering bullies whose sole concern was loot."[25] Now, however, Josephus saw the best troops of a regular army numbering a quarter of a million men. It must have dawned on him that nobody could hope to defeat them.

Having made a success of a difficult mission, Josephus went home to Judea. After Poppaea's death there was no point in staying at Rome. Yet his time there had begun his transformation into a Diaspora Jew who took a keen interest in Greek literature, while his visits to the imperial court had given him a firsthand knowledge of Roman politics and how to deal with Rome's ruling class. At the same time, his encounters with the Hebrew community had shown him that one could be both a Jew and a loyal Roman. Above all, he had seen the irresistible might of the legions.

4

The Jew Baiter

"It was [the procurator] Florus who gave us no option other than to fight the Romans, as we thought that it would be better to be destroyed at once instead of little by little."
JOSEPHUS, *JEWISH ANTIQUITIES*, 20, 257

JOSEPHUS SAILED HOME to Judea at some date during the first half of 66, no doubt expecting to be warmly congratulated. He had every reason to think that, together with his important contacts at Rome, his success should open up all sorts of opportunities that would enable him to aim at such prizes as membership of the Sanhedrin. But as soon as he reached Caesarea, he found a totally different climate from the one that existed when he had left Judea. A great deal had happened while he was away because of a man who, to use an anachronistic term, was one of the most baneful anti-Semites in history.

This was the new procurator, Gessius Florus, a Roman by blood although born in Greek Clazomenae on the coast of Asia Minor. He brought with him a promisingly named wife, Cleopatra, whose friendship with the Empress Poppaea had got him his post in Judea. Josephus says tantalizingly that she was "in no way different from [her husband] in wickedness" but gives us no further details.[1] Florus was a man who boasted about how he ill-treated his "subjects," punishing innocent Jews as if they were criminals, while practicing all kinds of robbery and graft. No one had more contempt for the truth or was better at telling lies. "He plundered whole cities and ruined entire communities, more or less giving official permission for anyone to turn bandit so long as he shared in the loot," Josephus tells us. "Because of his greed for money, complete districts were laid waste, many people fleeing from their homeland and taking refuge abroad."[2]

Florus had developed a devouring hatred for the people he ruled, possibly after trouble with Jewish communities in Asia Minor. It is clear that from the start he had made up his mind to do the Jews of Judea all the harm he could. As he tried to goad them into a rebellion against the Roman imperial authority that would provide him with the excuse he needed for retaliation, his behavior verged increasingly on insanity. The account which follows of the horrors he perpetrated is taken almost verbatim from Josephus's *Jewish War*. Even the hostile Tacitus admits that Florus pushed the Jews' patience beyond the breaking point.[3] Although Josephus had not yet returned to Judea, he spoke to eyewitnesses who had been caught up in these events, enabling him to recreate them for his readers.

Nobody dared to complain to the legate of Syria, Cestius Gallus, until he visited Jerusalem on the eve of Passover. Then a vast crowd begged him to remove Florus, "who stood beside him laughing." Cestius, an elderly mediocrity with no idea of how dangerous the situation was becoming, promised he would see that the procurator treated them fairly, after which he went back to Antioch. Florus accompanied him as far as Caesarea, hiding his fury. He also concealed his plan to make a war break out, since (if Josephus can be believed) he had decided that it was the only way to hide his crimes; if peace continued, the Jews would find a means of appealing to Caesar.

In reality, there was no point in making an appeal to the imperial lunatic at Rome. Nero was not even in his capital but wandering around Greece and pretending to be an actor. Before he went off on his holiday—and before Florus's arrival in Judea—in answer to a desperate plea from the Caesarean Jews for help against the Greeks, he sent back a rescript drafted by his secretary, Beryllus, who had been bribed by the city's Greek community.[4] The rescript deprived the Jews of every privilege they had secured over the years, giving complete control of Caesarea to the Greeks, who at once took the opportunity to build a row of shops and block access to a synagogue. Misguidedly, the Jewish elders then paid Florus a large sum of money to see that the shops were removed, but he simply pocketed the bribe and allowed the rioters to expel all Jews from the city. The Greeks' next action was to perform a parody of Jewish sacrifice outside the synagogue, using an upturned chamber pot as an "altar." When the elders complained to Florus, demanding their money back, he imprisoned them—on the charge of removing copies of the Torah from Caesarea. Understandably, his behavior caused outrage in Jerusalem. Josephus believed that the rescript was a major factor in causing "the miseries which befell our nation."[5]

Jerusalem became the scene of the procurator's next misdeed. Here he acted as if he had been encouraged to "blow the war into flame," seizing the enormous sum of seventeen talents from the Temple treasury, on the pretense that Caesar needed it, a deliberate affront to the entire Jewish people. In response, a mob rushed into the Temple, calling on Nero by name, imploring him to free them from Florus's government, while another group paraded a begging bowl around the city in cheerful derision, telling bystanders that the procurator was destitute and faint from hunger. Enraged by the insult, Florus marched on the city with a large detachment of troops, sending fifty cavalry ahead. When a big crowd went out to welcome the horsemen, hoping to placate Florus, the troops were ordered to disperse them with a charge.

On 16 May—the day after he arrived at the palace—Florus had his judge's chair placed on a platform outside, summoned Jerusalem's leading citizens, and demanded that all demonstrators be handed over to him, threatening that otherwise they themselves would be punished. In response, the citizens insisted that the city's population was peace-loving, apologizing for any insults and begging him to pardon the people who had caused the uproar. Inevitably, they explained, the crowd had included some stupid young hotheads, and while it was impossible to identify those who were guilty, every one of them was sorry for what he had done. For the sake of the nation and if he wanted to keep the city safe for the Romans, the procurator would be well advised to forgive the guilty few rather than punish a large number of innocent people.

Florus was infuriated by this reasonable appeal. His reaction was to let his troops loose on the Upper Market, telling them to sack the entire district and kill anybody they met. Jew-haters (most of them seem to have been Samaritans) who were eager for loot, they obeyed with unrestrained savagery, breaking into the houses, slaughtering every man, woman, and child they found inside. The inhabitants fled through the streets, hotly pursued, many more being cut down, while others were dragged before the procurator, who had them scourged and crucified. Josephus was told that, including infants in arms, over 3,500 people died that day. What was extraordinary, however, was the unheard-of way in which members of the Jewish ruling class, pillars of the imperial regime, were treated. "For Florus dared to do what no one had ever dared to do before, to have men of equestrian rank whipped before his judgment seat and then nailed to crosses, men who although they were Jews were also Roman citizens."[6]

King Agrippa II's sister, Berenice, was in Jerusalem to make a thirty days' thanksgiving for a blessing from God—abstaining from wine and shaving her head. (Although she had married her uncle and was rumored to sleep with her brother, in her own way she was devout enough.) She sent her master of horse and the captain of her bodyguard to Florus, begging him to stop the bloodshed, but he took no notice, while his soldiers deliberately tortured people to death in front of her. They even tried to kill her, but she escaped into her palace where she spent the night under the protection of her guards. Although Berenice had stood barefoot with her cropped head in front of Florus's platform, she had been ignored by him and was lucky to escape with her life.

Next day, mourners poured into the Upper Market, bewailing the dead and cursing the procurator. Knowing Florus's insane temper, the more important citizens and high priests implored the crowd of mourners not to provoke any further bloodshed, as they wept, tore their clothes, and heaped dust on their heads. The crowd dispersed, realizing the wisdom of this appeal and that they were in serious danger with such a madman in charge.

The last thing Florus wanted was for the demonstrations to die down. Sending for the high priests and the city's other leaders, he told them that the only way the people of Jerusalem could prove they were not going to revolt again was to go into the countryside and welcome two cohorts of soldiers marching up from Caesarea. At the same time he sent orders to his officers to cut down anyone who uttered a word against him. After much persuasion by the priests, a crowd marched out to meet them quietly enough, but when the troops ignored their greetings they shouted abuse at the procurator. Immediately one of the cohorts charged, chasing the panic-stricken mob back to Jerusalem, many of them being trampled to death while trying to get through the gates.

The soldiers burst into the city with them but were suddenly checked by the Jews, who seized whatever weapons they could find, hurling spears and tiles down from the rooftops. They also demolished the porticos between the Temple and the Antonia, making it impossible for Florus to launch a further raid on the treasury. Baffled, he withdrew the cohort that had been engaged, leaving the other, as requested by the city authorities, who promised to keep order. He then sent a report to Cestius at Antioch, claiming that the Jews had begun the fighting and started a revolt.

However, the Jews' leaders wrote to Cestius to explain what had really happened, as did Berenice. After consulting his officers, a very worried Cestius sent a tribune named Neopolitanus to investigate. He arrived at Jerusalem at the same time as Agrippa, a mob going out for miles to greet them, led by the dead men's wailing widows. Complaining to both men about Florus's atrocities, the citizens showed them the blood-stained Upper Market where the massacre had taken place, together with the looted houses. They also persuaded Neopolitanus to walk round the city with a single servant, so he would realize there was no hostility against Romans apart from Florus and his thugs. The tribune was convinced that no one in Jerusalem wanted a revolt, and before leaving he even prayed in his pagan way at the Temple, in the Court of the Gentiles. Apparently, he took back a reassuring report to Cestius at Antioch: If there were trouble-makers in the city, most citizens wanted peace and the continuation of Roman government.[7]

Meanwhile the Jews begged Agrippa and the high priests to send an embassy to Nero to denounce Florus, arguing that if they did not, the fighting would be taken as evidence of their guilt. Agrippa disagreed; perhaps he feared Nero might make matters worse. Despite the good impression received by Neopolitanus, Agrippa realized there was every likelihood of a full-scale rebellion. Deciding to make a speech, he asked his sister, Berenice, to support him by sitting in a window of the Hasmonean palace so that the crowd could see her watching while he delivered it. These two last Herodians hoped to appeal to any lingering loyalty to their dynasty.

Standing outside the Temple, he delivered a long, impassioned harangue. Josephus was not there to hear it, but almost certainly Agrippa gave him a copy of it years later, and although he polished the speech to look like something from the Greek classics, his version carries conviction. It also conveys Josephus's own considered view of the situation, which was probably that of most of the Jewish ruling class. What follows is the gist of Agrippa's speech.

"If I thought you all wanted to fight the Romans and that the honest and good hearted among you were tired of living in peace, then I should not bother to make a speech like this," said Agrippa. "But I realize that a lot of you are young men who have not known the horror of war, that others are over optimistic about gaining independence, and that selfish people hope to profit from it." He was well aware of how much they had suffered, how pleasant freedom from foreign rule must seem. Even so, they should submit. "I can see that the procurator ill-treats you." This did not mean that all Romans were ill-treating them, let alone Caesar; no one in Rome knew what was going on. Why make war because of one man when their much better armed ancestors had been conquered by Pompey with a small detachment of legionaries. Yet now they were proposing to challenge the full might of the entire Roman Empire.

"Just what sort of an army have you got, and what sort of weapons?" asked Agrippa. "Do you have a fleet to take control of the seas from the Romans, do you have the money to pay for the campaigns?" Then he listed in detail all the nations that had been conquered by Rome and how. "Despite the Britons living on an island as big as this entire continent, protected by an ocean, the Romans crossed the sea and crushed them—today, a mere four legions are enough to run the place." If the Jews went to war, the Romans would certainly burn down Jerusalem and exterminate the entire nation. "If you won't have pity on your wives and children, at least have pity on your capital and its holy walls, have pity on the Temple and the Sanctuary."[8]

At the end of his speech Agrippa and his sister burst into tears. Deeply moved, the people of Jerusalem shouted they had never had any intention of fighting Rome, but only wanted to fight Florus because of what he had done to them. Agrippa replied that they had already been fighting Rome, by not paying the tribute due to Caesar and by pulling down the porticos between the Temple and the Antonia Fortress. However, if they paid the tribute and rebuilt the colonnades, then that would be an end to it, since the Antonia was not Florus's business nor was he going to be paid the tribute.

The Temple porticos were repaired and the arrears of tribute owing to Caesar began to be collected from the villages. It looked as if Agrippa had managed to avert the war.

Then he overplayed his hand, by announcing that the Jews must continue to obey Florus until Rome appointed a successor. Terrified by the prospect of what Florus might do to them, a mob gathered in front of the king's palace, yelling abuse and throwing stones. In despair, Agrippa left Jerusalem for the safety of his border kingdom. Yet he was still hoping to defuse the situation by sending an embassy of rich—and no doubt very apprehensive—citizens to Florus at Caesarea with a message that advised the procurator to employ them if he wanted to collect the remainder of Caesar's tribute.[9]

It was plain that the peace party could expect nothing more from the king; he was obviously too committed to Rome.

5

War

"And the Lord discomfited them before Israel, and slew them with a great slaughter at Gibeon, and chased them along the way that goeth up to Beth-horon."

JOSHUA, X, 10

IN JULY 66 CE the disturbances at Jerusalem turned into a revolt that became a full-scale war of independence. The first, unmistakable sign was when Eleazar, captain of the Temple and son of Ananias ben Nedebaeus, the high priest—and the person once kidnapped by the *sicarii*—persuaded the priests who were in charge of the sacrifices not to accept further gifts from gentiles or to make any more offerings on their behalf. Obviously, Josephus knew Eleazar, whom he describes with a distinct lack of enthusiasm as "a very confident young man."[1] He may have learned his extremist views from the knifemen while he was being held as a hostage by them. Although Eleazar was the son of a high priest, many of his followers came from the poverty-stricken lower clergy, who bitterly resented the high priests and the upper class.

Josephus describes the critical turning point in the crisis: "The moment when our war with the Romans really began was when the [priests] refused to go on sacrificing on behalf of Caesar. Although many of the high priests and notables implored them not to stop the usual offerings for the [Roman] government, they remained obdurate. Why they were so sure of themselves was because there were such a lot of them, while they looked for leadership to Eleazar, the Temple captain."[2] What was particularly alarming was that Eleazar was a patrician, a member of the class on whose cooperation the Roman regime depended. He may well have been one of the young hotheads to whom Agrippa had alluded in his speech a few days before.

In the meantime, a band of Zealot *sicarii*, who wanted war and freedom at any cost, seized the great Herodian stronghold of Masada on the Dead Sea. They took it by treachery, slaughtering every Roman inside, and installed a garrison of their own, which would hold the fortress for the next seven years. This was a deliberate act of rebellion, even more unmistakable than the insult made to Caesar at the Temple.

At Jerusalem, realizing that a crisis had been reached, the high priests and notables called a public meeting at the "bronze gate" (the gate into the inner Temple or Court of the Priests). Led by Ananias, they pleaded frantically that the sacrifices in honor of Caesar be resumed. However, they were shouted down by the extremists, who included the Temple officials and lower clergy. Fearful that Rome was going to blame them, they sent delegations to Florus and Agrippa, insisting that they were guiltless of disloyalty to the emperor.

Many of the poor joined the rebellion, which took place at a time when fresh hardships were afflicting a country already made restive by savage taxation. It seems that Judea had suffered from a series of bad harvests and that more farmers than ever were losing their holdings. Many went to beg in Jerusalem where, despite the alms of the devout, people were already starving. Josephus tells us that 18,000 workmen had been laid off when the Temple was completed in 64 CE, though some found employment in paving the capital's streets with white marble. The Jews had become "two nations," the have-nots identifying Roman government with the rich. Significantly, the rebels burned down not only the palaces of Agrippa and Berenice and the house of the high priest Ananias but also the archives containing debtors' records. Josephus says they did so with the express purpose of winning over poor men to their cause.[3]

Weapons were available, if scarcely those of soldiers. Because of the threat from brigands and thieves, a fair number of Jews owned spears or swords. Apparently, the spears were of a type that if necessary could be thrown like javelins, while the swords were not much bigger than long knives and resembled the daggers used by *sicarii*. In addition, many must have possessed hunting bows and also slings for shooting birds. Later, these haphazard arms would be supplemented with weapons from the arsenals in the Herodian royal palaces as well as captured Roman equipment.

Florus did not even bother to answer the high priests' envoys, "as he had always meant to start a war."[4] Agrippa was horrified and immediately dispatched 3,000 cavalry to Jerusalem. When they arrived, the peace party joined them in the Upper City, while the rebels under Eleazar occupied the Lower City and the Temple. Seven days of slaughter followed, each side trying to drive the other from their strongholds with an exchange of spears, slingshots, and stones. The loyalists and Agrippa's men were out-numbered, and eventually Eleazar's men, aided by *sicarii*, drove them from the Upper City. Some of the high priests and notables hid in the sewers while others, including Ananias—father of the rebel leader—shut them-selves inside the Upper Palace. Two days later, on 17 August, the rebels stormed the Antonia, massacring the defenders. For the moment, the loy-alists held out in the Upper Palace.

A new leader now emerged: Menahem, a son of the Zealot Judas the Galilean and the *sicarii*'s current chief, seems to have seen himself as an-other Judas Maccabaeus. Accompanied by like-minded extremists and joined by a large number of bandits en route, he went to Masada, where he broke into the arsenal, taking any weapons needed to turn his followers into a formidable bodyguard. He then returned to Jerusalem, robed like a king, to assume command of the rebellion and organize the siege of the Upper Palace. Since his men lacked siege engines, they undermined a bas-tion, which they brought crashing down on 6 September. Those of its de-fenders who were Jews were allowed to withdraw unharmed, as were Agrippa's men. Most of the Roman troops managed to escape to the three great towers of King Herod's palace, but the rest were killed as they tried to reach safety. Next day, the high priest Ananias and his brother Hezekiah—two men who epitomized the old regime—had their throats cut by Menahem's men after they were caught hiding in an aqueduct.[5]

Drunk with success, especially at having killed Ananias, Menahem be-came impossibly arrogant, torturing and murdering opponents. People began to grumble that there did not seem to be much point in exchanging a Roman tyrant for a Jewish one, particularly for a man of such obscure background. One day, when he appeared in the Temple in royal robes, he was suddenly attacked by Ananias's son Eleazar and the Temple guard, the spectators joining in with stones until he and his bodyguard fled. Captured at Ophales, Menahem was tortured to death, along with his leading henchmen. A few escaped to Masada, among them someone of whom more will be heard—his kinsman, Eleazar ben Yair.

Menahem's royal pretensions are not without significance, however. Less than two hundred and fifty years earlier, Judas Maccabaeus had defeated a far more numerous enemy army of experienced soldiers with a makeshift guerrilla force. Why should God not intervene and save his chosen people once again? Clearly, Menahem had hoped to reincarnate the Maccabee monarchy. No doubt, he was unbalanced and had failed, but it is obvious that the memory of the first Maccabees remained very much alive and was still an inspiration to the Jewish nation.

What was left of the Roman garrison held out in the more or less impregnable towers of Hippicus, Phasael, and Mariamne. Losing his nerve, the commander, Metilius, asked for terms. It was agreed on oath that the troops' lives would be spared if they surrendered their weapons, but when they marched out and laid down their swords and shields, they were butchered on the spot. Only Metilius (probably one of the few genuine Romans among them) was spared, after begging to become a Jew and be circumcised in return for his life. Everyone knew that there was no turning back after a massacre on this scale. "The city was full of sadness, moderate men being appalled at the thought of having to pay for the rebels' crime," comments Josephus, adding, "These murders were committed on the Sabbath, the day on which Jews refrain from labor for reasons of religion."[6]

On the same day that the garrison in Jerusalem was cut down (17 September), the Greeks in Caesarea took the opportunity to slaughter their city's Jewish community, presumably with Florus's encouragement. On the Sabbath, when they were all in their homes or at the synagogues, 20,000 men, women, and children were killed within an hour. Florus caught the few who escaped and sent them to the galleys. The bloodshed spread, as Greeks massacred Jews throughout Judea and Syria. The victims included not just Hebrews but converts to the Jewish faith as well. At Ashkelon, 2,500 were killed, and almost as many perished at Ptolemais (Akka), while thousands more were murdered at Tyre, Hippos, Gadara, and other cities and in the surrounding villages. Yet nowhere had the Jews given their neighbors any possible grounds for suspicion.

This thirst for Hebrew blood also affected Egypt. After some vicious provocation by the local Greeks, the vast Jewish colony at Alexandria rioted so menacingly that the panic-stricken Roman governor sent his legionaries into the Jewish quarter of Alexandria known as the Delta, with specific orders to kill, loot, and burn the houses. The Jews put up a gallant resistance with what weapons they could lay hands on, but they were overwhelmed. The legionaries then proceeded to slaughter people of all ages "till the place overflowed with blood and 50,000 lay dead in heaps." Even the governor was shaken, calling off his men, but he could not stop the Alexandrians from savaging the bodies.[7]

These pogroms were partly due to a violent Jewish reaction to the news from Judea. Florus's calculated refusal to restrain the Caesarean Greeks from launching a pogrom had triggered a bloodbath, as the Jews attacked Greek towns and villages in revenge, killing large numbers of their inhabitants. Every city in Syria and non-Jewish Judea was split into two murderous armed camps, "the daytime spent in shedding blood, the night-time in fear, the latter being the more terrible." Besides revenge, loot was a strong motive on both sides. "It was quite usual to see cities full of unburied bodies, with those of old men and babies strewn all over the place, the women's corpses lying naked."[8]

In the midst of this mayhem, the Jews showed sound strategic sense. They captured the fortress of Cypros, which commanded Jericho, cutting the Roman defenders' throats and demolishing its fortifications. They also talked the enemy garrison at Machaerus into surrender, installing a garrison of their own at this reputedly impregnable fortress on the cliffs east of the Dead Sea.

∽

It seems clear that Josephus returned from Rome at about this time, during September 66 CE but before the pogrom at Caesarea, since otherwise he would have been murdered as soon as he stepped off the boat. He must have been horrified by the situation in Jerusalem.

> I found a lot happening that was completely new, with all too many people wildly enthusiastic at the prospect of a revolt against Rome. So I did my best to dissuade the men who were attempting to make us revolt. I tried as hard as I could to make them see reason. I told them to think about what sort of a nation it was they were going to fight, to remember that they did not have Romans' military training or the same unfailing good luck in war. I warned them not to be so reckless, not so crazy as to expose their land and families and themselves to the most dreadful danger. Using arguments like these, fully aware that a war of this sort could only end in disaster for us, again and again I tried to stop them. But it was no good. I lacked the powers of persuasion that might just possibly have shaken them out of their imbecility.[9]

Suddenly, he realized that he might be arrested and murdered out of hand, partly because of his plain speaking and partly because more than a few members of his class were already suspected of collaborating. Josephus probably looked very much the noble, in a silk tunic and wearing a gold ring. It was time for him to hide. The Antonia had already been captured so he took refuge in the inner court of the Temple, which he could enter because he was a priest. No doubt he disguised himself in cheaper clothing, taking care to avoid any smart acquaintances, since the lower clergy who staffed the Temple were staunch supporters of Eleazar and fanatically anti-Roman. The fact that he had been away for so long may have given him anonymity. He did not dare to emerge until Menahem and his friends disappeared from the scene.

> Then I felt safe enough to venture out of the Temple and was once again able to talk to important people [who mattered]—high priests and influential Pharisees. Naturally, we were all very worried. We could see the people arming and had no idea what to do because we had no way of stopping the rebels. Aware every moment of the day that each one of us was in real danger, we tactfully pretended to share their opinions, but at least we tried to suggest they should do nothing rash and ought to leave

the enemy alone until he attacked, so as to have the excuse of only using weapons in self-defense. While doing this, we were of course all hoping that Cestius was soon going to arrive with a large army and quickly put an end to the rebellion.[10]

At Antioch, Cestius Gallus realized that he had to act without further delay, as the Romans normally campaigned only between March and September. He assembled a formidable army, his best force being the Twelfth Legion Fulminata (the "Thunderer"), which may have numbered 6,000 men if up to strength, along with about 2,000 men from each of the other three legions stationed in Syria. He also took six cohorts and four troops of local recruits. (A cohort consisted of roughly 600 men.) In addition, he had 20,000 auxiliaries supplied by friendly potentates such as King Agrippa II and by the Syrian cities of northern Judea. Mainly light horse or bowmen, these native levies were of questionable value, but at least they could be relied on to hate Jews.

Accompanied by Agrippa who acted as his guide, Cestius marched down the coast to Ptolemais, from where he sent out a detachment to destroy the beautiful city of Zabulon, burning it to the ground, while he himself sacked the Jewish villages in the area. During his absence, however, a Jewish force attacked Ptolemais, killing 2,000 troops. He then marched on to Caesarea, where he set up his base. From here his men ravaged the surrounding country and put the villages to the torch, besides exterminating the entire population of Joppa—over 8,000 people—after surrounding the city by sea and land so that no one could escape. Finding Lydda empty of inhabitants, save for fifty who were butchered, he burned it to the ground.

The commander of the Twelfth Legion, Caesennius Gallus, advanced into Galilee with a strong detachment, receiving a warm welcome at the capital, Sepphoris. Even so, some guerrillas held out in the mountains in central Galilee and inflicted 200 casualties when the Romans approached. However, the legionaries quickly outflanked them, killing about 2,000 and ending armed resistance in the area—for the time being.

These tactics were designed to terrify Judea into abject submission, particularly Jerusalem, and were standard Roman practice. No doubt, Cestius expected he would have very little trouble when he reached the capital.

However, he had given all too clear warning of his approach and was in for a very nasty surprise.

Marching by way of Antipatris and Lydda and climbing Beth-horon, Cestius pitched camp at Gibeon, six miles from Jerusalem. He was accompanied by Gessius Florus. Although it was the Sabbath, the Jews attacked the Romans here, with such fury that they broke through their ranks and killed over 500 of them while incurring a loss of only twenty-two men on their side, before retreating into the city. A ferocious young man called Simon bar Giora—who subsequently came to play a major role in the war with Rome—fell on the enemy rearguard while it was ascending Beth-horon, inflicting further casualties and capturing a mule train laden with weapons.

King Agrippa II made a final, frantic effort to secure a peaceful solution, sending two of his men, who were well known in Jerusalem, to promise the Jews that Cestius would do his best to persuade Caesar to give them a complete pardon if they laid down their arms. Fearful that the offer might be accepted, the extremists deliberately killed one of the envoys and wounded the other, who barely escaped with his life by running away. If Josephus has told the truth, a great crowd of people in the city were so angry at losing this last opportunity of ending the conflict that they stoned the saboteurs of the king's peace efforts.

The legate now moved his headquarters camp closer to Jerusalem, up onto Mount Scopus ("Lookout Hill"), which was a mere three-quarters of a mile away from the walls. However, he did not launch an assault for another three days, as he was still hoping the city would surrender; in the meantime he sent out foragers to gather provisions. At last, on 4 October, he made a move and—no doubt much to his astonishment—was able to march his men into the Upper City without meeting any resistance, setting fire to Bezetha (the New City) and the timber market, before setting up a new camp outside Herod's Palace. Terrified, the extremists and their followers retreated into the Inner City and the Temple.

Had Cestius forced his way into the Temple at this moment, the rebellion would have been over. However, he was persuaded to postpone the attack by his quartermaster, who had been bribed by Florus, desperate to have a war. As it was, Ananus, son of Jonathan, sent a message to the legate, saying he would open the gates, but Cestius refused to believe that the message was genuine. Next day, the Roman assault began in earnest, but the hard-liners had regained their nerve and resisted fiercely. After five days of inconclusive fighting, the legate sent in his best troops supported by picked archers, attacking the Temple from the north side, yet the defenders beat them off time and again with a hail of missiles.

Finally, the legionaries adopted the Roman tactic known as the *testudo* (tortoise), which consisted of holding their shields over their heads so that any spears thrown at them glanced off harmlessly. Protected like this, they were able to undermine the wall and set the Temple gate alight. Some of the defenders fled while supporters of the Romans prepared to open the gate, led by Ananus ben Jonathan, who seems to have been a member of the ruling class. Josephus may well have been among them. "If Cestius had kept on for just a little longer, he would certainly have captured the city," he says. "But I think those criminal rebels had already made God take a deep dislike to both city and sanctuary, and that He would not allow the war to come to an end."[11]

The legate did not realize that his opponents had nearly abandoned hope or that he had so many supporters inside the city. Suddenly, he called off the attack. He withdrew from Jerusalem to his camp on Mount Scopus, as the defenders harried his rearguard, killing a substantial number of Romans. Next day, Cestius withdrew still further, again for no apparent reason. Led by Eleazar ben Simon, his enemies followed closely, throwing javelins from the roadside at his columns and cutting down stragglers, the lightly armed Jews being able to dodge their heavily equipped opponents. Sometimes the Roman formations disintegrated, making the soldiers still more vulnerable. Among the casualties were the commander of the Sixth Legion and a tribune, along with other senior officers. They also lost a great deal of baggage.

Withdrawal turned into retreat and retreat into a rout. Cestius attempted to make a stand in his fortified camp at Gibeon, but after two days he saw that he was almost surrounded by the insurgents whose numbers, now that they were winning, grew by the hour. On the third day, 8 November, he decided to pull out, killing all his pack mules except those that carried throwing spears and siege weaponry. As he and his men painfully descended the narrow, difficult road down from Gibeon to Beth-horon, the Jews kept up a constant hail of spears, inflicting more and more casualties. It was too steep for cavalry to have any chance of dispersing them; what is more, the legionaries could not keep their ranks, so their shields and armor failed to provide enough protection. Roman morale began to break, the men groaning and cursing. In contrast, the Jews were cheering. But for nightfall, Cestius and his whole army would have been butchered or taken prisoner.

During the night of 8 November, Cestius positioned 400 crack troops at what seemed to be a defensible site on Beth-horon, with orders that on next morning they should hoist emblems that would give the impression he and the army were still inside. Then, abandoning his siege weaponry, he and the rest of his men marched off as quietly as possible while it was still dark. The next morning, the Jews came up, overwhelmed and massacred the 400 legionaries, and then set off in hot pursuit of the retreating legionaries. But by then Cestius and the bulk of his troops had got too far ahead and were able to reach Syria in safety. Not since Varus's defeat by the Germans sixty years earlier had the armies of Rome experienced such a crushing defeat.

Singing with joy, the Jews returned to Jerusalem and a heroes' welcome. They carried the arms and armor stripped from the dead Romans, which could be used to equip their own men. They also brought back the siege weaponry and heavy artillery abandoned by the Romans in their flight, which included stone-throwing catapults for demolishing walls and large, quick-firing mechanical bows that shot a huge arrow capable of going straight through several men one after another. These, too, would be employed against the enemy in future battles. In addition, they seem to have captured Cestius's war chest, which contained a large sum of money.

During the recent engagement at Beth-horon the Jews had suffered surprisingly few casualties, despite fighting the legionaries at close quarters. On the other hand, it was plausibly estimated that the Romans had lost 5,500 infantry and 380 cavalry. Most impressive of all, we know from Suetonius that the poorly armed, amateur soldiers of Jerusalem had succeeded in capturing one of Cestius's "eagles," that of the Twelfth Legion Fulminata. A legion's eagle, it will be remembered, was a hallowed standard for which legionaries were supposed to give their lives rather than suffer the indelible disgrace of losing it. No one could deny that the Jews had won a victory worthy of the Maccabees.

6

Governor of Galilee

"How long shall I see the standard, and hear the sound of the trumpet?"

JEREMIAH, IV, 21

CESTIUS'S DEFEAT WAS an unmitigated disaster for Rome's military reputation and authority. The news might easily unsettle other parts of the empire, besides encouraging Parthia to attack. Above all, it had turned the Jewish revolt into a war of independence.

Already Judea was a free country again. There was no movement to restore the monarchy, however, since Agrippa II, the last surviving Herodian, was all too obviously a client of Rome and would never cooperate with the new regime. Instead, a kind of junta, a coalition of notables, emerged in October 66, led by Ananus ben Ananus, who was a former high priest (and had been responsible for the murder of James, the brother of Christ). The Sanhedrin met again, taken more seriously now that the Romans had gone. Coins were minted, thick silver shekels and large numbers of smaller denominations in bronze, which bore such inscriptions as "Jerusalem the holy" or "The freedom of Zion"—later changed to "The redemption of Zion." A fair number of Judea's ruling class rallied to the cause of independence, even if some of them had tried to open the capital's gates to Cestius. They had no wish to lose their beautiful mansions in Jerusalem or their lands, and they saw opportunities for increasing their power. The swiftness with which they formed a government shows that it was people like this who had organized the resistance to Cestius, handing out the weapons and dictating the strategy that defeated him.

There were some grounds for thinking the new state might be viable. As it was not on the Mediterranean littoral, it posed no direct threat to the Romans, who could well be deterred by the prospect of a long, difficult war and besieging a city stronger than Carthage. Not only did its walls look impregnable, but the surrounding Judean hills were ideal for ambushes; they provided cover for guerrillas and deprived large armies of room to maneuver. Moreover, as the Jews had shown under the Maccabees, they were one of the great fighting races of Antiquity when properly led. Nero's regime seemed to be weakening, while there was also the possibility that the Parthians might intervene, despite their king's timidity. It was not entirely unreasonable, therefore, to hope that Rome might agree to a looser form of suzerainty in order to save face and avoid paying for an expensive series of campaigns.[1]

Ananus's most powerful allies in the junta were Eleazar ben Ananias and Joshua ben Gamala—the friend of Josephus's father. An uncompromising fanatic, the son of the high priest recently murdered by Menahem, Eleazar still commanded the Temple guard. It was he who had been responsible for discontinuing the sacrifices for the well-being of the emperor and, although a member of the upper class, for burning the moneylenders' archives. His total commitment to war with Rome was beyond doubt. Even if his championship of the poor was inspired by a thirst for power, he had many followers who stayed loyal to him, especially the more radically minded among the lower clergy. On the other hand, Joshua ben Gamala seems to have been much less of an extremist, despite maintaining a formidable army of private retainers. Unlike Eleazar, he hoped for a compromise. Yet, however different their ultimate aims may have been, men like these worked together, providing Judea with a government.

Nevertheless, as soon as the legate had been chased back to Syria, "many of the most eminent Jews swam away from the city, as if leaving a sinking ship," says Josephus.[2] They suspected that utter ruin was coming upon their country and that it was likely to come soon. Some fled to the humiliated Cestius at Antioch, who sent them off to Nero, to inform him of the loss of Judea—with instructions to lay all the blame for starting the war on Florus and deflect the emperor's anger from himself.

Besides these upper-class pessimists, the entire Judeo-Christian community decided to leave Jerusalem. Writing in the fourth century, with access to accounts long since lost, Bishop Eusebius of Caesarea says they had been "warned by a prophecy to depart from the city before the war began and go to Perea, to the gentile city of Pella."[3] The little community's exodus meant the extinction of Judeo-Christianity and its Jewish ritual observances, their formal worship having until now been centered around the Temple, though they broke bread together in services at their houses.

The first really serious reaction to the defeat, however, was not against the Romans but against the Jews. At Damascus, thousands of Jews were herded into the public gymnasium where their throats were cut, during a massacre that lasted for an entire hour. Josephus says that the perpetrators did not dare tell their own wives beforehand because so many women in Damascus sympathized with the Jewish religion. Reports of the atrocity stiffened the determination of the Jews at Jerusalem to go on fighting for their liberty.

"People in the neighboring cities in Syria turned on and killed the Jews who lived among them, together with their wives, without the slightest provocation, since these folk had never even considered the possibility of rebelling against the Romans, nor had they shown any sign of disliking Syrians or of wanting to harm them," Josephus recalled.[4] After describing what he regarded as the worst of these massacres—at Scythopolis, where many thousands were butchered despite having demonstrated their readiness to fight for Rome—he tells us that he has recorded these atrocities "because I want to show readers that the war with the Romans was not so much because the Jews wanted one as because they had no other option."[5]

It is difficult to determine Josephus's actual behavior during these days since he wrote after going over to the Romans and after the Jews had been totally defeated. Although he had tried to prevent the revolt from breaking out, undoubtedly his own attitude toward the war had been changed by the pogroms. Yet if he felt it necessary to fight the legions, he did so very reluctantly. Having so much to lose, he always hoped for an agreement with Rome.

Meanwhile the independence party in Jerusalem prepared for war. Of those who still favored yielding to Roman rule, some were won over by argument, while others were bullied into accepting the new regime by threats of violence. A great public meeting was held in the Temple, attended by thousands, at which ten generals were chosen. To some extent the meeting seems to have been influenced—if scarcely dominated by—the Sanhedrin, despite the ingrained antipathy toward revolution of most of its members, whose families had prospered under the Roman regime.

Upper-class influence can be detected in the meeting's opposition to making a Zealot, Eleazar ben Simon, overall leader. No doubt, he had played an important part in defeating the Romans. In fact, the captured weapons and Cestius's war chest were still in his possession, and he had somehow got control of the treasury. The magnates were nervous about him, however, because he was a Zealot and had a bullying, dictatorial manner, while people were frightened by his arrogant bodyguard of fanatical knifemen. In the end, an urgent need for Eleazar's money, exploited by subtle political maneuvering on his part, prevailed, and he was put in nominal charge of all matters of state. In practice, he was bypassed by the Sanhedrin and had little influence on policy—for the moment.

Among the ten generals appointed at the meeting in the Temple was "Josephus, son of Mattathias," who was made governor of both the Galilees, with the strongly fortified city of Gamala as his headquarters. (The phrase "assistant generals" used in *The Jewish War* indicates that there were plenty of others.) It may seem surprising that he did not flee to Antioch, since he later wrote that he had always known how the war would end. At this stage, however, he was not so sure, and many of the new government's leaders were his friends, such as Joshua ben Gamala, who may have secured his appointment.

Many people were better suited for the post than Josephus, who was going to meet with fierce criticism in Jerusalem as well as in Galilee. He is fairly reticent about this in *The Jewish War*, but in his so-called autobiography he provides more detail. Yet what seem to be inconsistencies in the two books are not so much contradictions as changes in emphasis, the two accounts being complementary.[6] Sometimes unconvincing, often boastful, he offers a wonderfully vivid picture, besides giving extraordinarily frank insights into the workings of his mind.

His patrician background may perhaps seem to make him a surprising choice for the post of governor of Galilee at a time when the social order was starting to fall apart. Yet, for the moment, Ananus's junta and the Sanhedrin maintained considerable influence, while many generals were of aristocratic origin—notably Ananus himself and Joseph ben Gorion, who were joint governors of Jerusalem, with responsibility for strengthening the city walls. Patricians still commanded respect, even if it was diminishing. Significantly, soon after his arrival in Galilee, Josephus wrote to the Sanhedrin, asking them for further instructions.

What ordinary people in Jerusalem did not realize was that while ostensibly preparing for war with Rome, more than a few rich aristocrats were concealing their true reasons for joining in the rising against the *Khittim*. In reality, they wanted to take it over, defuse it, and then negotiate a compromise peace. They had too much to lose by gambling on an outright victory, and in any case, they were anxious about the mob. Their secret agenda is hinted at by Josephus in a key, if slightly ambiguous, passage in the *Vita*:

> After Cestius's defeat, aware that the bandits and revolutionaries were alarmingly well armed, the Jerusalem notables suspected they might be in serious danger because they themselves lacked weapons, which in fact was what happened. When they learned that so far nowhere in Galilee had revolted against Rome and that much of it was still peaceful, they sent myself and two other priests, Joazar and Judas, both reliable men, to persuade anyone who was about to revolt to lay down his weapons and to convince him of the need to use them on behalf of the nations' leaders. The idea was that [the Galileans] . . . should keep their weapons ready for whatever might happen, while waiting to see what the Romans were going to do.[7]

Although Josephus does not admit as much in *The Jewish War*, he understood that his real job was to find men who would defend the magnates while they were building up a power base from which to negotiate with the Romans. He sympathized totally with his fellow patricians' last ditch attempt to take over the revolution and avoid a social upheaval and, at the same time, to put an end to the war. Although he never lost sight of these secret objectives and never had the slightest intention of attacking the Romans, once hostilities had become inevitable he started to organize the defense of Galilee in earnest. His companions, Joazar and Judas, seem to have gone back to Jerusalem, leaving him in sole control.

He tells us in *The Jewish War* that as soon as he arrived in Galilee his first step was to gain the population's good will, by sharing his authority and giving orders only through the "Galilaioi"—the Galileans.[8] He selected seventy mature, experienced men to form a local Sanhedrin that would administer the province. Appointing seven magistrates in each city to hear minor disputes, he reserved serious cases such as murder for trial by himself and the seventy. "I made them my friends and travelling companions," he says. "I consulted them about cases I tried, and asked them if they approved of the sentences I gave. I did my best to avoid being unjust through hastiness, and always refused to take bribes."[9] In reality, as we know from the *Vita*, the seventy were the old regime's principal magistrates, whom he kept near him as hostages.

Just how chaotic was the situation is revealed by Josephus's frank admission that he bought off brigands. "Realizing I had no chance of disarming them, I summoned the toughest bandits and persuaded the [country] people to pay them, explaining that it was cheaper to pay small sums than have their farms raided. I made the bandits take an oath not to enter the district unless invited or if their pay was in arrears, and then sent them away with strict orders against attacking the Romans or their neighbors. My overriding concern was peace in Galilee."[10] It looks as if he was posing as the only man who could control them, hoping to secure both their support and that of the peasants, in a situation that bordered on anarchy.

In reality, he was practically powerless, and his task of keeping Galilee peaceful and stopping it from going to war was an impossible one, further complicated by the presence of so many Greeks in the cities. Nowhere was this more evident than at Sepphoris, the capital where for a short time Josephus established his headquarters. Its population was almost entirely Greek-speaking, while it was deeply proud of the Greek surname bestowed on it by the Romans—Avtokratoris, "of the Emperor"—and disliked being ruled by a Jewish governor who had been appointed by a rebel junta at Jerusalem.

"I found all the Sepphorians terrified about what was going to happen to their city, as the Galileans [of the surrounding countryside] were planning to plunder it because they were pro-Roman and had been in touch with Cestius Gallus, the legate, assuring him of their loyalty and fidelity. I managed to reassure them, however, by persuading the locals not to attack [the Sepphorians], and also by letting them stay in contact with a number of their fellow citizens who were being held hostage by Cestius."[11] In addition, he allowed them to fortify the city against the peasants, in the vain hope that their attitude toward him would soften, which was a bad mistake. There is absolutely no truth in his claim to have taken Sepphoris twice by storm. Elsewhere, he openly admits that he tried to take the city on three separate occasions but was beaten off each time.

Matters were scarcely less difficult for him at Tiberias on the shore of Lake Gennesaret. Until quite recently it had been a center for Greek merchants, but by now its population was overwhelmingly Jewish since most of the Greeks had fled. They were divided over what to do. Some of them, clearly the richer ones with plenty to lose, were secretly determined to stay loyal to Rome while another group—"which consisted of the most insignificant people in the place"—were clamoring for war. A third group led by Justus son of Pistus—a Jew despite his name—pretended to urge caution but really wanted revolution. According to *The Jewish War*, Justus whipped up the mob at Tiberias by appealing to their long-standing hatred of Sepphoris.

"He was clever at rousing the rabble, his charlatan oratory making him a match for an opponent with wiser ideas," is how Josephus—no doubt the opponent he has in mind—describes Justus. "He had some small knowledge of Greek literature, which he later used to write a history of this time, hoping to disguise what had really happened by twisting the facts. During my account, I shall produce evidence of the man's depravity and show how our ruin was largely due to him and his brother. On this particular occasion, after persuading the citizens [of Tiberias] to revolt, and forcing others to do so against their will, Justus marched out with his supporters and set fire to villages around Gadara and Tiberias."[12] In reality, Justus seems to have been a secret moderate who, just like Josephus, was ready to welcome an accommodation with Rome. The two men's enmity had more to do with personal rivalry than political differences.

Another nuisance was the archon or chief magistrate of Tiberias, Jesus ben Sapphias, who is described contemptuously by Josephus as "ringleader of the party of the sailors [the lake's fishermen?] and the destitute class."[13] He tells us that Jesus was "a scoundrel who had a flair for throwing everything into confusion, and was unrivalled for stirring up sedition and revolution."[14] When the Sanhedrin ordered the demolition of a Herodian palace nearby because it contained pagan sculptures, Jesus promptly burned it down, since its golden roof indicated rich plunder. An angry Josephus recovered most of the loot that survived the blaze—Corinthian candelabra, "royal tables," and a large amount of uncoined silver—intending to restore it to King Agrippa II, whom he did not want to antagonize. Meanwhile, Jesus and his followers cut the throats of the few Greeks misguided enough to remain in Tiberias.

The motives of these local bosses were bewilderingly mixed. On the one hand, they wanted to make whatever profit could be made now that law and order had broken down; rich pickings were available from bribes, protection rackets, and plunder. At the same time, they realized they had to keep in with the government at Jerusalem while the rebellion lasted, since they might be targeted for elimination. Yet even if they hoped to benefit from the revolution, the shrewder knew it was imperative to secure a position for themselves that might help them to survive when the Romans reoccupied the country.

There were other problems for Josephus besides party bosses. From Antioch, Cestius Gallus, waiting for reinforcements before making a major move, was threatening Galilee's northern border, and from a base at Ptolemais on the coast, Placidus, who was a particularly daring commander, was menacing the province with two cohorts of infantry and a squadron of horse. Sulla, captain of King Agrippa's bodyguard, was raiding across the northeastern border, while Varus, a former minister who had turned against the king, was attacking all and sundry.

At the head of a mob of "mercenaries," Josephus galloped to and fro, skirmishing with Roman sympathizers or brigands, but without much effect. There was danger from the peasantry, who tried to storm and plunder non-Jewish towns. Cities fought each other, Sepphoris with Tiberias, Tiberias with Taricheae, hostile factions squabbling in their streets. Over everything loomed the shadow of Rome's vengeance. Understandably, many cities wanted to invite the Romans back, if only as an insurance against their reprisals. Sepphoris eventually succeeded in persuading Cestius to install a Roman garrison behind its walls—by now repaired with Josephus's permission.

He did his best to prepare the two Galilees against the full-scale Roman invasion he knew was inevitable. Secretly hoping to make peace, he needed something with which to bargain. Yet he had no chance of building a properly united opposition. Most of his supporters were the country people, not because they loved him, as he claims so smugly, but because they thought he might protect them against the rapacious city folk whom they feared and hated, and because he gave the impression of being able to tame the bandits. The Taricheans supported him since they thought he would take their side against detested Tiberias. None of these two groups had anything in common.

He explains that he concentrated on places nature had made defensible, such as Tiberias and Jotapata, where he strengthened the ramparts, and Mount Tabor. He built walls in front of the caves near Lake Gennesaret in Lower Galilee and around the rock called Acchaberon in Upper Galilee. Among the other places he fortified was Sepphoris, where the inhabitants were allowed to raise the height of the ramparts. At Gischala the party boss was also allowed to rebuild them on his own initiative. However impressive all these preparations may sound, in reality they were no more than cosmetic and would prove to be useless against Roman siege engines.

Josephus then recruited over "100,000 young men"—10,000 would probably be nearer the truth—whom he armed with any weapons available. He says that he tried to impose discipline by appointing a high percentage of NCOs and instituting a proper command structure, with centurions, decurions, and tribunes. The troops were taught now to maneuver to the sound of trumpet calls such as the "advance" or the "retreat," how to extend an army's flanks and to wheel around, how to send a victorious flank to the help of a flank in trouble. He told them that courage and physical toughness were essential, stressing that they were going to fight men who had conquered the entire inhabitable earth with these qualities. They would have to refrain from their favorite pastimes (robbery, looting, and stealing from their own countrymen) if they were to be of any use in combat.

Perhaps he employed ex-soldiers to advise him, yet one cannot help suspecting that many of these measures existed only in his imagination. He was writing after the war, when he had gained the military experience that he lacked when it began. Throughout, he portrays himself as a born general, a portrayal that has more to do with his vanity and the conventions of Greek historiography than with reality.

He claims that he finally assembled what he considered an adequate force—60,000 infantry, 250 horse, and about 4,500 mercenaries. As so often with Josephus, these figures are likely to be wild exaggerations. One guesses, too, that his "army" was a pitifully ill-armed rabble, little better than a mob, whose sole assets were the bravery that came from an unswerving belief in their faith and nation, who would never stand a chance against the legionaries. His best troops were his "mercenaries," men of the type whom he calls bandits—in Greek, *lestai*. The "army" that accompanied him on a day-to-day basis, and enforced his rule, must, at largest, have consisted of about two or three hundred brigands. They formed his so-called bodyguard.

In the meantime, Galilee's growing disorder was assuming nightmarish proportions, the greatest problem continuing to be the party bosses. The most dangerous of these was Yohannan ben Levi—better known as John of Gischala—who was probably a small landowner, though he is often described as a merchant. Once a supporter of Roman rule, he had changed his mind and become a fervent Zealot after the Romans encouraged the Greeks of Tyre and Gadara to sack his local town of Gischala and then burn it to the ground. In response, he armed the men of Gischala, driving out the Greeks.

At first John was on good terms with Josephus, who entrusted him with refortifying Gischala, but later he fell out with "this treacherous person," one of the most formidable foes he ever faced. Josephus saw people purely in terms of black or white so that his character sketches never quite convey the full depth of a man's personality. "The most cunning and unscrupulous of all men who have ever gained notoriety by evil means," is how he begins his portrait of John. Perhaps inspired by the historian Sallust's account of Catiline, the great Roman rebel, his full description is almost comically abusive:

> He began life hampered by lack of money. A hardened liar, always plausible, he prided himself on skill in deceit, tricking even his close friends.

Pretending to be humane, he never had any qualms about committing murder if he thought it might be profitable, while he systematically furthered his insatiable ambition by criminal activities. Originally a bandit working alone, he had a rare talent for thieving, which was why he was able to find so many followers, only a few of them at first, but increasing in proportion with his success. He chose the type of man who knew how to avoid being caught, tough and determined, preferably with a military background, and eventually built up a gang of 400, mainly outlaws from Tyre and its neighboring villages. With their support, he laid waste all Galilee, plundering the poor who were helpless because of the looming war.[15]

No one should accept an enemy's account unreservedly, and some see John of Gischala very differently. The novelist Lion Feuchtwanger credits John (whom, perhaps not inaccurately, he calls "this Galilean squire") with a strikingly attractive personality, while *The Jewish War* cannot conceal that he was an exceptionally brave man and a fine soldier. It is conceivable that his plotting against Josephus was inspired by a conviction that if he took over command, there would be a better chance of saving Galilee from the Romans; according to Josephus's own account, John found supporters from among all classes. It even looks as though Josephus's two principal lieutenants, Joazar and Judas, thought that John would be preferable. Far from being a mere brigand, he was of much higher social status than *The Jewish War* or the *Vita* would have us believe, and his powerful friends at Jerusalem treated him as an equal.[16]

One of John's coups was to corner an entire year of Galilee's production of oil by persuading Josephus to let him have a monopoly, arguing that otherwise Jews in Syria would have to buy "pagan" oil. He then sold the Galilean oil for eight times what he paid, although *The Jewish War* omits to say that he probably used the money to strengthen Gischala's defenses. Soon he was planning to overthrow Josephus and take his place, ordering his men to raid still more savagely. With a bit of luck, the general might turn out to be among the victims or, if he escaped, might be blamed for failing to catch a gang that was inflicting misery far and wide. He spread rumors that Josephus was secretly plotting to hand Galilee over to the Romans.[17]

The citizens of Sepphoris, who, as has been seen, were not so secretly loyal to Rome, grew alarmed when Josephus decided to visit them and paid a brigand chief called Jesus to assassinate him. Just before Jesus arrived at the city from his base near Ptolemais with 800 bandits, one of his followers revealed the plot. Separated from his men by a ruse and arrested, he made a complete confession, but Josephus pardoned him. He also forgave the Sepphorians. He was in no position to punish either the city or the bandits.

John saw an opportunity to overthrow Josephus when some young men held up King Agrippa's steward and robbed him of valuable baggage that included silver cups and 600 gold pieces. Finding difficulty in disposing of their plunder, they brought it to Josephus, who was at Taricheae. He immediately confiscated the stolen baggage, intending to restore it to its owner, the king, whom he realized might be a useful friend in any negotiations with the Romans. In response, the robbers went to every city and village in the province, claiming Josephus was about to betray them all. John appears to have been behind these demonstrations, which gathered strength, while outwardly remaining on good terms with him.

The rumor that Josephus was planning to hand the country over to the Romans spread throughout Galilee, and thousands gathered in the hippodrome at Taricheae to protest. Repeatedly, they demanded his stoning or burning. The clamor was whipped by John of Gischala and by an old enemy, the chief magistrate Jesus ben Sapphias, who stepped forward dramatically with a copy of the Torah in his hands. "Perhaps you're selfish enough not to be disgusted by Josephus, fellow citizens," he shouted. "But at least you can still remember your Law, which your commander was planning to betray and for its sake alone you ought to abominate the crime and punish such an impertinent criminal."

Jesus then led a band of armed men to Josephus's house, intending to kill him. Waking the governor, the sole member of his bodyguard who remained told him they were coming and advised suicide. Instead, he put on black clothes, sprinkled dust on his head, hung his sword round his neck, and, avoiding Jesus, went to the hippodrome. Here, a few people, mainly Taricheans, felt sorry for him, but most of the mob were country folk who disliked his taxes. They yelled that they wanted their money back and told him to admit he was a traitor. Throwing himself on the ground and bursting into tears, he made such an impression that the mob prevented some soldiers from killing him. "Fellow citizens, if I deserve to die, I shan't ask for any mercy. But at least, please let me tell you the truth before my death." Then he promised, with heroic untruthfulness, to confess everything:

> I have no intention of sending all this money to Agrippa or of keeping it for myself. And I am certainly not going to treat your enemy as a friend of mine, nor am I going to profit from your loss. But I have noticed, you Taricheans, that your city has much more need of fortifications and of being made safe than any other city in the area, and has to find the funds for building a proper wall. I was worried that the citizens of Tiberias or some other city might decide to appropriate the money for their own use, so I decided to keep it back and build a wall for you. But if you don't care for the idea, then of course I shall hand over what was brought to me so that you can divide the lot up between you. I have tried to do my best for you, so why punish a man who merely wanted to do you a good turn?

The Taricheans cheered this "confession" and, as he had hoped, they and the Tiberians started quarreling with each other. Above the din, he went on shouting that they could do better than be angry with someone who was only trying to help them. Eventually, most of the crowd drifted away, and he went home, no doubt with considerable relief. (Josephus gives two slightly different accounts of this incident.[18]) However, 2,000 of them suddenly returned, waving weapons and shouting menaces outside his house, which they threatened to burn down. In response, he invited their leaders to come in and discuss their grievances. As soon as the men were inside and the door was shut, he had them seized and soundly flogged by his bodyguards with the terrible Roman whip (studded with lead and drawing blood with each stripe) "until their guts showed through their flesh," he writes with obvious pleasure. In addition, he tells us in the *Vita*, he had a hand cut off from the biggest of the leaders and hung around his neck. (It has to be said that this revolting punishment was fairly standard practice.) Then he had them thrown out into the street, more dead than alive, their friends bolting in horror at the sight.[19]

Undeterred, John of Gischala hatched a new plot. While Josephus was away at a village in Galilee called Cana, John appeared at Tiberias, after writing a friendly letter to him to say that he was coming to take the hot baths. Encouraged by Justus ben Pistus, he then tried to make the inhabitants hand over the city to him. However, Josephus returned unexpectedly with 200 troops and John hid in his lodgings, pretending that he was ill. Dismissing all save a handful of his escort, Josephus went to the stadium and from the top of a wall began to tell the crowd about some important news that he had received. Suddenly, one of his soldiers yelled that John's thugs were coming up behind him. "The swords were at his throat" when, just in time, he leaped down from the wall, ran to the lake, and jumped into a boat, taking refuge at Taricheae.

According to Josephus, not only the Taricheans but the entire people of Galilee were so angry at this attempt to murder him that he had to stop "tens of thousands" from marching on Gischala, where John had taken refuge, and burning the plotter and his city. John sent a letter vehemently denying all knowledge of a plot, "ending with oaths and horrible curses, by which he hoped to convey an air of sincerity."[20] Josephus then announced that he had discovered the names of John's supporters in every city in Galilee and that he was preparing to burn the house of anyone who did not leave his party within five days. As a result, 3,000 men rushed to offer their swords to Josephus.[21]

In contrast, the citizens of Tiberias went over to King Agrippa, inviting him to occupy their city, evicting Josephus and his bodyguard as soon as a handful of the king's horsemen rode in. He responded by collecting all the boats on Lake Gennesaret, some 230, manning each one with only four sailors, and then took his armada across the water to Tiberias, anchoring far out, so that the Tiberians could not see that the little vessels were virtually unmanned. Then he sailed his own boat to near the shore. Believing a huge army was about to attack them, the horrified citizens threw down their weapons and surrendered. Josephus then asked for a delegation with whom he could negotiate and on one pretence or another tricked the entire senate of 600 men, together with about 2,000 citizens, into coming on board his boats.

While being put ashore at Taricheae, they shouted that the instigator of the revolt had been Clitus, "a rash and headstrong youth," so Josephus ordered one of his bodyguards to amputate the young man's hands. When the guard dared not go in among the huge crowd of prisoners, Clitus

begged to be allowed to keep one, and after Josephus had grudgingly
agreed, he cut off his left hand with his right, using his sword. Josephus
tells us that he felt extremely proud about the way in which he had
crushed the Tiberians' revolt "without any bloodshed."[22]

Then he asked the Tiberian council to dinner. Among the guests was
his old enemy, Justus, along with his father, Pistus. "During the meal, I
said I knew very well that the Roman army was terrifyingly effective, but
kept quiet about it because of the brigands"—by which he meant extremists.
(He was saying that everyone present realized that Rome would reconquer
Judea.) "I suggested they should be as discreet as I was and be patient. I
also advised them not to criticize my government, as they were unlikely to
find another general as tolerant as myself." That was not all he had to say
during this cheerful entertainment. "In addition, I reminded Justus how,
just before I arrived from Jerusalem, the Galileans had cut off his brother's
hands for forging letters." Finally he recalled how the people of Gamala
had murdered Justus's brother-in-law. Clearly in a good mood, he gave orders the next morning for the release of his Tiberian prisoners.[23]

His cheerfulness was soon dispelled by a crisis to which he devotes several pages of the *Vita*. John of Gischala had sent his brother, Jonathan, to
Jerusalem to obtain the intervention of Simon ben Gamaliel, who appears
to have been his friend, if not a very close one. It also seems that Joazar and
Judas, Josephus's two lieutenants, had returned to the capital and severely
criticized the governor of Galilee.

A Pharisee whom even Josephus describes as "a man of illustrious family," Simon, and his ally Gorion ben Joseph had considerable influence in
Jerusalem, and they persuaded the authorities to replace Josephus with
John as soon as possible.[24] They agreed about the governor's shortcomings
(he claims they were bribed), accepting allegations about him that appear
to have included corruption, luxurious living, and stealing. "Tyranny,"
which presumably meant threatening behavior, was another charge, to
some extent borne out by the many times Tiberias had rebelled. There also
seem to have been insinuations that he was intending to hand the province
over to the Romans. But instead of replacing him with John of Gischala,
they decided to install a commission.

As a result, four commissioners from Jerusalem, three of them Pharisees and all highly respected, were sent to Galilee to arrest or kill the gov-

ernor. One was Joazar, Josephus's former lieutenant. Financed from the public treasury, they rode to the province with a thousand armed men. Luckily for Josephus, his father had learned of their mission and sent a letter to warn him. Reassured by a dream worthy of a prophet that he was destined to stay in office and lead the fight against the Romans, and heartened by having been begged by the Galileans to remain—at least he says they begged him—he assembled an army on the pretext that it was needed to fight Roman raiders from Syria. Then he waited for the commissioners to arrive. When they came, they wrote and very politely asked him to join them on an expedition to punish John of Gischala but to bring only a few men.

While Josephus was at dinner, their letter was delivered by an insolent young officer who did not even bother to salute and told him to be quick about writing an answer:

> However, I asked him to sit down and join us for dinner. He refused. So I held the letter in my hand without opening it, talking to my companions about other things. I soon rose from the table and, after saying goodnight to most of them, invited four close friends to stay, telling my servant to bring some wine.
>
> When no one was looking, I opened the letter, saw exactly what the writers were up to, and sealed it again. Holding the letter as if I had not read it, I ordered the soldier to be given twenty drachmas for his travelling expenses. He took the money, thanking me.
>
> Guessing from his reaction that greed was the best way of getting the better of him, I then said, "If you would like to drink with us, you can have a drachma for every goblet of wine you drink." He was only too pleased to accept, and in order to win as much money as possible drank so deeply that he got very drunk indeed. Unable to keep a secret any longer, he at last told me, without even being asked, all about the plot that was brewing and how his superiors had sentenced me to death.[25]

The commissioners' attempts to lay hands on the wily governor of Galilee dragged on for weeks, at times degenerating into farce. They had no help from John of Gischala, who wanted the governorship for himself and who never forgave Simon ben Gamaliel for conceding to the commission;

the rejection may have given him a lasting hatred for the aristocratic junta at Jerusalem and the entire ruling class. Nor did the Galilean peasants, who formed the bulk of the governor's supporters, have any time for these haughty Pharisees.

The quarry arranged for crowds to boo the commissioners wherever they went, much to their fury, while when they tried to send letters around the province asking for support, he had the couriers arrested and put in chains. Attempts to kidnap him failed—one in a castle, another in a synagogue, and a third at a feast. When they persuaded the Tiberians to revolt, Josephus captured one of the commissioners who organized the uprising, by offering terms and then seizing the man around the waist when he came to negotiate. After this coup he marched into Tiberias with 10,000 troops and imprisoned anyone who was known to be hostile to him. It was the end of the commission.

Although Josephus survived, it had been a humiliating episode. It meant that not only throughout Galilee but in Jerusalem as well, there were influential people who had decided that the governor was not up to his job. Pretending that it had all been a plot by John of Gischala, boasting of his resourcefulness and of the supposed loyalty of the Galileans toward him, he uses all his skill to disguise the affront in the *Vita*. Even so, toward the end of his few months in Galilee, if his account is correct, it really does look as though he had outwitted his opponents. The commissioners had left, John of Gischala was confined to his little city, and Justus of Tiberias had taken refuge at King Agrippa's court. It also seems that Josephus had cowed restive cities, such as Tiberias.

"In those days, I was about thirty years old, a time of life when, even if you are wholly respectable, it is not easy to avoid being slandered," he says in the *Vita*, referring to his Galilean period.[26] "Yet I never molested women, while I refused all the presents offered to me as I didn't need them. I suppose I kept some of the loot captured from Syrian cities in the area and admit that I sent it back to relations at Jerusalem." But he was sure his conduct had been beyond reproach. His self-esteem is almost ludicrous. "The Galileans were so fond of me that when their cities were stormed and their wives and children sent off to the slave market they were far more worried about what had happened to me," he claims complacently.[27] Yet it is unlikely that the notoriously boorish Galilaioi felt much

in common with a rich patrician from Jerusalem who, like many well-bred
Jews, had difficulty in understanding what they were trying to say to him
in their thick accents.

"I took Sepphoris twice by storm, Tiberias four times and Gabara
once," he says, hoping to impress us. He adds that he never punished any
of these cities for rebelling.[28] Not only are most of these claims patently
untrue, but the statement is an admission that he was unable to assert his
authority over Galilee, which by now must have been in hopeless disorder.
Despite the glowing account he gives of his military achievements, he was
clearly no good as a field commander—which, since he had had no military experience, was scarcely surprising. His inadequacy explains why there
were so many revolts against his administration, and why John of Gischala
never gave up hope of replacing him.

In fairness, it has to be said that at least one modern historian is inclined to believe that he had been a success and takes his pretensions at
face value. E. M. Smallwood thinks that by spring 67, when a new Roman
offensive opened, Josephus had established his authority over all Galilee
except for Sepphoris.[29] Not everyone will agree with her, despite her impressive scholarship.

He had to suffer a further humiliation. The citizens of Sepphoris—
which, it will be remembered, was the Galilean capital—wrote to Caesennius Gallus, commander of the Twelfth Legion and Cestius's deputy at Antioch, asking him to send them a Roman garrison. This duly arrived, and
Josephus was unable to dislodge it. Sepphorians preferred security under
the Romans, however oppressive, to freedom under an inept Jewish governor. Yet he claims, blandly and untruthfully, that "Everything had calmed
down in Galilee by now," after describing how he outwitted the citizens of
Tiberias with his armada. "The people stopped quarrelling and got ready
to fight the Romans."[30]

They were certainly getting ready to fight at Jerusalem, where the walls
were being strengthened and every wealthy man who was not a secret supporter of the Romans was acquiring an arsenal for himself and his servants.
The noise of weapons and armor being forged rang out all over the city.
Most of the young men were enthusiastically training as soldiers, disrupt-
ing the normal pattern of everyday life, but the more balanced among the
citizens were very gloomy indeed, realizing what lay ahead and bewailing

their fate. There were omens that could only spell disaster, although fire-brands were trying to give them an optimistic interpretation.

Even before the Romans arrived, the mood in the Jewish capital was divided. On the one hand, there were those who believed their city might soon be facing destruction but made up their minds to fight to the end. On the other hand, there were the optimists, who argued, not entirely without reason, that King Herod's fortifications made Jerusalem capable of surviving the most determined siege. What was certain, however, was that the junta at Jerusalem had no time to help a man who remained governor of Galilee despite their wishes, especially after the commissioners had reported how insultingly he had outwitted them. Josephus was now on his own and had to fend for himself.

7

The Return of the Legions

"For a nation is come up upon my land, strong, and without number, whose teeth are the teeth of a lion."

JOEL, I, 6

"WHEN NERO WAS told of the Roman disaster in Judea, as one might expect he was very shaken and bewildered, although he did his best to hide it," Josephus tells us, perhaps echoing the description of a courtier who had been present.

> He lost his temper, saying that what had happened was entirely his commander's fault and had nothing at all to do with the enemy's generalship. Believing as he did that someone who bore the whole burden of empire should show contempt for disturbances of this sort, he always feigned indifference to reversals of any kind. Just how worried he was, however, could be seen from the pains he took in trying to mend matters. After debating with himself who would know best how to deal with the east when it was in such a mess, and be able to put down the Jewish rebellion and stop the trouble from spreading to other countries, he decided that only Vespasian could do the job properly.[1]

Fifty-seven years old, Titus Flavius Sabinus Vespasianus, an obscure Sabine from the little village of Reate (Rieti), was far from being a patrician and spoke with an uncouth accent. A no-nonsense sort of man, tough, shrewd, and efficient, with a caustic wit, a soldier's soldier who always led from the front and had been wounded several times, he was liked by his troops despite being a ferocious disciplinarian. According to Tacitus, he often marched on foot at the head of his army (despite his gout), marked out the night's camp each evening, ate whatever was put in front of him, and dressed as a ranker.[2] If he appeared to be a mediocrity at this stage of his career, he was at least an experienced one, having campaigned in Germany and Britain, where Suetonius says he fought in thirty battles, captured twenty towns, and conquered the Isle of Wight.[3] Even so, running short of money, he had abandoned military life to deal in mules.

Ironically, Nero had developed a deep dislike for Vespasian, who in any case was hardly a kindred spirit. After falling asleep while the emperor was singing, he had very nearly been executed because of his lack of appreciation. Suetonius tells us that on the day after the concert he was refused admission to the imperial presence and banished from court. He was more or less in hiding at an out-of-the-way town in Achaia, fearing the worst, when messengers came to offer him the governorship of Syria with command of an army.[4] Having been on the retired list for some years, the offer must have come as a surprise, but he accepted with alacrity.

Crossing the Dardanelles, Vespasian went as quickly as possible to Antioch where he took over command of the Fifth Legion and the Tenth Legion (Macedonica and Fretensis) from Cestius Gallus, whom he replaced as legate of Syria. He had sent his son Titus to Egypt, to bring the Fifteenth Legion (Apollinaris) from Alexandria, while he was reinforced by auxiliary troops from client states, including the whole of King Agrippa II's little army. Eventually, he assembled a force numbering over 45,000 men—Josephus says it was 60,000—the best being twenty-three cohorts of legionaries and six squadrons of regular cavalry. This was more than had been used in the recent conquest of Britain. It was an indication of how seriously Rome was taking the Jewish threat. According to Suetonius, Vespasian overhauled the discipline of every single unit.

The Jews did not wait for the new Roman general to arrive but decided to attack the Greek city of Ashkelon on the coast, which was garrisoned by only a single cohort and a squadron of cavalry—less than a thousand soldiers. Still elated by Cestius's defeat, "like people blown into flame by good fortune," a large, overconfident army led by Niger the Peraite, Silas of Babylon, and John the Essene marched out from the capital.[5] But while their objective was inadequately garrisoned, they forgot that it had strong fortifications and possessed an exceptionally resourceful commander, Antonius.

When the Jews reached Ashkelon, they rushed headlong at the city, but instead of sheltering behind its walls, Antonius drew up his horsemen outside. Then he charged. Undisciplined, badly armed, and on foot, the Jews did not stand a chance. Many ran, to be pursued and slaughtered. Others fought bravely until evening, suffering 10,000 casualties, which included two of their leaders. The Romans lost only a few men. Undiscouraged by the sight of so many comrades lying dead on the battlefield, the Jews made another attack the next day, led by Niger the Peraite, but were cut to pieces. Niger and some of his troops took refuge in a tower at a village called Belzedek, which the Romans promptly fired. They thought they had succeeded in killing Niger, but he jumped down through the flames and hid in a cave, emerging three days later when his men were tearfully searching for his corpse. His miraculous survival delighted the Jews, who felt proud to have such a commander. But it was the last time they attacked a Roman garrison.

Vespasian marched out from Antioch with his army, along the sea road down to Tyre and then to Ptolemais where he went into winter quarters. He installed a garrison at Sepphoris, under the tribune Placidus, a thousand horse and 6,000 infantry camped on the plain outside the city. An unrealistic attempt by Josephus to recapture his capital failed; not only did he have too few troops, but the Sepphorians did not want him back. Although it was not the campaigning season the Roman cavalry raided far and wide throughout the winter of 66–67 CE, burning crops and villages, driving off cattle, sending the wretched 'am ha-arez off to the slave markets. "Everywhere, Galilee was filled with fire and blood," we are told in *The Jewish War*. "The only refuge for the inhabitants being hunted for their lives was inside the cities that Josephus had fortified."[6]

For the moment, people felt safe behind city walls. Realizing this, Placidus decided to storm Jotapata, the strongest of the cities, which was only a few miles from Sepphoris, hoping its capture might frighten the others into surrendering. However, learning that he was on his way, its citizens ambushed his troops and routed them with a hail of javelins— although the Romans withdrew in such good order that they lost only seven men.

Bringing the Fifteenth Legion with him, Titus joined his father at Ptolemais where they wintered together, training their army in siege warfare. Vespasian's experience of besieging and storming hilltop forts in Britain was going to be useful, even if Galilean mountain towns would prove tougher nuts to crack. By the spring of 67 the Romans were ready. In *The Jewish War*, Josephus gives us a picture of their army as it marched out from Ptolemais to conquer Galilee:

Lightly armed native horse and bowmen rode in front, guarding against sudden assaults by the enemy and always ready to search any suspicious looking thickets that might conceal an ambush. After them, wearing full armor, came a force of horse and foot, then ten men from each century carrying camping equipment besides their own, then pioneers with tools for leveling road surfaces or clearing a way through woods, to save the troops from being worn out by marching. Then followed the general's carriage and those of other senior officers, along with a strong cavalry escort. He himself came next, marching at the head of a picked body of horse and foot soldiers, with a troop of pikemen. Then came the legions' special cavalry, each legion having a hundred and twenty horsemen of its own. Next, the mules with the siege engines and other heavy weaponry. After these marched the senior officers, commanders of cohorts and tribunes, with an escort of crack troops.

Then came the eagles, those standards which are borne at the head of every Roman legion, since they consider the eagle to be the king of birds and the strongest, a symbol of victory and an omen they will always win, whatever the odds against them. These sacred battle emblems were followed by the trumpeters, and in their train marched the main army in cohorts, six infantrymen abreast, with a centurion to see they kept in step. Camp servants followed the infantry, leading the pack animals which carried the legionaries' baggage. A vast host of mercenaries came after the Roman soldiers, followed by a rearguard composed of heavy and light infantry with a large body of horse.[7]

Vespasian knew all about psychological warfare; he restrained his men from attacking while he prepared to overwhelm the cities of Galilee. He guessed that the spectacle of such a huge, well-equipped army would deter them from fighting, and he was right. Josephus admits that mere rumors of the approach of this gigantic war machine, as it clanked along at a carefully regulated pace toward his own makeshift army, in camp at Garis, four kilometers from Sepphoris, were enough to rout the Galileans. The men he had taken such pains to train bolted before the enemy came in sight. Devastated by their desertion, he decided the war was already lost and, with the few troops who remained at his side, took refuge in Tiberias.

Vespasian's reconquest of Galilee started with Gadara, which he found almost without defenders. Storming the little city at the point of the sword, he slaughtered not just the young men but the old, with all its women and children. Besides burning down the city, he methodically put to the torch every small town and village in the area, killing anyone who was foolish enough to stay within reach.

The people of Tiberias were panic-stricken when Josephus arrived, suspecting that their once confident governor would never have run away had he not been convinced the war was lost. They were quite right. He knew exactly what was going to happen, and that the only chance was to try and make peace. However, he insists he would have died many times over rather than dishonor his post as army commander by reaching a cowardly understanding with its enemies against the wishes of his government. Instead, he sent a full report to the leaders at Jerusalem by fast messenger, in the hope that it might persuade them to negotiate without delay.

One need not believe the claim he made years later that he always felt sure the Romans would give him a pardon. In those days, it was more likely that they would crucify him, and he must have been living in fear, desperately trying to find a means of changing sides. He cannot have had much confidence in the Tiberians, who had given him such trouble, but he knew of another Galilean city on an almost impregnable site with very strong fortifications, where he might be safe. It was so formidable that Vespasian had made a point of besieging it after demolishing Gadara. Quietly abandoning Tiberias to its fate, in May 67 Josephus slipped into the hill city of Jotapata, just after the Roman army had pitched camp nearby. He informs us, in his selfless way, that he did so "to raise the drooping spirits of the Jews," but his real motive was almost certainly that he thought it stood a better chance than Tiberias of surviving a siege. However, he was going to find that he was caught in the city like a rat—albeit a resourceful, smooth-talking rat—in a trap from which there was no possibility of escape.

8

The Siege of Jotapata

"In the morning thou shalt say 'Would God it were even!' and at even thou shalt say, 'Would God it were morning!'"

DEUTERONOMY, XXVIII, 67

JOTAPATA WAS CERTAINLY the safest place in Galilee, hidden away in the mountains and practically invisible until you reached it. Perched around a precipice, guarded on three sides by ravines so deep that the bottom was out of sight, it could be attacked only from the north, where the lower part of the city sloped down the mountain and then up to a slight ridge. At this strategic point, another wall had recently been built, on Josephus's instructions, to defend the ridge. The approach road through the hills was scarcely better than a goat track, just about adequate for men on foot but not for horses or even for mules, and the little mountain city must have seemed impregnable to those who had never encountered Roman sappers. Its one grave weakness was the lack of a spring inside its walls so that it depended for water on rain stored in its cisterns.

Our sole source for the siege of Jotapata is what Josephus cares to tell us in *The Jewish War*, since he does not make any mention of it in the *Vita*, and no other history of the period contains any reference to Jotapata. It has to be remembered, too, that as always he was writing some years later, with two very different audiences in mind: the Romans whom he had joined during the war and the Jews whom he had abandoned. In addition, he was trying to portray his behavior in the best light possible, as that of a heroic commander fighting against impossible odds.

Whether he liked it or not, he was in command and had to fight the Romans. If he attempted to escape, the Jotapatans would try to kill him, and even if he succeeded he stood a fair chance of being caught by enemy patrols who would give him short shrift. In *The Jewish War* he portrays himself as the gallant and determined leader, the *strategos* (general) who was always resourceful, always undismayed. In reality, during the forthcoming siege he became increasingly desperate to negotiate but was never given the opportunity.

Yet even if some of his account in *The Jewish War* is obviously distorted, most of it is plausible enough and carries conviction, in particular when he is not describing his own actions. There is another reason to believe that the broad outline of the siege is correct: when Josephus was writing his history, he knew that it was going to be closely read by the man who had been the commander of the Roman army in the siege. This was the eagle-eyed Vespasian, who lent him his notebooks of the Palestinian campaign. A substantial number of details, especially those concerning the Roman army—such as troop numbers and the names of the enemy commanders—can only have come from Vespasian's notebooks.

Jotapata's strength made it a priority for Vespasian. If he succeeded in taking the place, no other Galilean stronghold could think itself impregnable. Moreover, he knew that large numbers of fanatical Jews were in the city. When a deserter told him the governor of Galilee was there as well, he was delighted and thought it divine providence. "The man whom he considered his cleverest opponent had shut himself up in a self-appointed prison," Josephus modestly records.[1] The Roman general's first move was to send Placidus and the decurion Ebutius, "an exceptionally brave and resourceful officer," with a thousand men to surround the city and ensure that the governor did not escape. "He thought he would be able to capture all Judea if only he could get hold of Josephus," says *The Jewish War*.[2] This sounds like boasting, yet it may be true since he knew that Vespasian was going to read the account.

On 21 May, a few hours before Josephus reached Jotapata, Vespasian had arrived there with his entire army. He chose a small hill about three-quarters of a mile north as the site of his camp so that it was within full view of the defenders, whom, he hoped, would be terrified by the sheer number of besiegers. His first action was to fence the city off with a double line of infantry and another of cavalry, preventing anyone from getting in or out.

Next day, the Romans launched a full-scale assault. Some of the Jews tried to stop the attackers before they reached the walls, but Vespasian engaged them at long range with archers and slingers while he led his infantry up a slope to where the walls were easiest to climb. Realizing the danger, Josephus rushed out with his entire garrison and drove the legionaries back from the walls. The fighting went on all day, the defenders losing seventeen dead and six hundred wounded, while thirteen Romans were killed and many more wounded. The Jews were so encouraged that the next morning they again sallied out and attacked the enemy. Sorties and savage hand-to-hand fighting continued for five days, with many losses on both sides. When a lull at last ensued, the Romans had inflicted such heavy casualties that the Jews began to lose heart.

Even so, the Jews had fought effectively enough for Vespasian to realize that their city's walls were a much more serious obstacle than he had appreciated. After consulting his senior officers, he ordered the construction of a siege platform next to the section of the wall that looked the weakest. His troops set about cutting down every tree on the neighboring mountains and gathering big stones and sacks of earth. Layers of wooden hurdles protected them from the javelins and rocks that rained down as they built the platform.

At the same time, the Roman siege artillery, a hundred and sixty "scorpions," fired nonstop at the walls, together with the catapultae and the stone projectors. There seem to have been two types of scorpion—a big, repeating crossbow, and a smaller, portable version of the catapulta. Mounted on carts, catapultae had multiple strings of twisted catgut and shot armor-piercing bolts or stone balls at very high velocity. Stone projectors (onagers) were huge mechanical slings that hurled boulders, barrels of stones, or firebrands in bundles. This artillery was so effective that some defenders were too frightened to go up on to the ramparts. Nevertheless, some particularly gallant Jews made sorties again and again, pulling off the hides, killing the sappers beneath them, and knocking down the platform.

In response, Josephus built up the wall opposite the platform until it was thirty feet higher, using shelters covered in the hides of newly slaughtered oxen to protect his workmen against missiles. The moist skins gave but did not split when hit and were more or less fireproof. He also added wooden towers along the wall together with a new parapet. The Romans were taken aback by these measures, while the Jews took fresh heart and stepped up their sorties at night, raiding and burning the siege-works.

Irritated at the siege's slow progress and impressed by the defenders' pugnacity, Vespasian decided to starve Jotapata into submission, so he pulled back his troops while continuing the blockade. The city had all the food it needed, but not enough rain fell to replenish the cisterns, and water had to be rationed. However, when Josephus saw that the Romans suspected the inhabitants were suffering from thirst, he made them hang heavy garments from the walls, dripping with water. Vespasian was so discouraged that he resumed his daily assaults on the walls.

Despite a close blockade, for a time Josephus was able to communicate with the outside world and obtain at least some of the supplies that he needed. There was a narrow gully, so nearly impassable that the Romans did not bother to guard it, down which he sent couriers disguised by sheepskins on their backs. But eventually this stratagem was discovered, and the city became completely cut off.

What is fascinating about Josephus is how he sometimes lets us see into his mind, in a way that is almost akin to honesty. As he admits, he had gone to Jotapata for his own safety, but now he began to lose his nerve. "Realizing the city could not hold out much longer and that his life might be in danger were he to stay, Josephus made plans to escape with the local notables," he blandly informs us.[3] He had no qualms about leaving its people to be butchered. Hearing rumors of his plans, a large mob gathered and begged him not to abandon them. "It was wrong for him to run away and desert his friends, to jump from a ship sinking in a storm, in which he had embarked when everything was calm," they cried. "By leaving, he would destroy the city—nobody would dare go on fighting the enemy if they lost their one reason for confidence."[4]

Without mentioning that he was worried about his own safety, Josephus replied that he was leaving the city for their sake. If he stayed, he could not do them any good even if they survived, while should the place be stormed he would be killed pointlessly. If he got away from the siege, however, he would be able to do a lot to help, since he could raise a new Galilean army, a huge one, and draw off the Romans by attacking elsewhere. But he really did not see how he could aid the people of Jotapata simply by staying put. It would only make the Romans intensify the siege because what they wanted more than anything else was to capture him.[5]

This eloquent appeal had no effect. The citizens of Jotapata were determined that he should stay; children, old men, and women with babies fell down in front of him and clung to his feet, wailing. They all felt they would be saved if he remained in the city. Realizing that if he stayed they would think he was answering their prayers, but that if he tried to leave he would be lynched, he graciously agreed to remain. He even claims that what made up his mind was pity for them. "Now is the time to begin the struggle when hope of safety is there none!" he declaimed nobly. "What is really honorable is to prefer glory to life by doing heroic deeds that will be remembered from generation to generation." Then, so he informs us, he immediately led a sally against the Romans, killing several of their sentries and demolishing some of the siege works. For the next few days and nights, "he never left off fighting."[6]

The legionaries had withdrawn from the front line, waiting for the moment they could mount a full-scale assault. The scorpions and stone throwers kept up their fire, as did the Arab archers and Syrian slingers, inflicting many casualties. The only way the Jews could respond was by repeated sallies, exhausting their strength. By now, the assault platforms had almost reached the top of the walls, so Vespasian decided it was time to use a battering ram. This was a huge baulk of timber like the mast of a ship, its end fitted with a massive piece of iron in the shape of a ram's head, which was slung by ropes from scaffolding on wheels. Repeatedly pulled back by a team of men, then hurled forward, the iron head could demolish most sorts of masonry. While the Roman artillery stepped up its bombardment, the enemy hauled the ram into position, protected by hides and hurdles. Its first blow made the whole wall shake. "As though it had already fallen down, an awful shriek rang out from those inside," recalls Josephus.[7]

He tried to lessen the ram's impact by letting down sacks filled with chaff, but the Romans pushed them aside with hooks on long poles. Recently built, the wall began to crumble. However, the Jews rushed out from three different sally ports and, taking the enemy by surprise, set fire to the ram's protective superstructure with a mixture of bitumen, pitch, and brimstone, which destroyed it. "A Jew stepped forward whose name deserves to be remembered," says *The Jewish War*.[8] He was Eleazar ben Sameas, born at Saab in Galilee. Lifting an enormous stone, he threw it from the wall on to the ram, knocking off the head. Then, leaping down among the Romans, he seized the head, which he carried back to the wall, where he stood waving it until he collapsed, mortally wounded by five javelins, writhing in agony but still clutching his prize.

The besiegers rebuilt the ram and toward evening started to batter the same section of wall. Panic broke out among the Romans when Vespasian was wounded in the foot by a spent javelin (which shows he must have been standing dangerously close to the wall). As soon as they realized he had not been seriously hurt, they attacked with real fury. Josephus and his men fought throughout the night, sometimes sallying out to attack the team working the ram, although the fires they lit made them an easy mark for enemy artillery that was invisible in the dark. Clouds of the scorpions' monster arrows cut swathes through their ranks, while rocks hurled by the ballistae demolished part of the ramparts and knocked corners off the towers. The lethal power of this weaponry is gruesomely described by Josephus; for example, he wrote that a man standing near him had his head torn off by a stone and flung over 600 yards and that when a pregnant woman was hit in the belly, the child in her womb was thrown 300 feet.

The siege machines made a terrifying clatter, and the endless whizzing of the arrows and stones fired by the Romans was no less frightening. The sinister thud of dead bodies hitting the ground as they fell down off the battlements was equally dispiriting. Women inside the city were shrieking incessantly, while many of the wounded were screaming with pain. The area in front of the wall flowed with blood, while the corpses were heaped as high as the ramparts. To cap everything, the noise was made even more dreadful by the echoes from the mountains that surrounded the city.

Toward morning the wall finally collapsed under the ram's ceaseless battering. After letting his men have a brief rest, Vespasian got ready to launch his assault at daybreak. Dismounting the pick of his heavily armored cavalrymen, he stationed them three deep near the breaches, ready to go in as soon as the gangways were in position. Behind them, he placed his best foot soldiers. The rest of the horse remained mounted, in extended order farther back, to cut down anyone trying to escape from the city once it had fallen. Still farther back, he ranged the archers in a curved formation with bows at the ready, together with the slingers and the artillery. Other troops were ordered to take ladders and attack undamaged sectors of the wall, to draw off defenders from the breaches.

Realizing what was coming, Josephus placed the older men and walking wounded on the part of the wall that was still standing, where they were more protected and could deal with any attempts at escalade. The fitter men he positioned behind the breach, while groups of six—drawn by lot and including himself—stood at the front, ready to bear the brunt of the assault. He ordered them to plug their ears to avoid being frightened by the legionaries' war cry and to fall back during the preliminary rain of missiles, kneeling under their shields until the archers had used up their arrows, and then to run forward as soon as the Romans pushed their gangways over the rubble.

"Don't forget for one moment all the old men and all the children here, who are about to be horribly butchered, or how bestially your wives are going to be put to death by the enemy," he exhorted them. "Then remember the fury that you feel at the idea of such atrocities and use it in killing the men who want to commit them."[9]

When daylight came and the women and children saw the three ranks of Roman troops menacing the city, the great breaches in the walls, and all the hills around covered by enemy soldiers, they raised a last, dreadful, despairing scream. Josephus gave orders for them to be locked in their houses to stop them from unnerving their menfolk. Then he took up his post in the breach. Strangely, he had prophesied to some of those around him that the city would fall and that he would be taken prisoner—predictions that were plausible but scarcely good for morale.

Suddenly, the serpentine Roman trumpets sounded their booming summons to battle, the legionaries bellowed their war cry, and the sun was blotted out by missiles—javelins, arrows, scorpion bolts, slingshot, and a hail of stones from the onagers. Josephus's men, remembering his instructions, had plugged their ears, and they sheltered under their shields. As soon as the gangways went down, they charged forward to meet the attackers. They had no reserves, however, while the enemy, who had a seemingly inexhaustible supply of fresh troops, formed a tortoise with their big, oblong shields and began to push forward over the main breach.

Josephus had expected this, however, and was prepared. He ordered boiling oil to be poured down from the sections of wall that flanked the breach onto the tortoise. Leaping and writhing in agony, the legionaries fell off the gangways, their close-fitting armor making it impossible to save them from an excruciating death. When the Jews ran out of oil, they threw a slippery substance—boiled fenugreek—on to the gangways, which made it hard for new waves of attackers to keep their balance, some falling over and being trodden to death. Early that evening Vespasian called off the assault.

He then ordered that the three assault platforms further along the wall should be raised much higher, equipping each one with a fireproof, iron-plated siege tower that was fifty feet tall. His archers, slingshot men, and javelin throwers were able to shoot down at the defenders in comparative safety, and at close range, from the tops of these towers, which also mounted the big repeating crossbows.

In the meantime, Vespasian did not confine himself to besieging Jotapata. He sent 3,000 troops under Ulpius Traianus, commander of the Tenth Legion—and father of the future Emperor Trajan—to sack the town of Japha seventeen kilometers away, whose people had joined the revolt, and he sent his son Titus to help him with additional troops. Together, Trajan and Titus killed over 15,000 Jews, taking another 2,000 prisoner. At the same time, Sextus Cerealis, prefect of the Fifth Legion, marched into Samaria, which despite its traditional hostility to Jews looked as if it was on the verge of rebellion, and slaughtered more than 11,000 Samaritans who had gathered on Mount Gerizim

On the forty-seventh day of the siege of Jotapata, the assault platforms overtopped the walls. A deserter informed Vespasian that the defenders had become too exhausted to put up much of a fight and that sentries often dropped off to sleep in the early hours of the morning. Just before dawn the Romans crept to the platforms, Titus being one of the first to climb over the walls, accompanied by a tribune, Domitius Sabinus, with some men from the Fifteenth Legion. They cut the throats of the watch and then entered the city very quietly, followed by the tribune Sextus Calvarius, Placidus, and other troops. (Josephus must have obtained these details from Vespasian's campaign notebooks.)

Within a short time the Romans had captured the citadel on the edge of the precipice and were sweeping down into the heart of Jotapata, yet even at daybreak the defenders had not realized that their city had fallen. Most were still fast asleep, having collapsed from fatigue, while a dense mist enveloped everything. The few who were awake were too tired to be alert. Only when the Jotapatans saw the whole Roman army running through the streets and killing everybody it met did they understand that it was all over.

The city quickly turned into a slaughterhouse. The legionaries had not forgotten what they had suffered during the siege, especially the boiling oil. The weapon they used was their principal sidearm, the "gladius" or short, doubled-edged Roman thrusting sword (more like a big knife than a sword), which was ideally suited for massacre. They drove the terrified crowds down from the citadel to the bottom of the hill through the narrow streets, so tightly jammed together that those who wanted to fight could not raise their arms. When they were able, some of Josephus's best men cut their own throats in despair.

A few held out in one of the northern towers but were overwhelmed, seeming to welcome death. The legionaries suffered only a single casualty. A Jotapatan who had hidden in a cave shouted up to a centurion called Antonius that he wanted to surrender, asking him to reach down and help him out, but when Antonius did so he was stabbed in the groin from below with a spear. Having killed everybody they found in the streets or houses, the Romans spent the next few days hunting down defenders hiding underground. During the siege and the storm they killed at least 40,000 Jews. (This is the figure given by Josephus, who for once may not be exaggerating.) The only prisoners they took were about 1,200 women and children.

Even so, the little city of Jotapata had put up an astonishing resistance. It was a heroic achievement to hold out for nearly eight weeks against the most efficient and best-equipped army in the world. Once again, the Jews had shown that they knew how to fight as if by instinct and that despite their lack of any sort of military training and their pitifully inadequate weaponry, they could be formidable opponents.

Although Josephus may have been a disaster as governor of Galilee in peace time, during the siege of Jotapata he had shown himself to be a gallant and resourceful commander—even if at one point he had thought of running away and deserting his men. His leadership of the city's defense was one of the great triumphs of his life.

But where was he now?

9

The Cave and the Prophecy

"And it shall come to pass, that he who fleeth from the noise of the fear shall fall into the pit; and he that cometh up out of the midst of the pit shall be taken in the snare."

ISAIAH, XXIV, 18

THE STORY OF HOW Josephus persuaded his fellow fugitives to kill themselves is the most equivocal of his entire career. Some historians find it sinister. Yet it is more likely than not that he was innocent of any wrongdoing. We only know about the episode from what he himself tells us in *The Jewish War*. Had he thought that it might harm his reputation, he could have chosen not to include it in the book. He does not mention it in the *Vita*, his apologia, which implies that he did not think it needed any explanation.

The Roman legionaries tried particularly hard to find Josephus, because they hated him as the rebel leader who had inflicted so much mischief on them during the siege and because—under the delusion that his capture would help to win the war within a matter of weeks—their general had given specific orders for him to be taken prisoner. Searching everywhere, they turned over all the dead bodies, ransacked the houses, and went down into the city's cellars and caves, but without success.

At the moment when the city was stormed, aided by a providence that must have been supernatural, despite being hemmed in by the enemy he managed to escape by jumping down into a deep pit, out of which a large cave opened. The cave was completely invisible from above and inside it he found forty notables [of Jotapata] with supplies that would last for a long time. During the following day he remained hidden there, since the enemy was stationed all over the city, but when night fell he climbed up in order to look for some way of escape and see where they might have posted sentries. Everywhere was being so closely watched by the troops searching for him that he had to go back into the cave. For two days he outwitted his pursuers.[1]

On the third day a woman in the cave went up and was caught by the Romans. Questioned, she told them where the governor was hiding. Vespasian at once sent two tribunes to the pit, Paulinus and Gallicanus, with other officers. They shouted down, asking him, politely enough, to come up and telling him not to be afraid—his life would be safe. However, after killing and wounding so many of their comrades, he expected to be put to a spectacularly horrible death, and in any case he knew that Romans frequently broke their word. He declined the invitation.

Vespasian then sent a third tribune called Nicanor, an old friend of Josephus, who explained that his commander had no wish to punish him but only wanted to save the life of a brave soldier, adding that Vespasian would never use a friend to trick a man. Infuriated at the idea of the enemy general going unpunished, the legionaries began to yell that he ought to be burned in his cave. Nicanor stopped them. He wanted to take him alive. Then Josephus saw a possible means of escape.

"Suddenly he remembered the dreams he had sometimes dreamed at night, when God showed him the future calamities that were going to strike the Jews as well as what would happen to the Roman emperors," *The Jewish War* tells us. "As an interpreter of dreams, he understood how to disentangle the real meaning of matters that were expressed by God in ambiguous terms, while he knew a good deal about the prophecies in the sacred books, since he was a priest himself and the descendant of priests."[2]

He claims that he became divinely inspired and, bearing in mind the terrible things he had dreamed, prayed to God. "Since it has seemed good to you who created the Jewish nation to level it with the dust, and since all their prosperity has passed to the Romans, and since you have allowed my spirit to have knowledge of the things to come, I willingly give myself up to the Romans and am happy that I am allowed to stay alive. I am not going over to the Romans and I am certainly not a traitor. I do this because I am your servant."[3]

This is a key passage, even if written years later. Skeptics question his foreknowledge of what lay ahead for Judea and Rome and his assertion that he had been an "interpreter of dreams." Yet he is more than likely to have heard of the popular rumors about a new world ruler. Moreover, it is possible that Nicanor had insinuated that he might make himself useful to Vespasian by looking into the future, since Jews in Rome had a reputation for soothsaying. Whatever inspired him, that sharp, resourceful mind had stumbled on a way for its owner to talk himself out of a very unpleasant situation.

"There had spread over all the Orient an old-established belief that in those days [the end of Nero's reign] men were destined to come out of Judea, who would rule the world," so Suetonius informs us.[4] This is what Josephus must have heard, while it was common knowledge that Nero's regime was growing shaky. Nor had he forgotten what he had learned of the Essene seers when a young man. Although any Jew knew that his priesthood did not give him special powers of seeing into the future, the idea might convince Romans.

He accepted Nicanor's invitation, asking to talk to Vespasian as soon as possible. Unfortunately, his friends in the cave had no intention of letting him go. To have an old friend who was a Roman centurion with a Greek-sounding name—they had probably spoken in Greek—seemed bad enough in itself to these straightforward Galilean hill men. But from what they could gather, they suspected that their leader was thinking of entering the enemy's service, which was downright treason. Josephus records his comrades' efforts to dissuade him from surrendering:

> The laws God gave our ancestors make such a thing impossible, the laws of God who provided us Jews with a spirit that despises death. Josephus, do you love living so much that you're ready to live like a slave? Have you lost all self-respect? How many men did you persuade to die fighting for

liberty? You won't deserve to be called a man and everybody will despise you for allowing yourself to be spared by the people you fought so fiercely, if you really are ready to accept it from them—provided they're in earnest. Perhaps the Romans' awful victory has made you forget who you are, but we are here to see that our forefathers' honor is not insulted. We will give you our own right hands and a sword, and if you are ready to die properly, then you shall die as a Jewish general. But if you refuse them, you can die as a traitor.[5]

It is likely that from the start these rough provincials had distrusted this rich aristocrat from Jerusalem. Now they threatened him with their swords, promising they would cut him down if he tried to surrender to the Romans. He must join them in a mass suicide. Frightened that they might attack him, before killing themselves, Josephus tried to talk them into a more reasonable frame of mind—"like a philosopher." His reply, which he puts in *The Jewish War,* is too long to quote in full, but even if composed in retrospect, it must repeat some of the things he said.

"What makes us so frightened of going up to the Romans?" he asked. "Is it death? If so, why are we afraid of it when we've made up our minds to kill ourselves—we only suspect the enemy might kill us. Or are we scared of being made slaves? Well, just now we're not exactly free." Then he argued that suicide was a sin. "The souls of men who act against themselves in this mad way are shut up in the darkest hole in Hades while God punishes their children, blaming them for their fathers' sin. God hates such a deed and the crime is punished by our lawgiver [Moses]—the law demands that the bodies of suicides should never be exposed until the sun has set before they are buried, yet we are allowed to bury the corpses of our enemies much sooner." There is no need to doubt his sincerity in questioning what he called "self-murder." Many rabbis disapproved of suicide. No doubt, Zealots preferred it to captivity—as they were to show at Masada—but Josephus did not subscribe to the Fourth Philosophy.

"I am not going over to the Romans because I want to betray myself," he ended. "I would be as stupid as a deserter if I did—they do it to save themselves while I should be doing it to destroy myself. Yet in a way I should rather like it to be a piece of Roman treachery. If they kill me after giving their word to spare my life, I shall die happy, since it will show up their falseness and their lies, and be worth even more than winning a victory."[6]

His speech caused uproar, and he describes himself as being like a wild beast at bay surrounded by huntsmen. "They were infuriated by Josephus," he admits frankly. "They ran at him from all sides with drawn swords, calling him a coward, and were only too keen to thrust at him." The scene in the cave must have been a nightmare, the former governor trying desperately to dodge the sword blades in the darkness, ducking and pleading. In the end, he somehow managed to calm them down.[7]

Even so, he was still committed to a suicide pact. "Since we are all determined to die, let us draw lots about how we do it," he announced, neatly gaining control of the situation. "The one who draws the first lot will die by the hand of the one who draws the second lot, until we have worked our way through all of us—nobody ought to die by his own hand as it would be unfair if a survivor was left to change his mind and stay alive after everybody else was dead." The forty calmly allowed themselves to be killed in turn, until only Josephus and another man remained. "Disliking the prospect of being condemned by lot out a choice of two or of shedding the blood of a fellow Jew, he soon talked the other man into abandoning the pact and persuaded him to go on living."[8] But he had only won the right to climb out of the cave and face the Romans.

"It happened by chance or by God's providence" is how he explains his survival.[9] Some commentators are not so sure, convinced that he rigged the draw. It has been suggested that this was a circular count rather than simply drawing lots and that he might have fixed the result by using a formula that mathematicians unjustly call the "Josephus count."[10] Yet we only know what went on in the cave at Jotapata because Josephus chooses to tell us. If he had thought there was anything sinister he would never have told the story, while clearly he was proud of having tried to prevent his companions from "murdering themselves." Nor does he appear to have been accused by his enemies of having done anything wrong in the cave, although they must have read *The Jewish War*.

There were many men who were prophets in first-century Judea, all of them convinced that they possessed the gifts of another Jeremiah or Isaiah. Nor did the Roman dismiss such foreknowledge out of hand; they had their own pagan oracles. It was in this context that Josephus claimed to have dreams in which he saw how the war would end and who was going to rule Rome. Although he never actually describes himself as a prophet, before the conflict was over, he too would be comparing himself to Jeremiah.

Throughout the summer of 67 CE Vespasian must have been an extremely worried man. Only the previous autumn Emperor Nero had forced his best general, Domitius Corbulo, to commit suicide, although Corbulo had routed the Parthians, ridding Rome of her biggest danger in the East. Admittedly, the aristocratic Corbulo was destroyed for having relations who had political ambitions. Suetonius, in his *Lives of the Caesars*, explained why Vespasian had been chosen: "because of the obscurity of his family and lineage there was no need to fear him."[11] Yet Nero might easily come to the conclusion that he was not so harmless after all. Every senior commander feared the emperor. (Later, his successor, Galba, said that when he had received letters from Rome, he had always wondered if they contained Nero's orders for his death.)

Almost as alarming, the emperor was growing increasingly unpopular. There had been a botched attempt at a coup in 65, involving members of the Praetorian guard, and another, perhaps successful coup must have seemed far from unlikely. If it happened, it meant civil war of a sort unseen for a century, with the dilemma of choosing the right side in order to survive. More than a few strong men were likely to fight each other for Nero's place, while the Roman aristocracy still sighed for a republic. The future was full of danger. Even so, Vespasian was determined to win this war, whatever might happen at Rome, and in the circumstances Judea was much safer than Italy.

Taking so much trouble to coax the enemy general out of the cave shows the value he set on taking him prisoner. Josephus himself admits that it was too high: "he thought the war would be more or less over, once Josephus was in his hands."[12] Yet the former governor of Galilee possessed a good deal of information that would be extremely useful to the Romans. Not only was his topographical expertise—later, evident in his writings—and his knowledge of the baffling Judean landscape vitally important for their strategy and tactics, but to some extent he would be able to make informed guesses at what the Jewish leaders were thinking at Jerusalem.

At the very least, as an enemy commander he would be a welcome or-
nament for a spectacular procession through Rome in the event of Vespasian being awarded a triumph after a successful campaign. However, this
was far too optimistic a calculation to weigh heavily with such a realist,
since Nero was most unlikely to reward him in such a way. On balance, it
is likely that Vespasian had not yet made up his mind whether to execute
the prisoner as soon as he had been debriefed or send him back to Nero to
show that the campaign in Judea was going well.

Josephus cannot have known what to expect when, led by the centurion Nicanor, he was dragged into the Roman general's presence. Legionaries flocked around the general and his prisoner, struggling to get a
better view, demanding that he be put to death. We may question his
claim that all the officers felt sorry for him. No doubt, he felt he stood a
good chance of being nailed to a cross, the standard penalty for anyone
who rebelled against Rome. However, we know that he had already
thought of a plan that might just work, his only hope of survival.

He saw, sitting on a curule chair with a folding seat, the invariable
camp stool of a Roman commander, a stocky, bald man with a beaked
Roman nose whose lined forehead and tightly compressed mouth gave
him an oddly tense expression. (Suetonius says that Vespasian always
looked as though he were suffering from constipation.[13]) Yet, judging from
the surviving portrait busts and from coin profiles, if it was an alarmingly
tough face, it was also a noticeably humorous one. In the eyes of Roman
aristocrats he was "not quite a gentleman," and he seems to have lacked
their frozen hauteur.

Next to Vespasian stood his lieutenant, his twenty-seven-year-old elder
son, Titus. Not so tall as his father but with the same nose, he was, despite
having a plump belly, a handsome and dignified young man with a kind
expression. Yet for all his smile, it was obvious that Titus, too, was very formidable indeed.

Knowing the Roman cult of dignity, Josephus looked as unconcerned
as possible when he was pushed forward. If one can believe his account,
this had its effect on Titus, who immediately felt sorry for him, and it
made some of the other Roman officers feel the same way. The prisoner
begged to be allowed to say something in private to Vespasian, who told

everybody except Titus and two senior officers to leave them, and then
Josephus appealed to his captor:

> You may think you have done no more than take Josephus prisoner, but
> I am here to tell you something of vital importance, Vespasian. Had I not
> been sent to you by God, I should have obeyed the Jewish Law and killed
> myself—I know how defeated generals ought to die. So why send me to
> Nero, then? Because Nero and those who will follow him are not going
> to survive. Vespasian, you shall become Caesar and Emperor, you and
> your son here. Put me in chains, keep me close to you, because you, Cae-
> sar, are not only my lord, but the lord of land and sea, the lord of all
> mankind. Guard me carefully so that I can be punished if I have said
> anything that has not been decreed by God.[14]

Always skeptical, Vespasian at first suspected that he was lying to save
his life. So did the two officers. "I'm surprised you did not prophesy to the
people of Jotapata that their city would fall, and that you failed to foresee
you were going to be taken prisoner," one of them retorted unpleasantly.
"Or are you just talking nonsense in a futile attempt to escape what is
coming to you?" It was his most dangerous moment.[15]

"But I of course I prophesied that Jotapata would fall, on the forty-
seventh day, and that I was going to be captured alive by the Romans,"
answered Josephus.[16] Vespasian then ordered that other prisoners be questioned about this—presumably female prisoners, since the men had all
been slaughtered. When the Roman learned that these predictions really
had been made by Josephus, he began to take them more seriously, and
there was no more talk of sending him to Nero. Vespasian agreed with
Titus that he should be spared, giving orders for him to be kept in close
but comfortable confinement.

One distinguished modern historian suggests that Josephus invented
the prophecy later and inserted it in *The Jewish War* in order to conceal the
extent of his collaboration with the Romans.[17] Yet this seems highly unlikely. Although he almost certainly supplied the Romans with vital information, it is surely taking skepticism too far to doubt that he made some
sort of prediction to Vespasian.

It must be remembered that he was not alone in making such a prediction. As has been seen, Suetonius mentions in his *Lives of the Caesars* how a rumor had been circulating for years in the East that new rulers of the world were about to emerge in Judea. Time and again, prophets and "magicians" in Judea had foretold the coming of a messiah. Might he not be a gentile instead of a Jew? Rabbi Yohanan ben Zakkai told Vespasian he was going to become emperor, just as Josephus had done. There were pagan omens, too. Both Tacitus and Suetonius mention how Vespasian consulted the oracle of Ba'al on Mount Carmel. "While he was offering sacrifice there and pondering over his secret ambitions, Basilides, priest of the shrine, carefully examined the entrails of the sacrificial victims and then told him, 'Whatever you are planning, whether it is building a house, enlarging your estates or increasing the number of slaves you own, it is certain that a mighty dwelling, immense territory and a whole host of men have been given to you.'"[18] Both Vespasian and Titus took this sort of foreknowledge very seriously indeed.

Describing how he prophesied before Vespasian, Josephus takes care to remove the incident from the climate of messianic expectation that was widespread among his fellow countrymen. He does so to conceal Jewish resentment at the Roman occupation so that he can argue that most Jews had been against the war but were manipulated by a handful of extremists who prevented them from making peace.[19]

Josephus's prophetic utterance before Vespasian was more than a guess about the political situation at Rome or a cynical calculation that it might turn out to be useful for Vespasian's reputation. He genuinely believed he possessed some sort of prophetic gift, and later he became convinced that he was a prophet in the full, Old Testament sense of the word. The only plausible explanation for his survival after Jotapata is that he really did make his prophecy about the future of the Roman Empire, and it was so convincing that Vespasian and Titus decided it might come true. There is no other good reason for the favor they showed him. His belief in his powers as a prophet also explains his behavior on many occasions during the subsequent course of the war.[20]

10

Josephus the Prisoner

"Boast not thyself of tomorrow, for thou knowest not what a day may bring forth."

AFTER CAPTURING JOTAPATA, Vespasian withdrew with two legions to Ptolemais and then Caesarea Maritima. A third was sent to the Greek city of Scythopolis, ten kilometers away. No doubt, his weary troops hoped that the campaigning season of 67 CE would end earlier than usual, since they had been savagely mauled and felt that they needed time to recuperate. Their tough old general did not have room for such a luxury.

When the legions marched into Caesarea, a mob of Greeks swarmed around them, howling for Josephus's execution, but were ignored by Vespasian. During the next few months, he must frequently have questioned his prisoner. If one reads between the lines of *The Jewish War*, it very much looks as if Josephus kept on repeating the prediction that had saved his life besides using every trick he knew in trying to convince his captors of Jewish mastery of the occult.

In his *Jewish Antiquities*, Josephus mentions a performance that he no doubt laid on to impress them. "I saw a fellow Jew called Eleazar casting out a demon in front of Vespasian, his sons and his tribunes," he tells us. "This is how he did it. Under the nose of the possessed man he put a ring enclosing a root recommended by Solomon and, as the man sniffed it, pulled the demon out through his nose: when the man fell down, he commanded the demon to leave him, calling on Solomon and reciting spells."[1] Eleazar may have been an Essene, and the magic root was probably the phosphorescent and presumably foul-smelling baaras plant, which supposedly grew near Masada and is described in the seventh book of *The Jewish War*.

Although Vespasian kept Josephus under close guard, he gave him new clothes and valuable presents.[2] At Caesarea Maritima, he was probably housed in the governor's pleasant white palace by the sea and was more comfortable than he had been for months. He recalled that the climate was as genial in winter as it was suffocatingly hot in summer. As time went by, his captivity was relaxed, and his chains were taken off. "Vespasian showed in all sorts of ways how much he respected me," Josephus tells us proudly.[3] He even gave him a wife, although he already had one at Jerusalem (of whom nothing is known), ordering him to marry her. She was "one of the women taken prisoner to Caesarea, a virgin and a native of that place."[4] That is all he says about her, but since she had avoided being sent to the slave market, we may guess that she must have been good-looking and desirable. She left him after his release.

Nonetheless, he cannot have failed to see that his life was still in danger. If Nero survived, Vespasian was not a man to forgive what he would see as deception. We can guess too that his relations with Roman officers, apart from Vespasian and Titus, were strained. Admittedly, as a fluent speaker of Greek who knew Rome, he had more in common with them than with his recent comrades, the hillbillies of Jotapata. They may even have respected him as a patrician: it is revealing that Suetonius places him among the *nobiles*, the highborn. Even so, they distrusted an enemy commander who had defected and always remained suspicious. This early period as a prisoner, never knowing whether the next day would be his last, must have been nerve-racking for Josephus.

Most Jews regarded him as a traitor, a man fighting against his own country. At first only rumors of the fall of Jotapata reached Jerusalem, since there were no survivors to tell the tale. Many people refused to believe that it had fallen. When the rumors were confirmed, Josephus was said to be among the dead. He possessed a dry wit and records with amusement how the news "filled all Jerusalem with sorrow . . . the wailing did not cease for a whole month, people hiring professional pipers to play laments in the streets." They mourned him more than friends and family. After all, he had been one of the nation's leading generals. Sorrow turned to rage, however, when it became known that not only had he survived, but he was being unusually well treated by the Romans. He notes dryly that he was called a coward and a deserter and that the inhabitants' eagerness to take revenge on him made them keener than ever to fight the legionaries.[5]

Yet we can assume that there were exceptions among what have been called his fellow upper-class moderates, those Jews for whom he later wrote the *Vita*.[6] They included people still inside Jerusalem. As the Roman army remorselessly ground forward, they came to agree with his view that the war was hopeless and that the Jewish nation had been taken over by a fanatical minority. Men like this secretly sympathized with his going over to the Romans and wished they were able to follow his example.

Identifying potential Jewish allies and trying to understand their attitude would have been of real interest to Vespasian during his conversations with Josephus. We know that these were frequent from his statement in the *Contra Apionem*: "While I was a prisoner, Vespasian and Titus demanded my constant attendance on them, at first in chains."[7] Presumably, they recognized a pragmatist rather than a renegade in the turncoat general, someone who could be extremely helpful. Nor is it too much to suspect that these two Romans took a liking to the Jewish patrician, which was to find expression in future favors.

Meanwhile, Josephus got to know Vespasian well, developing genuine admiration for this soldier who fought as hard as he marched. Despite his grim face, the general in private life was an exceptionally good-natured man, tolerant of criticism and even jokes at his expense, seldom bearing a grudge. He was pleasant company, fond of laughter. We know from Suetonius what his tranquil routine as emperor would be, and it cannot have been so different when he was at Caesarea Maritima.

He rose early, just before daybreak, and after reading letters and official reports, received his friends. While they were greeting him, he dressed, putting on his own shoes. Having dealt with any business, he went for a drive and then took a nap, sleeping with one of the concubines whom he acquired when [his wife] Coenis died. After his rest, he had a bath and then dined. They say he was never in a better mood or readier to grant favours than at such times, and members of his household waited for them if they wanted to make a petition.[8]

For all his love of a quiet life, Vespasian was never idle. Although his army was so badly in need of a rest, before July was over he marched out from Caesarea to deal with the seaport of Joppa farther down the coast, which, despite having been sacked by Cestius, had turned itself into a pirates' nest. Fugitives from Jewish cities destroyed in the recent campaigns had settled here in large numbers, and many took to stealing boats to use as privateers, preying on the local merchant shipping and making communications between Egypt and Syria increasingly hazardous. They also endangered the export of grain from Alexandria on which the citizens of Rome depended for their bread.

When they heard that the Roman army was approaching, the pirates took refuge on board their boats. However, Joppa is not a natural harbor, and when a violent storm (called "the black north wind" by Josephus) blew up during the night, there was no safe haven in which to shelter, and the ships were driven onto the rocky shore or collided with each other. Some of the pirates killed themselves in the belief that dying by the sword was less painful than drowning, while others were dashed into bloody fragments by the rocks. A ghastly screaming could be heard above the roaring of the wind and the waves. The description in *The Jewish War* is so vivid that one can only conclude that Josephus was present on Vespasian's staff and heard the noise for himself. Later, over 4,000 mangled bodies were washed up onto the nearby beaches.[9]

The next morning, Vespasian marched into a deserted Joppa at the head of his legions, without opposition since nobody was left alive. After razing it to the ground, he left a detachment of cavalry in a fortified camp on the former acropolis, defended by a handful of infantry. The cavalry were given specific orders to ride out and devastate the surrounding countryside, destroying the local cities and villages, which they did every day for a month—reducing it to a desert. The Romans had recovered control of the entire coastline.

Vespasian then led his troops to the northeast to visit King Agrippa II at his capital in the Golan, Caesarea Philippi. Apart from a few cities, the king's lands lay outside Jewish territory, as he and his subjects were Idumeans. While nobody could have been more civilized than Agrippa, the Jews regarded Idumeans as barbarous descendants of Ishmael, even if they were fellow believers, a distinction that perhaps made the Idumeans more acceptable to the Romans. Vespasian spent three weeks at Caesarea Philippi, resting his troops and being entertained lavishly. *The Jewish War* refers to "feasting," so it is likely that Agrippa gave some good parties, and Josephus, as Vespasian's expert on the natives, would have been there to enjoy them. The Roman general got what he wanted from Agrippa: license to crush the Jewish rebels who had recently taken over the king's cities of Tiberias and Taricheae.

Vespasian's three legions pitched camp three miles away from Tiberias, but in view of its walls. The decurion Valerian was then sent forward with six horsemen to offer terms to the citizens. Dismounting, so as to look more peaceable, Valerian said he knew very well that the Tiberians loved peace and that he realized they had been forced into rebellion by a small minority. (Josephus must have told him.) While he was speaking, Jesus ben Sapphias—Josephus's old enemy—made a sudden sortie with his thugs, and Valerian had to run for it, leaving his horses behind. However, Tiberias's notables went out to Vespasian, begging him not to blame the city for the behavior of a few lunatics, and Jesus fled to Taricheae. The next day, after breaking down the south wall to facilitate their entry, the Romans marched in without violence. Vespasian promised the citizens that they would be safe so long as they remained loyal to King Agrippa.

He then moved his camp to between Tiberias and Taricheae. Reinforcements were pouring into Taricheae, and although no new general had taken Josephus's place, its garrison obviously meant to fight. Protected by a hill behind it and by walls, the city seemed strong enough, with a fleet of boats on Lake Gennesaret ready to evacuate the defenders should things go wrong. The irrepressible Jesus ben Sapphias attacked the Roman camp as it was being built, trying to demolish the fortifications. Outnumbered, he was easily beaten off, and withdrew to the boats from where his bowmen shot at the Romans on the shore.

Vespasian now learned that the enemy had gathered in large numbers on the plain before Taricheae, and he sent his son with a cohort of 600 picked legionaries to disperse it. The enemy force was bigger than anticipated, so Titus asked his father for more troops. While waiting for them, he cheered his men with a rousing speech, telling them they were better armed, better disciplined, and more experienced than the Jews. Their opponents were brave alright, but it was a crazy sort of bravery; they might be fighting for their country's liberty, whereas he and his men were fighting for glory. "Don't let me down, and keep in mind that God will be helping my attack. Remember, we're better than they are at close quarters."[10]

In response to his request, Ulpius Traianus came up with 400 cavalry, while Antonius Silo occupied the hill behind Taricheae with 2,000 archers, keeping the enemy bowmen too busy to help their fellow citizens outside. Then Titus charged into the Jews on the plain. The Jews fought well enough, but being poorly armed and without shields, they had no defense against the Roman cavalry's long lances. They broke, bolting for the city, and were cut to pieces or trampled down as they ran, many being headed off and slaughtered. Inside the walls, uproar ensued between the citizens who wanted to give in and the fanatical rebels who had taken refuge in the city and were determined to go on fighting.

Guessing what was happening, Titus saw his chance and cheered his men on again. "Now's the time!" he yelled. "Why are we waiting, comrades, when God is handing the Jews over to us? We are going to go inside and win! Can't you hear them quarrelling?"[11] Then he jumped on his horse and led a charge along the shore, riding through the lake's shallows to burst into the city where it was unfortified. The usual massacre began, but he called it off fairly soon. Jesus ben Sapphias and his gang got away into the countryside, while large numbers of diehards took refuge in the boats on Lake Gennesaret.

Vespasian soon arrived, and after placing guards around Taricheae with orders to kill anyone who tried to leave, he set about dealing with the boats, building big rafts. The Jews' craft were very small, and they had no chance of landing since the shore was closely watched by horsemen. When the rafts were ready, manned by legionaries and spread out in a long line, they sailed toward the enemy. Desperately, the Jews threw javelins and stones, which had no effect on armored men. Their boats were boarded, rammed, or forced on shore. Many were speared in the water or shot with arrows; those who tried to climb on the rafts had their heads or hands cut off. The whole lake was colored with blood and choked with bodies, not a single fugitive escaping. For weeks a dreadful stench came from the shore, which was littered with rotting corpses. Including those who had already perished in the city, the dead amounted to 6,500.

Vespasian had no desire to hand back a deserted, valueless Taricheae to Agrippa. Seated on a curule chair on a platform in the center of the city, he gave orders for the locals to be separated from the newcomers who had led the rebellion; the former were pardoned, while the latter were told to go to Tiberias and take their goods with them. Although the road was guarded by soldiers to make sure they did not run away, they went cheerfully enough, convinced that their lives had been spared. When they reached Tiberias, however, they were herded into the stadium where the old and sick, numbering about, 1,200, were butchered, while 6,000 strong young men were put in chains and sent as navvies to dig Nero's canal at Corinth. Of the remainder, amounting to nearly 40,000, over 30,000 were sold in the slave markets. Those from Agrippa's territory were returned to their king, who then sold them off as slaves in just the same way.

According to Josephus, Vespasian had been a little uneasy about duping the refugees into believing they would be spared. "His war council overcame his scruples, arguing that nothing wrong could ever be done to Jews"—meaning that Jews did not possess the right to be considered as human.[12] However impressive and likeable he may have seemed, Vespasian, like so many great Romans, had an evil side and was no stranger to treachery.

Titus, who does not seem to have shared his father's uneasiness, was very proud of having captured Taricheae and, in particular, of the battle on Lake Gennesaret. Ships would feature prominently in his triumph at Rome in 71 CE, and there are references to it on some of his father's coins.

By now it was September. After the fall of Taricheae, nearly all the Galilean cities and fortresses still in rebel hands surrendered. There were three important exceptions: Gamala, Mount Tabor, and Gischala. Although the Roman campaigning season had in theory come to an end, and it was time to take up winter quarters and rest his battle-weary legions, the iron-willed Vespasian was determined to complete the job before the year was over.

The best fortified of the surviving Jewish strongholds was the seemingly impregnable Gamala in the Golan, on the far side of the lake from

Taricheae. In fact, Gamala was even more inaccessible than Jotapata. (It was the birthplace of Judas the Galilean, founder of the Zealots.) So vivid is the description of the city in *The Jewish War* that the reader realizes how familiar Josephus must have been with the city, as governor of Galilee as well as during the siege.

At the top of what he calls a high mountain, Gamala was built on a rough spur like a hump on a long neck, and thus its name, which meant "camel." Surrounded on three sides by deep, impassable ravines, there was a slightly more accessible approach on one side, although the inhabitants had carved a huge, slanting trench out of the rock to defend it. The houses were built all along the mountain face, crowded above each other, so that the city looked as if it were hanging in midair and about to topple down at any moment. The mountain top served as a citadel while, unlike Jotapata, there was a spring at the far end of the city and a well inside the walls, which supposedly ensured an adequate water supply. Not only was the place almost impregnable, but during the previous year Josephus had made it even stronger with trenches and subterranean passages.

The Romans had given Gamala to King Agrippa II, but its people refused to submit to him and remained stubborn supporters of the rebellion. The city's capture and its return would not only please Agrippa but destroy an important rebel center that was menacing Galilee. Even so, after all the heavy casualties inflicted on Vespasian's men during the long and grueling siege of Jotapata, one can only wonder that he felt so confident about his ability to capture such an eagle's nest. However, he had the former commander of Jotapata by his side to advise him and read the defenders' minds.

Because of the strength of its mountaintop site, the people of Gamala were far more convinced that they could hold out against a siege than the Jotapatans had been. There were fewer fighting men in their city, but they relied on its natural defenses. Agrippa's troops had been besieging them for the past seven months without making any progress.

When Vespasian arrived on 24 September with King Agrippa, he found that his normal practice of surrounding a besieged city with a ring of soldiers was ruled out by the terrain. Instead he placed sentries and lookouts at each convenient point, besides occupying a nearby hill. As soon as the legionaries had pitched their camps on the hill and fortified them, he set about constructing assault platforms. One was built by the Fifteenth Legion at the eastern end, facing the city's highest tower, while another was constructed opposite the town center. The Tenth Legion filled in trenches and ravines. Agrippa went up to the walls to try and persuade the defenders to surrender, offering good terms, and begging them to listen to reason. They refused to hear him, and one of their slingers hit the king on the right elbow with a lucky shot. The Romans were shaken by such a savage response. If these men would try to kill a distinguished fellow countryman who had their best interests at heart, then they were going to put up an unusually bitter fight.

The assault platforms were completed in a surprisingly short time by the legionaries who had done the same job at Jotapata. They started to bring up artillery. Chares and Joseph, the city's leaders, ordered the men of Gamala onto the ramparts, although they were already losing heart— partly because their supposedly inexhaustible water supply was running dry, partly because of insufficient stocks of food. Throwing javelins, they managed for a time to slow down the legionaries who were hauling the siege engines forward, but when the scorpions and stone-throwers were in position and began shooting, they abandoned the walls and took cover in the city.

The besiegers now used battering rams to breach the walls in three places and poured in "with a mighty sound of trumpets and clash of arms, and of soldiers shouting."[13] For a moment, it looked as if Gamala had fallen. Fighting desperately, its citizens were pushed back into the upper part of the city.

Then, everything went wrong for the Romans. Unexpectedly, the defenders charged downhill from the upper city, hurling back their astonished enemies. Jammed into the steep, narrow streets that twisted along the mountainside, the legionaries were unable to benefit from superior weaponry. Trying to escape, they started jumping onto the flat roofs of the low houses, but as more and more did so, the rickety dry-stone shanties fell down, causing further deaths; some were killed by falling beams, some broke their legs, others were suffocated by the dust, and a few even stabbed themselves. The wreckage gave the citizens plenty of stones to throw, while they snatched up swords from dead and dying enemies. Clouds of dust made it hard to see, and Romans killed each other by mistake. In the murk, it was difficult for them to find their way out of the city.

Upset at seeing his men suffer so many casualties and anxious to regain control of the situation, Vespasian pushed forward—instead of retreating—amid the confusion into the upper city, accompanied by a handful of officers. Suddenly, he too found himself cut off. Always a fighter, he managed to rally enough troops to form a tortoise, taking his place in the front line. Holding their shields in front or above them, beating off their enemies, they retreated step by step until they were outside the walls.

The Romans had suffered severe losses, their most important casualty being the distinguished decurion Ebutius, who had "done very great mischief to the Jews" in the recent campaigns. Others managed to escape death through sheer good luck. "A centurion named Gallus and ten soldiers, isolated in the fighting, went and hid in a house," Josephus informs us. "That evening, still in their hiding place, he and his men who were Syrians [Aramaic speakers] could hear the owners talking at supper about what the citizens meant to do and in particular about what they were going to do to Romans. During the night, he and his comrades emerged and killed the lot, escaping back to their camp."[14]

The legionaries were thoroughly dejected. They had never been routed in such a way before; moreover, they had nearly suffered the disgrace of losing their general. Vespasian explained to them in a tactful speech what had gone wrong. He reminded them that as soldiers they must expect casualties. Like all ancient authors, Josephus cannot help turning the speech into an oration, but as he was present, his version may be fairly near the truth. It certainly sounds like the sort of thing Vespasian would have said to his troops:

A lot of Jews have been killed by us and now we are paying back part of what we owe to fate. Just as it's stupid to be puffed up by winning, so it's silly to be disheartened if things go wrong. The change from either mood can be a quick one, and the best soldier is the sort who's steady in bad times and cheerfully struggles on to put things right. What occurred just now had nothing to do with inadequacy on our side or Jewish bravery, but happened because it's a tricky place, which worked in their favor and slowed us up. Your mistake lay in being too excited and not thinking—you should never have followed the enemy to the top. After capturing the lower city, you ought to have lured them down into a stand-up combat, but by trying to win a victory as quickly as possible you forgot about safety. Our successes come from training and discipline. Impetuosity and lack of self-control are not Roman qualities, they are mistakes made by barbarians, and they're usually made by Jews. It is up to us to rediscover our natural fighting skills instead of being angry or depressed by this small set-back. You can cheer yourselves up by using your own right arms in the proper way. Because that's how you are going to avenge your dead comrades and punish the men who killed them. And it's my job to be the first into action and the last out."[15]

Wiser folk in Gamala fled down pathless ravines that had been left un-guarded or along secret passages. For a moment, Josephus reveals his pity for them. "They realized there was no longer any chance of making terms, no way out," he tells us. "Their food was almost gone—they were very frightened, and in despair."[16] Many began to die of starvation. Even so, most of the population held on. In October, after what sounds like super-human digging, three troopers of the Fifteenth Legion undermined a tower and opened another breach. One of Gamala's two leaders, Joseph, was killed trying to defend it, while the other, Chares, died of shock in his sickbed when he heard the news. Wary after their previous setback, the Romans did not send in a storming party just yet.

Then, in the fourth week of October, Titus rejoined his father. Shortly after his arrival, with 200 horsemen and a few legionaries, Titus raced into the city through a breach before the guards were able to intercept him. He was quickly followed by his father who attacked with every man at his dis-posal. "Everywhere you heard the endless groans of the dying while the en-tire city was deluged with the blood that was pouring down the slopes."[17]

All the defenders who were able fled with their families up to the "citadel." No more than a bare mountaintop, it was soon crowded with terrified men and women, frantically hurling stones or rolling rocks down on to the Romans. Suddenly a storm began, the wind blowing the be-siegers' spears into the faces of the defenders, who were barely able to keep their foothold on the mountain. The legionaries pushed on relentlessly, stabbing with their short swords and throwing babies into the ravines. Many people jumped into the void to escape them, clutching their wives and children in their arms. No prisoners were taken, the sole survivors being two nieces of one of Agrippa's senior officers. Five thousand Jews died at Gamala. Even so, they had killed four thousand Romans.

While Gamala was being besieged, Vespasian had sent Placidus with 600 cavalry to eliminate the Jewish garrison at Mount Tabor, between Scythopolis and the Great Plain. Two thousand feet high—characteristically, Josephus says 20,000—its summit was a plateau three-quarters of a mile long. At first sight, this, too, seemed impregnable, but no doubt Josephus had explained to Vespasian the place's weak point—lack of water—which was why he thought a small force could deal with it. The garrison came down, pretending to ask for terms, but hoping to catch the Romans off guard. As soon as they attacked, Placidus and his men galloped off into the plain. When the enemy pursued, he wheeled around to massacre them. Those who got away fled to Jerusalem, while the inhabitants of Mount Tabor surrendered in return for their lives and water.

By the end of October 67, both Gamala and Mount Tabor had been captured, and the Romans were ready to go into winter quarters. Now only one stronghold in Galilee remained in Jewish hands—Gischala in the extreme north of the province.

Josephus was lucky to be alive, and being a prisoner gave him plenty of time for reflection. It must have been during this time that he decided the God of Israel had abandoned his people because of their impiety and was using the Romans as an instrument of divine punishment. Nothing could save the Jews.

11

John of Gischala Comes
to Jerusalem

"The words of his mouth were smoother than butter, but war was in his heart: his words were softer than oil, yet were they drawn swords."

PSALMS, 55, 21

ALL THAT WE KNOW about Yohannan ben Levi—John of Gischala—comes from Josephus who, as we have seen, hated him for trying to take his place as governor of Galilee—not to mention several determined attempts at murder. Obviously, it is very hard to tell what is true in an enemy's testimony. Yet John was an uncompromising patriot who believed passionately in Jewish freedom, and he was convinced that the Jews could win the war. Admittedly, he was unbalanced by a little too much confidence in his own abilities, and he had few scruples about killing anybody who stood in his way.

Josephus says that although most of the inhabitants of Gischala (Gush Halav) were peace-loving farmers interested only in their crops, a large band of brigands had moved into the little city and that some of the city's notables were "sick of the same distemper." They had been encouraged to revolt, he explains, by John, an insanely ambitious intriguer, very clever at getting what he wanted, who knew how to be all things to all men. "It was common knowledge that his reason for being so keen on the war was that he hoped to make himself a dictator." The "malcontents" in the city had chosen him for their leader, and although the majority of the population would have liked to send a message saying they were ready to surrender, Gischala prepared to fight the Romans.[1]

Vespasian had taken two of his legions back to Caesarea, sending the third (the Tenth Legion) to Scythopolis. There was adequate food for his men in both cities, and being very much aware that they were in need of a rest, he wanted to build up their strength during the winter in preparation for the huge effort that would be required for the capture of Jerusalem. Not only was the nation's capital built on a naturally strong site but its walls were unusually solid and defended by fanatics. Any shortage of manpower had been made good by refugees who were flooding into the royal city. The prospect worried even Vespasian. Josephus comments that he trained his legionaries as though they were wrestlers.

In a remote area up in northeastern Galilee, Gischala had no strategic value. Its importance was purely symbolic, as the last stronghold in the province still in Jewish hands. Titus set off to capture the place with a mere thousand horsemen and, after reconnoitering, decided that it could easily be taken by storm. However, this would mean massacring its population, and for the moment at least, he seems to have been sick of bloodshed. Hoping to persuade its defenders to surrender, he rode up to the walls, which were crowded with men yelling defiantly.

Just what are you hoping for? Every other Galilean city has fallen, and far stronger ones than yours fell at the first assault, yet here you are, stubbornly holding out by yourselves. All the cities that have accepted Rome's terms are safe, keeping their goods and their way of life, and these terms are still on offer, despite your impertinence. Wanting "liberty" may be all very well, but trying to resist when there's no hope is ridiculous. If you turn down my very generous offer, which I make in all good faith, then you are going to learn what war means. As a defense against Roman siege engines, your walls are a joke. If they think they can depend on them, then the last of the Galilean rebels are about to discover they are vain and conceited slaves who have already been taken prisoner.[2]

According to Josephus, none of the locals dared to reply. In any case, they were not even allowed onto the walls, which were entirely manned by bandits who guarded the gates to stop anybody from going out to surrender or letting in enemy horsemen. John took it on himself to answer Titus. He was satisfied with the terms and would make everybody else in the city accept them, he shouted. But Titus must let the Jews observe the Sabbath, when they were forbidden by their Law to use weapons or conduct negotiations. Even Romans must be aware that Jews ceased from all labor on this day, and anyone forcing them to break the Law was as guilty as those who broke it. The delay could not hurt Titus because the only thing the Jews could do during the night was to try to escape, which he could easily prevent by camping all around the city. The Jews would gain from staying true to their traditions, and it would look more gracious if he respected their ways.

"This was the work of God who saved John so that he might bring destruction upon Jerusalem," comments Josephus, "just as it was God's doing that Titus was convinced by his excuse for a delay and decided to camp further off at Cydasa."[3] Cydasa was a well-fortified Syrian village with a long history of anti-Jewish activity. Just how small a place Gischala must have been is shown by the suggestion that Titus should surround it with a thousand men.

That Sabbath night, when the Romans had left the city unguarded, John fled south to Jerusalem, accompanied not only by his men but by several thousand local folk, a long and dangerous march through Galilee and Judea, much of it through territory controlled by the enemy. "Run for your lives," he told them. "Once we're in a safe place, we can revenge ourselves on the Romans for what they are going to do to the people we have to leave behind."

Unfortunately, after several miles the women and children could not keep up, and guessing that Titus would soon launch a relentless chase, John was forced to leave them behind amid the screams of wives who begged their husbands to stay. Terrified of being caught by the Romans, some were trampled down trying to run after John's men or were lost in the desert. This description is based on the account given in *The Jewish War*. The detail that several thousand of the locals tried to leave with John contradicts Josephus's statement that most of the inhabitants wanted to surrender. Nor does he give John credit for a gallant attempt to evacuate everybody loyal to the cause of Jewish freedom.

The next morning, Titus and his cavalry rode up to the gates of Gischala, which were opened at once, as the inhabitants and their families greeted him as a liberator. At the same time they told him of John's escape. Titus sent several squadrons of cavalry in pursuit, but he had gained too big a start. After a grueling forced march, John reached Jerusalem safely early in November with most of his little army. However, the Romans killed 6,000 of the noncombatants who had set out with him, dragging back to Gischala as prisoners nearly 3,000 women and children. Although angry at having been tricked, Titus was surprisingly merciful, taking the view that threats were a better deterrent than executions. He merely demolished part of the city wall and left a garrison.

Greeted enthusiastically by the crowds at Jerusalem, John and his men insisted that they had not run away but had withdrawn to fight on more favorable ground. "It would have been a waste of time to risk our lives by trying to defend Gischala or any other badly fortified little town," they explained. "We wanted to keep our weapons and our numbers to defend the capital." Even so, Jerusalem was horrified by the fall of Gischala and by so many refugees being killed or taken prisoner during the retreat. John tried to cheer them up. The enemy was much weaker than anyone realized, and their siege engines had breached the ramparts of Galilee's little cities only with the utmost difficulty, he claimed. "Even if the Romans grow wings, they won't be able to get over the walls of Jerusalem."[4] This went down well with younger men, making them keen to fight, but the older and wiser sensed that they were in terrible danger.

Law and order had broken down in all the cities of Judea before their recapture by the Romans, *The Jewish War* tells us. Each family was divided by politics, quarrelling bitterly, with fighting in the streets between those who were eager for war and those who wanted peace. Gangs of bandits terrorized the well-to-do, breaking into houses and ravaging the countryside. Finally, their leaders joined together and took their men into Jerusalem in search of better pickings. Already overcrowded, its population swollen by starving refugees, the capital grew nightmarish, especially for its richer citizens. Robbery, murder, and every imaginable crime were chronic, not just at night but in full daylight.

Josephus's picture is exaggerated, since he belonged to the class most at risk. The majority of the men he calls bandits are likely to have been illiterate young peasants, '*am ha-arez* who had lost their farms rather than professional criminals. Admittedly, even if they did not understand the finer points of the Fourth Philosophy, they agreed wholeheartedly that it was sinful to pay taxes to Rome, and some of them were levelers. Nevertheless, not all of the "rebels" were peasants. More members of the upper class joined them than Josephus says; they were attracted by the party's heady mix of idealism, courage, and refusal to compromise.[5] What they all had in common was a thirst for Jewish freedom, while they prided themselves on their zeal for religion—the source of their adopted name.

What Josephus does not mention is the impact of the loss of Galilee, which showed everybody just how much their ruling class had failed them. It was during this time that the Zealots began to coalesce into a revolutionary movement. Although there were plenty of aristocrats among them, those of humble origin suspected them of being lukewarm in their devotion to the nation's cause, of wanting to compromise. It looks as if more than a few people were thought to be potential collaborators because of their class. Josephus's defection may well have fueled these suspicions.

Suddenly, the unruly element seized Antipas, a man of royal blood and great influence who was in charge of the public treasury, together with two other distinguished nobles, Levias "a person of importance" and Sophas, the son of Raguel, putting them in chains. All three were rich grandees with armed retainers who might attempt a rescue, so they were speedily put to death. The deed was done by a Zealot called John, son of Dorcas, "one of the most bloody minded of them all."[6] Taking ten other thugs, he went to the prison where the three were confined and cut their throats. The news caused an uproar throughout Jerusalem. Everybody was worried about his own safety, as if the city had been taken by storm. The reason given for the "executions" was that the men had been in close touch with the Romans and were plotting to surrender Jerusalem to them, an accusation that may well have had some basis, although *The Jewish War* implies that it was trumped up and that the real motive was class hatred. Using the alleged plot as a pretext and insisting they were the saviors of the people and of liberty, the Zealots took over the Temple, which they turned into a fortress.

What outraged Josephus still more, however, was the way in which levelers among the Zealots forced the election of a new high priest of humble background, although it was an office that for many years had been a hereditary preserve of the great families. His name was Phannias ben Samuel, and he came from the village of Aphthia, "a man who not only lacked descent from high priests, but was too boorish to understand the meaning of the high priesthood." In *The Jewish War*, Josephus tells us with horror how this "ignoble, low born man" was brought in from the countryside, taken into the Temple, dressed up in the vestments, and told how to play the part and goes on to say that the Zealots thought that both the man and his election were a joke.[7]

Although Phannias did not have distinguished ancestors, he was nonetheless descended from Aaron, the first high priest, and therefore he was entitled to call himself *ha-Kohen*. Instead of being a peasant, as Josephus contends, he worked as a stonemason, which was a perfectly decent calling for a member of the lower priesthood. Moreover, one source claims that he had married a daughter of the Nasi—the Sanhedrin's president.[8] Until the fall of the city, he donned the high priest's miter and breastplate on Yom Kippur. Even so, Phannias's election foreshadowed class war. In political terms, however, he turned out to be a complete nonentity who never made any attempt to influence events.

The Zealot leader at this time was a man of upper-class background, Eleazar ben Simon, who had emerged during the battle with Cestius the previous year, and it was he who had suggested occupying the Temple. Despite a parade of idealism, Eleazar was in reality just a gang boss with a "tyrannical temper." It is unlikely that the Zealots possessed a coherent strategy until John of Gischala took over the leadership, which was some considerable time after his arrival in the capital. It was John who declared war on the old establishment and led the Jewish "revolution," although at first he concealed his aims.

The leader of the Jewish establishment was Ananus ben Ananus, senior among former high priests. Four of his brothers had held the office, and he epitomized the magnates of Judea. He still presided over the junta, though he was weakened by the disappearance of his ally Eleazar ben Ananias, which historians cannot explain. In Josephus's opinion, Ananus was a man of very shrewd judgment, who might have saved the city. No doubt, he had arranged the murder of James, the brother of Jesus, but he knew how to control his savage streak. Rallying the citizens against the extremists in the Temple, he quickly found allies among the elite, notably another ex-high priest Joshua ben Gamala, together with Gorion ben Joseph and Simon ben Gamaliel. The four made speeches all over the city, buttonholing everybody they met in the streets.

They held meetings at which they rebuked the citizens of Jerusalem for not standing up to people "who called themselves 'zealots' as if they were zealous for doing good instead of practicing depravity."[9] One of these meetings drew a particularly big crowd of people who complained about the occupation of the Sanctuary and about so much robbery and blood-shed. They were too frightened to do anything since the Zealots were such tough customers. However, during the meeting Ananus made a long, elo-quent speech that shows his views were close to those of Josephus, who no doubt inserted his own opinions into the version he gives us. The speech marked the last chance of reaching some sort of settlement with the Ro-mans—of escaping from a war bound to end in annihilation.

"I wish I had died before I had seen the house of God so full of abom-ination, at seeing sacred places that ought to be inviolable being trodden by the feet of blood-stained murderers," began Ananus, standing in the midst of a huge crowd. He was in tears as he spoke, frequently glancing meaningfully in the direction of the Temple. Angrily, he rebuked his lis-teners for permitting the Zealots to arm themselves and dominate Jerusalem, for allowing them to put Antipas and his friends in chains, and then torture and murder them, and for letting them establish a tyranny. How could they bear to see their holiest possessions trampled on by such criminals? "You really are pitiful creatures!" he told his audience. "Why can't you rise up and throw them out?" He added, "Or are you waiting for the Romans to come back and rescue our holy places?"

"We are in the middle of a war with Rome—I am not going to specu-late whether it's likely to do us any good and be to our benefit—but I am asking you to try and remember the whole point of the war," he contin-ued. "Surely it's about freedom? Then why are we refusing to let ourselves be ruled by the masters of the known world when we are putting up with these thugs in our own backyard?"

"Now that I've mentioned the Romans, I might as well say everything that came into my mind on the subject while I was talking and what I re-ally think of them. It is this. Even if they somehow succeed in conquering us—and may God forbid that it should all end in such a way—we cannot be asked to suffer anything much worse than what these wretched men have been doing to us."

Subtly, Ananus went on to suggest some of the advantages that might result from making peace. "The Romans have never overstepped the boundaries that are laid down for those who don't share our religion, they have never outraged our sacred customs, and they have always kept well away from our Holy of Holies, showing not only respect but genuine awe. In contrast, these men who were born in our country and brought up in our customs, these men who call themselves Jews, dare to walk around hallowed precincts when their hands are still stained with the blood of fellow countrymen. . . . In plain language, I'm telling you that the Romans might even turn out to be the real upholders of our Law instead of the enemies who are within our walls."[10]

He ended by begging the crowd to fight to the death to save the Temple, for the sake of their wives and children, and for the honor of God. Josephus comments sympathetically that Ananus was a realist who knew how difficult the struggle would be but was prepared to risk everything. His speech was a rousing success, his listeners shouting that the Temple must be recovered at once and demanding a leader. Immediately, Ananus started to collect weapons and to arm his new followers.

Learning that Ananus was organizing an army, the Zealots suddenly charged out of the Temple and attacked his supporters. An increasingly vicious battle ensued in the streets outside, first with stones and javelins, then at close quarters with swords. Although the moderates were badly armed, rage gave them the strength they needed to beat back their opponents. Finally, they stormed the outer court of the Temple, blockading the Zealots in the inner court. However, the devout Ananus refused to break down the sacred doors. Instead, he had 6,000 men chosen by lot, who mounted guard in the colonnade. Josephus notes grimly that many of the richer moderates hired substitutes to mount guard in their place. Yet for a moment it looked as if the moderates had won the day and that the Zealots would soon be starved into surrender.

The man who destroyed the moderates was John of Gischala who, Josephus reports inaccurately and ungenerously, "ran away from Gischala."[11] In retrospect, it is clear that ever since his arrival in the city, John must have been plotting to overthrow the junta because he realized they were planning to make peace with the Romans. Convinced that the war was just, he was no less certain that he was the one man to win it. He identified the Zealots as the only party who, despite their shortcomings, were committed to the war and decided to become their leader. He saw his chance in the struggle with Ananus.

Pretending to be on the moderates' side, John made a point of spending every hour of the day with Ananus, especially while discussing matters with his officers, in addition to passing much of the night with him when he was inspecting the watch. John then sent secret messages to warn the Zealots inside the Temple of any schemes to attack them. Eventually, Ananus and his advisers grew suspicious and wondered whether he was the source of the enemy's uncanny knowledge of all their plans. There was no proof of his guilt, however, and he had many friends in high places who trusted him. Instead of being arrested, he was made to take an oath of loyalty, which he did so convincingly that he was subsequently allowed to attend the meetings of Ananus's council. He was even entrusted with negotiating with the Zealots and offering them terms.

Once inside the Temple, John reminded the Zealots how often he had risked his life to save them, by sending information about Ananus's plans. He told them that they were in great danger. Ananus, he lied, had persuaded his party to send an embassy to Vespasian, inviting him to come and take possession of Jerusalem. In the meantime, Ananus was arranging a purification ceremony for the following day, so that his men could get into the Temple and attack them. There were so many of the moderates, said John, that he did not see how the Zealots could possibly hold out. They had only two choices—to beg for mercy or find help from elsewhere. If they chose the first, they could expect to be slaughtered by Ananus's followers in revenge for their own killings.

John's speech in the Temple, as recorded in *The Jewish War* is unimpressive, but it is only Josephus's unenthusiastic reconstruction and based on hearsay or even guesswork.[12] It is likely that he spoke very differently, and indeed brilliantly. Elsewhere, even Josephus admits that he was a most effective orator, for his speech achieved everything he wanted. It was now that John of Gischala became the Zealot leader and was able to start, if not a revolution, at least a reorganization, which he hoped would win the war.

12

The Zealot Revolution

"Princes are hanged up by their hand; the faces of elders were not honored."

LAMENTATIONS OF JEREMIAH, V, 12

IT WOULD BE FASCINATING to know precisely how Josephus was able to find out so much about what was happening at Jerusalem. It is reasonable to suppose that the Romans had spies all over the city, working undercover, whose reports he must have helped to assess, and almost certainly he was already interrogating defectors—we know that he did so at a later date—since his own experience made him ideally qualified to judge their motives. His re-creation of what went on inside the Jewish capital is built around his old enemy, John of Gischala, whom, as always, he portrays in an unflattering light.

There is no reason to doubt that the Zealots were convinced by John's speech. For a time, their leader remained the thuggish Eleazar ben Simon, whom they followed because of his unjustified reputation for shrewdness. His second-in-command was Zacharias ben Phalek, another Jerusalem man of priestly family. John told these two that Ananus had singled them out for particularly savage punishment—another lie. Terrified by John's warning that Ananus was planning to hand the city over to the Romans, the Zealots—probably at John's suggestion—called in Idumeans from the desert country south of Palestine. A letter was sent off at once to their rulers, saying that unless they came quickly, Jerusalem would soon be in Roman hands again.

The Idumeans, those wild sons of Ishmael, reacted "like madmen," gathering 20,000 men—no doubt an exaggeration—and racing to Jerusalem.[1] Ananus's followers saw them coming and barred the gates of the city, so that when they arrived they found themselves shut out. They yelled abuse from outside the walls, accusing Ananus of rank treachery and of selling Jerusalem to the Romans.

Joshua ben Gamala, the high priest next in seniority to Ananus, answered the Idumeans from a wall tower with a lengthy speech, saying that the accusations were a lie put about by the Zealots, whom he denounced. "There is groaning and wailing everywhere in this place because we suffer so much from the activities of these wretched men, who have been impertinent enough to move their banditry from the countryside and remote little towns into our city, the heart of the nation. They have moved not just into the capital but into the Temple, which they have turned into their headquarters."[2] Joshua refused to let the Idumeans inside the walls unless they laid down their weapons.

The Idumean leaders were affronted by his insisting that they should lay down their arms, while in any case their men were angry at not being admitted at once. An Idumean general shouted back, "I am not surprised that the defenders of freedom are locked up in the Temple when people like you keep their kindred out of a city that belongs to all of us while they prepare to let in the Romans." He ended his tirade by promising that until they were admitted, he and his troops would camp outside.[3]

The Idumeans grew angrier still when a violent storm blew up during the night. Torrents of rain swamped them in their bivouacs, where they had to shelter under their shields. Many in Jerusalem saw the storm as an omen of disaster. They were justified. While the sentries in the Temple colonnades and at the city's gateways were busy keeping dry, Zealots stole past them and sawed through the bars of one of the gates, the noise muffled by the wind, rain, and thunder. Then they opened the gates to the Idumeans, who ran through the city to the Temple.

Together, Idumeans and Zealots launched a joint attack on the area around the Temple, as its inhabitants ran for their lives. A frightful shrieking broke out among the women nearby, while the Zealots joined in yelling the Idumean war cry. "The shouting on all sides was made still more terrifying by the howling of the storm."[4] Naturally ferocious, the Idumeans gave no quarter. When day broke, the outer court of the Temple was flooded with blood. There were already 8,500 dead, but the Idumeans went further afield, rampaging through the city, looting houses, and killing everybody they saw. The high priests who had led the moderates were hunted down, and the bodies of Ananus and Joshua were thrown over the walls.

"I am not mistaken when I say that the city's destruction began with the death of Ananus, when the Jews saw their high priest, guardian of their safety, murdered in the middle of Jerusalem and that from this day on may be dated the overthrow of her walls and the total ruin of the Jewish state," is Josephus's mournful comment.[5]

The death of Ananus did not end the bloodshed. The Zealots and Idumeans continued to butcher people "as though they were a herd of unclean beasts," the poor being cut down on the spot.[6] After the massacre was over, for days young noblemen were routinely arrested, fettered, thrown into prison, and then murdered in what *The Jewish War* portrays as a purge of the upper classes, stating that they were offered their lives "in the hope that some of them would go over to the Zealots, but that they preferred to die rather than join these criminals."[7] For the moment they were spared and then, after being scourged and racked until nearly dead, they were hacked to death. Those arrested during the day were killed at night, their bodies thrown out to make room for fresh prisoners. Relatives dared not mourn for them. Josephus claims wildly that at least "12,000" young nobles died in this way.

This is almost certainly a distortion of what took place; probably a mere handful were killed. Although there was an element of class resentment during the war, Josephus takes every opportunity to exaggerate it. A selfish aristocrat, he believed that the only real Jews were the nobles—nobody else mattered—and his biased version of events claims that all of them wanted peace with Rome. He tries to convince us that it was impossible to be both a patrician and a Zealot, when there is plenty of evidence that this was not the case.

Josephus paints a picture of a city from which every man of breeding and substance wanted to escape. Yet whatever *The Jewish War* may tell us, modern scholarship has revealed that many of the upper class joined the Zealot Revolution and did so with fanatical enthusiasm.[8] The sheer number of well-born defenders whom he names during the siege leads one to suspect that his picture is a deliberate distortion. If magnates were persecuted, it was more from a desire to lay hands on their wealth than from class enmity. Mock tribunals were set up, including an imitation Sanhedrin of seventy judges. A "show trial" was conducted at the Temple, accusing the wealthy Zacharias ben Baris of corresponding with Vespasian and plotting to betray Jerusalem.[9] No proof was produced, the real reason for the charges being a wish to destroy a dangerous opponent and get hold of his money. Zacharias demolished the case against him and then listed the crimes of his accusers amid howls of rage. When he was acquitted by the "president," two men immediately cut him down and threw his body into the ravine below the Temple, shouting, "You've had our verdict too, with a better result!" After this, the so-called Sanhedrin was chased out of the courtroom with blows from the backs of swords.

The Idumeans soon learned that the alleged plot to surrender Jerusalem to the Romans had never existed and that Ananus and his friends had been innocent of any collaboration with the Romans. In private, a Zealot revealed the origin of the slander, explaining that the "defenders of freedom" were eliminating opponents in order to consolidate their control. Not too proud of themselves after their own bloodthirsty behavior, most of the Idumeans soon left the city and returned to their homes, much to everybody's surprise. Before leaving, they freed about 2,000 prisoners, the majority immediately taking the opportunity to escape from the city.

The Idumeans might have become a restraining influence had they stayed. Now that they had gone, the Zealots had a free hand. They stepped up their purges, liquidating not only every man of noble birth they distrusted but any potential opponent with an outstanding record as a soldier who did not share their views. According to *The Jewish War*, "they killed the first sort out of envy, the second from fear."[10] One of the magnates whom they murdered was Gorion ben Joseph, an outspoken critic of their activities, while among the warriors was Niger of Perea, who had distinguished himself fighting against Cestius and then become the hero of

Ashkelon. Niger, too, may have died for speaking out too freely. While he was dragged through the city on his way to the place of execution, he showed his scars to the crowd and, as he was being slaughtered, called down the vengeance of the Romans on his murderers, together with famine, plague, and war—besides shouting that he hoped they would all end by killing each other.

The Zealots had unleashed a class war that some modern historians compare to the Jacobin terror in France during 1793.[11] People were executed for the slightest reason. Those who tried to escape attention by avoiding their new masters were charged with arrogance, those who treated them too familiarly were charged with contempt, and those who fawned on them were charged with being plotters. The most trivial accusation brought the same penalty as the most serious—death. Only the poor were free from the daily fear of execution.

The death of Ananus and the attacks on Judea's ruling class confirmed Josephus in his view that the Zealots were murderous fanatics and that the Jewish people's only hope lay in a Roman reconquest. "The city was prey to the three greatest of all evils, war, tyranny and faction, so that its citizens . . . ran away from their own fellow countrymen to look for protection among foreigners, finding safety with the Romans instead of with their kindred," is how he describes Jerusalem at this stage.[12]

This is the picture Josephus chooses to give, because he wants to convince readers of *The Jewish War* that, like himself, every member of his class rejected a war against Rome, which was stirred up by a handful of lowborn fanatics. Yet it cannot be an altogether accurate picture. By his own account many members of the magnate families stayed behind to fight the Romans. Although many of Judea's nobles were killed by their fellow countrymen, research indicates that a surprisingly large number of them became enthusiastic Zealots.

Josephus is convincing, however, when he says that each day people tried to escape from Jerusalem, despite the fact that the gates were watched and anyone caught was executed on suspicion of going over to the Romans. Not everyone wanted to be trapped in a besieged city. The dead were piled in heaps along the roads just outside, their bodies left to putrefy beneath the sun. However, the rich were usually able to bribe the guards.

Outside the capital, the *sicarii* who had occupied Masada since the start of the war began raiding far and wide. During Passover they attacked the little city of Engedi, storming in to kill 700 women and children after their menfolk had fled, looting the houses and carrying off the crops—if *The Jewish War* can be believed. In addition, they supposedly plundered every village within reach of the fortress, reducing the entire area to a desert. Recruits flocked to them from all over the country. Elsewhere brigandage had broken out all over Judea, with gangs hiding in the desert after robbing their own villages. They pooled their strength and joined forces to attack cities, inflicting casualties of a sort that were normally experienced only in wartime, before vanishing into the wilderness with their loot. Almost certainly, most of those who died were killed because they were lukewarm in the fight against Rome.

Meanwhile, John of Gischala had become dictator of Jerusalem, gathering around him what Josephus portrays—or caricatures—as a private army of murderous psychopaths. Ignoring the wishes of fellow Zealots, he reached decisions and gave orders without consulting anyone and seems to have been obeyed because everybody was terrified of him. According to *The Jewish War*, his haughtiness alienated a substantial number of his followers, who feared that he was planning to make himself a king on the model of the Maccabees or even of the Herods. Predictably, he soon quarreled with the ferocious Eleazar ben Simon, who was not willing to take orders from him. The movement split into two mutually hostile factions, Eleazar's installing itself in the inner courtyard of the Temple. Both sides watched each other suspiciously, sometimes coming to blows, although for the moment they managed to avoid outright civil war.

In fairness, it has to be said that fanatical extremists like the Zealots needed a strong leader such as John. Even *The Jewish War* admits that some of them followed him out of sheer affection, which the author characteristically attributes to his skill "at using deceit and pretence to win support." Yet he was by no means without statesmanlike qualities. He urged Mesopotamian Jews to persuade the Parthians to attack the Romans. Meanwhile, he strengthened fortifications and stored food for the coming siege. Even Josephus has to confess that "many people were attracted by his energy of body and mind"—which can only mean dynamism accompanied by a magnetic personality.[13] John of Gischala's dominance survived unchallenged from spring 68 until spring the following year. Despite his tendency toward tyranny and his followers' proneness to use their swords, what has been called his "revolution" was limited to imposing Zealot ideals on the citizens with a certain amount of bloodshed. Although by now the new Jewish state was restricted to the capital and a few cities in the province of Judea, it still functioned with reasonable efficiency. Coins with optimistic inscriptions continued to be struck, and there was no interruption of the daily ritual of sacrifice at the Temple.

13

The Reconquest of Judea

"Go not forth into the field, nor walk by the way: for the sword of the enemy and fear is on every side."

JEREMIAH, VI, 25

UNDERSTANDABLY, THE ROMANS at their headquarters in Caesarea Maritima were delighted by the news of near civil war inside Jerusalem, seeing it as heaven-sent. Vespasian's war council told him that he ought to attack without delay. "Providence has helped us by making the enemy fall out with each other, but things could change very quickly," they advised. "The Jews may easily grow tired of quarrelling or come to regret all the killings, and form a common front again."[1]

Vespasian disagreed. "You're making a bad mistake about our next move," he answered.

You're much too keen on showing the enemy how formidable and well armed we are, forgetting about strategy and casualties. If we attack the city now, the effect will only be to re-unite our opponents, who can use their full strength against us. If we wait for a bit longer, however, we shall have a lot less of them to fight, as it looks as if a fair number are going to be killed in the faction fighting. God is a much better general than I am and, by the way he is handing over the Jews to the Romans without any effort on our part, he is giving our army a bloodless victory. Since our enemies are busy dying by their own hands and suffering from the worst handicap imaginable–civil war—the best thing that we can do in the circumstances is to stay as spectators instead of taking on fanatics who welcome death and are already busy murdering each other. If anyone here thinks a victory is spoiled if it's won without a fight, then he had better understand that a success won with delaying tactics is always infinitely preferable to risking disaster by letting a battle begin too soon.[2]

Vespasian's officers accepted his assessment, and just as he had expected, the Zealots became even more divided into factions. He made sure that he was kept fully informed of developments in Jerusalem by regularly interrogating any refugees who managed to avoid the guards at the gates. When he began the campaigning season of 68, his legions marched out from Caesarea as if he intended to besiege the capital. In reality, his priority was to overrun the rest of Palestine until not a single city remained in Jewish hands apart from Jerusalem—a strategy of isolation.

His first objective was the province of Perea, the rugged, mountainous province east of Galilee. Crossing the Jordan, he advanced on Perea's capital, Gadara. Although it was strongly fortified and contained Zealots who wanted to fight, the city's notables and its wealthier citizens secretly sent a deputation to meet him with a promise of immediate surrender. Rich men, they had no wish to suffer the fate of the Galileans. The Zealots realized what had happened only when they saw the Romans approaching. There was no time for them to prepare a defense, so, after lynching Dolesus—the leader of the notables who had organized the surrender behind their backs—and mangling his corpse, they fled from the city. Those who remained demolished the fortifications, cheering Vespasian as he marched in. He left a garrison of both infantry and cavalry to protect them in case the patriots should try to return to Gadara.

Vespasian did more than merely leave a garrison behind, however. He sent that highly experienced tribune Placidus after the patriots, with a force of 3,000 legionaries and 500 horsemen—which shows there must have been a sizeable group of Zealots at Gadara. Seeing cavalry in the distance, the fugitives realized they were being pursued and took refuge in a large fortified village called Bethennabris, where they armed the young men, making them promise to fight by their side. When the Romans came up, they charged out to attack. Placidus's men fell back, luring the Jews away from the walls until the cavalry could cut them off and shoot them down at leisure. A large group rushed at the legionaries, "hurling themselves like wild beasts on their enemies' swords."[3] Poorly armed, with no body armor, they were cut down in droves.

Placidus blocked their retreat with his cavalry, his men using javelins and arrows to lethal effect. Only the most determined of the Zealots were able to cut their way back to Bethennabris. Its inhabitants managed to shut the gates, but the Romans launched assault after assault, before storming the village in the evening and slaughtering everybody they caught inside, a fair number fleeing into the surrounding hills. After looting the houses, the legionaries set fire to them, reducing the place to ashes.

Enough survivors escaped from Bethennabris to spread word that the whole Roman army was coming. Terrified, the region's entire population fled toward Jericho, but their escape was prevented by the Jordan River, swollen by rain and no longer fordable. Drawing up his troops on as broad a front as possible, Placidus attacked the fugitives on the river bank, massacring 15,000 while "an incalculable number" threw themselves into the Jordan and drowned. Over 2,000 were captured, besides countless donkeys, sheep, oxen, and camels. *The Jewish War* tells us that although the disaster was no worse than others suffered by the Jews, it appeared more serious because the countryside was strewn with dead bodies, and the corpses floating in the Jordan made the river impassable. Exploiting the general terror, Placidus overran towns and villages in the area, slaughtering fugitive patriots wherever he found them. In a short time, he reimposed Roman rule on all Perea as far as the Dead Sea, except for the fortress of Machaerus.

Meanwhile, Vespasian had more to worry him than Palestine. In the middle of March 68, Julius Vindex, the governor of Gaul, and a group of Gallic chieftains had revolted against Nero, supported by Sulpicius Galba, governor of Nearer Spain, and by Salvius Otho, governor of Lusitania. Although the revolt was crushed within two months by the legions from

Germany, Nero's regime began to look increasingly fragile. Not only was the emperor's behavior unacceptable, despite his rushing back to Rome at the end of 67 after his long holiday in Greece, but the government was running short of money. The long war with the Parthians from 54 to 63 CE had cost Rome huge sums, as had the British rebellion in 60 CE, while the Jewish war was also costing a great deal as it dragged on. Quite apart from the enormous expense of putting them down, revolts meant that taxes went unpaid, and in consequence less cash was available to keep the Roman population in idle pleasure—to pay for "bread and circuses." Subject provinces were asked to pay even heavier levies, causing discontent all over the empire. If the imperial authority collapsed, the entire Roman world would be in turmoil. It might even disintegrate.

"Vespasian had already foreseen that civil war was looming, recognizing the terrible danger into which it would plunge the empire, and in the circumstances he decided that if he could settle the problems in the east as soon as possible, it would help to calm down the mood in Italy," Josephus informs us. "This was why he had been so busy during the winter in garrisoning all the villages and smaller towns that he had conquered."[4] In addition, we can guess that after Vindex's abortive rebellion, Vespasian had grown even more nervous that Nero might decide to order his own liquidation, as he, too, was an army commander who could be a potential rival. Yet at this date the thought of becoming emperor does not seem to have crossed his mind.

In such uncertain times, the best course of action was for him to be seen as doing his job properly, by crushing the Jews without further delay. He abandoned his former policy of waiting for the Zealots to weaken themselves by civil war and embarked on a campaign that was designed to prepare the way for the siege and capture of Jerusalem. At no time dilatory, he showed extraordinary energy (although he was nearly sixty) once he had decided to cow the province of Judea into submission.

While Placidus was reconquering Perea, leaving Traianus in overall command of the operation, Vespasian marched back to Caesarea Maritima and inland down to Antipatris where he restored Roman rule in two days. After this, he devastated the surrounding region "with fire and sword" for miles around, destroying every village as he went. Having conquered the territory around Thamna, he marched on Lydda and Jamna, killing or enslaving the inhabitants and replacing them with deserters from Jerusalem, who included men from the upper classes.

He left the Fifth Legion (Macedonia) in a fortified camp at Emmaus, so that it could block the approaches to Jerusalem, before going on Bethleptepha southwest of the capital, burning it to the ground and laying waste the surrounding countryside—which involved slaughtering everything that moved. Marching even further south, across the Judean border into Idumea, he captured two important villages, putting 10,000 of their inhabitants to the sword and enslaving another thousand.

He then went north through the hills to Jericho, most of whose inhabitants ran into the surrounding mountains when they heard he was coming. Those foolish enough to risk staying behind were massacred, with a few exceptions. He showed signs of a scientific bent by selecting prisoners who could not swim, tying their hands behind them, and throwing them into the Dead Sea to see if they would float—which they did "as if a wind had forced them upward." In spirit, the experiment anticipated some of those by the Nazis, the prisoners presumably being put to death after their ordeal.[5]

Vespasian was soon joined by Traianus with all the troops from Perea, reinforcements that enabled him to establish fortified camps at Jericho and Adida, each with a garrison of legionaries and auxiliary cavalry. In addition, he sent Lucius Annius to the city of Gerasa with a small mixed force of horse and infantry. Annius stormed it at his first attempt, massacring a thousand young men, enslaving any of the rest he could catch and then, after allowing his soldiers to loot the houses, setting fire to the city—a process he repeated at all the surrounding villages.

The aim behind all this activity was to isolate Jerusalem, which Vespasian planned to blockade on every side with a ring of strong points. (Josephus's knowledge of the local topography must have been useful when choosing the sites for these.) Each step in his recent campaign had been designed to make absolutely sure of his communications, by methodically eliminating every center of opposition on the coast and in the countryside, so that no enemy force remained that could interrupt his supply lines. Until now, he had deliberately left the enemy capital alone. However, it seemed clear that the moment was fast approaching when he would at last be ready to deal with it.

About this time, during the spring of 68, a particularly interesting deserter arrived in the Roman camp, probably when Vespasian had returned to Caesarea. This was an elderly judge from Jerusalem, a former merchant—and former pupil of Hillel—named Rabban Yohanan ben Zakkai, who was to become famous throughout Judea for his learning. There are several versions of what took place, but on the whole they agree. Yohanan shared Josephus's view of the war, about which he had grown increasingly unhappy, either because he was against it or because he believed in a compromise peace. In the end he escaped from the capital in a coffin, after being nearly stabbed to death by a guard who stuck his sword inside to make sure that the body really was a corpse.

When he saw Vespasian, Yohanan shouted in Latin, "Vive Dominus Imperator!"—"Lord Emperor, live for ever!" Apparently he did so in front of a large crowd, since an alarmed Vespasian answered that he was not emperor, and Nero would have him killed if he heard about it. Yohanan then told him he was going to be a king, as there was a tradition that the Temple would surrender only to a king, and that a prince would cut down the forests of Lebanon. He quoted Isaiah, "he shall cut down the thickets of the forest with iron, and Lebanon shall fall to a mighty one"(Isaiah, 10, 34). Rabban Yohanan, who knew how well Josephus's prophecy had been received by Vespasian, also asked for permission to set up a rabbinic school near Jamnia (Yavneh), a town in the coastal plain where many of those who had fled from the city had been allowed to take refuge.[6] Ironically, his school was to become a subtle, intellectual rebellion against everything represented by Rome.

Although it has been suggested that the story of his prophecy was included to cover up some kind of sordid bargain, perhaps an offer of covert collaboration, there is no good reason to suspect that Yohanan contributed to the war against his fellow countrymen.[7] He was just the sort of cultivated Jew who was welcomed by the Romans in their longsighted efforts to divide their opponents and rebuild a pliant ruling class who would cooperate with them after the war. However, it was almost certainly his prophecy that ensured his freedom.

Before this, other Jews of less distinguished background than Rabban Yohanan's, whose names have not survived, had prophesied that Vespasian was going to rule the world. Their predictions had now been strongly supported by someone far more impressive, further confirmation of the accuracy of Josephus's much earlier prophesy, which was now about to be borne out by events.

On 9 June 68, after the entire army—including the Praetorian guard—rebelled, Nero cut his throat on hearing that he had been outlawed by the Senate as a public enemy and was going to be executed "in the ancient fashion"—flogged to death.[8] The seventy-three-year-old Galba was proclaimed emperor, and in the autumn Vespasian sent Titus to Rome to swear allegiance and ask for orders, as his command had lapsed automatically at Nero's death. He was forced to abandon his plans for besieging Jerusalem.

14

Simon bar Giora

"A man of strife and a man of contention to the whole earth."
JEREMIAH, XV, 10

I N THE MEANTIME, Jerusalem was facing fresh and extremely serious
trouble of a new sort, in the person of Simon bar Giora. "A young man,
a Gerasene by birth, perhaps not quite so cunning as John who was then
in control of the city, but much fiercer and far more daring," is how Josephus curtly describes Simon in *The Jewish War*.[1] As always, however, one
must be careful in accepting at face value his description of an enemy.

Simon's obscure origin and the fact that he had been born at the little
city of Gerasa made him an object of contempt to the snobbish Josephus,
who portrays him as a bloodstained tyrant from the gutter, yet perhaps it
was not all that far from the truth. He was half-Greek, his father having
been a convert to the Jewish faith. Admittedly, one modern historian,
Martin Goodman, has argued, unconvincingly, that he was a member of
the ruling class.[2] However lowly Simon's background may have been,
never for a moment did Josephus underestimate this ruthless leader, who
was always resourceful and always able to arouse the deepest loyalty. The
Romans saw him as their most dangerous opponent.

Josephus and his friends would have every reason to hate him. In their
eyes, Simon and John of Gischala were the two evil geniuses of the war,

Simon being the worst. Yet in his own terrible way, Simon was very much a Zealot. Probably, his hatred for the Judean magnates was inspired not so much by his humble origin or a leveling instinct, as by what he saw as their betrayal of the nation, their long-standing failure to resist Roman occupation and their readiness to collaborate. His extraordinarily rapid rise to power, which could only have happened in a situation where the social order had broken down, deserves a full description.

During the short period when the late lamented Ananus had run Jerusalem, the wily old high priest had recognized at once that despite his youth, Simon bar Giora was very dangerous indeed. This was apparent from the disturbingly aggressive way in which he was behaving. Before he could become any more of a threat, Ananus had him thrown out of the toparchy (administrative district) of Acrabatene after discovering that Simon was trying to build up a power base in the area by ingratiating himself with the peasants.

After his expulsion from Jerusalem, he took refuge with the Zealot *sicarii* at Masada by the Dead Sea. At first the knifemen were suspicious and would only let him stay in the outer courtyard of the fortress, with his womenfolk, barring him from their quarters in King Herod's former palace, but he was an unusually congenial companion, a sympathetic listener, and his magnetic personality and unfeigned devotion to the Zealot cause impressed them. Soon they were allowing him to go on their cattle raids around Masada. Enormously ambitious, he quickly grew dissatisfied with this way of life, especially after hearing that his old enemy Ananus had been killed and that the Zealots had taken over the capital.

When his new friends, the *sicarii*, refused to leave Masada and help him with what must have seemed preposterously ambitious plans, he went up into the hill country, where he gathered an army of sorts by promising freedom for slaves and plunder for men who were already free. At first it was a villainous, ill-armed rabble, but it quickly acquired good weapons and discipline, learning to fight well under such an unusually gifted commander. As soon as it grew big enough, he started to attack and loot poorly defended mountain villages, and his success attracted a steady stream of recruits. In a short time he was strong enough to go down into the lowlands and raid towns. He was so effective that even men of rank began to join him, and his dynamism won him many supporters. Josephus, in *The Jewish War,* comments, "He no longer had a mob of slaves and robbers, but an army of soldiers who obeyed him as if he were their king."[3]

Now that he possessed sufficient troops, Simon overran the toparchy of Acrabattene and the surrounding region as far south as Great Idumea. He fortified a village called Nain with a rampart, making it his headquarters, and he used the caves in the nearby valley of Pharan as storehouses for the corn he had plundered or as barracks. Here he trained and drilled his followers. Instead of concealing his intention of attacking Jerusalem, he told everybody.

As he had hoped, the Zealots in the capital grew alarmed and dispatched a force to crush him before he became too powerful. But Simon easily routed it, chasing the survivors all the way back to Jerusalem. Since he did not have the resources to storm the city, he decided to neutralize the Idumeans and prevent them from coming to aid his enemies, as they had assisted John. He marched south with 20,000 men, all properly armed. Hearing that Simon was on his way, the Idumeans hastily assembled their best troops, about 25,000 in all, and managed to intercept him at the border.

After a hard-fought but inconclusive battle, Simon withdrew to Nain, where his soldiers recuperated. Then he invaded Idumea again, pitching camp at the village of Tekoa, from where he sent an officer called Eleazar to the Idumean garrison of the nearby fortress of Herodium to demand its surrender. Eleazar was admitted, but as soon as they heard his insolent request, the garrison chased him around the ramparts with drawn swords until, seeing no hope of escape, he threw himself from the wall into the ravine below and was killed. Even so, the Idumeans were shaken by Simon's self-confidence. They decided to find out how strong his force was before risking a battle.

Jacob, one of the Idumean commanders, volunteered to reconnoiter. Setting out from Olurus, the village where the Idumean army was encamped, he went to Simon and offered not only to betray his comrades but to help with the conquest of all Idumea in return for a position of influence. Expert at exploiting treachery, Simon readily agreed to his terms, promising even better rewards, and gave a splendid feast for him. Jacob returned to Olurus, demoralizing his brother officers with inflated reports of the size of Simon's army, spreading gloom and despondency, and suggesting that the only hope of saving their lives lay in surrender. He then sent secret messengers to Simon, telling him to attack without delay. As soon as he advanced, Jacob and his friends leaped on their horses and fled, screaming that all was lost. The entire Idumean army bolted in panic.

Having won a bloodless victory, Simon advanced south into Idumea, plundering Hebron—not yet destroyed by the Romans—where he found the grain he needed to feed his large army. Now over 40,000 strong, his forces were more formidable than ever and included heavily armed infantry. Next he ravaged all Idumea, looting towns and villages, turning the countryside into a wasteland. "As the passage of locusts through the woods is marked by trees without leaves, so nothing save desert remained in the wake of Simon's army," comments Josephus.[4] "Some places they torched, others they razed to the ground."

The Zealots in Jerusalem grew more worried than ever, but they lacked the confidence to risk a full-scale battle. Instead, they ambushed Simon's troops in the mountain passes. After capturing Simon's wife in one of these ambushes, they expected him to surrender and beg for her release. However, far from being demoralized and surrendering, he was enraged. "Advancing on Jerusalem like a wounded wild beast unable to avenge himself on the hunters who have wounded him, he vented his fury on everybody he met," *The Jewish War* informs us. "Any human beings that were found wandering outside the walls, usually harmless old people in search of herbs or firewood, he had seized and tortured to death, barely able in his rage to stop himself from gnawing at their corpses."[5]

He sent some of them back into the city alive, but with their hands cut off. They were told to inform the authorities that, by the God who reigns over all, Simon bar Giora had sworn that unless his wife was given back to him without delay, he was going to smash his way through the walls and would kill everyone inside, whether old or young, guilty or innocent. Not just the population but even the toughest Zealots became so terrified by his ferocity that they released his wife at once. After recovering her, Simon returned to making what was left of Idumea into a desert. Many of the starving Idumeans tried to take refuge in Jerusalem, and those of them who were caught en route, generally simple peasants, were put to death on his express orders. By now, as he had intended, the Jews were more frightened of him than of the Zealots or the Romans. Having finished his work of devastation, he came back to Jerusalem and surrounded its walls.

Meanwhile, inside Jerusalem, John of Gischala had rewarded the Zealot army for their support by letting them do what they liked, and as a result, discipline had broken down. Looting the houses of the rich, murdering men, and raping women had become widespread. According to Josephus, out of sheer boredom Zealot troops had turned to homosexuality, dressing in women's clothes, using cosmetics and scent, and putting kohl under their eyes. "They rolled around the city as if it were a brothel," *The Jewish War* tells us, "defiling it with their impure lust. Even so, while they may have tried to look like women, they still had murderers' hands. Tripping along with mincing steps, they would suddenly revert to being warriors, drawing their swords from beneath their gaily colored cloaks and running through any passer-by whom they happened to meet."[6]

One suspects, however, that this picture of a Jerusalem terrorized by murderous homosexuals stems entirely from Josephus's imagination and is another example of his determination to slander the Zealots. Many of them were devoutly religious, well aware their faith taught that homosexuality was sinful. It is possible that something of the sort described took place, but, if so, it was probably an isolated incident that later was blown up out of all proportion. It is also conceivable that from sheer poverty, many of the more humble Zealots were unable to distinguish between the clothing of rich men and rich women—for them a silk robe was a silk robe.

Nevertheless, it is clear that life in Jerusalem under the rule of John of Gischala could be very unpleasant for anyone who did not belong to the Zealot garrison. Yet the leader outside the walls was even more bloodthirsty than the one within, killing everyone who tried to leave. For the time being, Simon had put an end to any hope of escaping to the Romans.

Despite the way in which John was indulging them—or perhaps because of it—a substantial number of the Jerusalem garrison eventually turned against him. He was already opposed by Eleazar ben Simon and his group, and the more levelheaded troops must have realized that such a chaotic army had little prospect of saving the city when the Romans finally decided to attack. The first to rebel against John's regime were a group of

Idumean refugees in the spring of 69 CE. Besides disliking the way in which he was running Jerusalem, they were revolted by his cruelty. During the ensuing battle, they killed several Zealots, driving the remainder into the royal palace that had become John's personal residence. Built by Gapte, a kinswoman of the King of Adiabene, it was also where John stored his loot. After chasing the Zealots out of the palace and into the Temple, the Idumeans set about plundering John's treasure.

While the Idumeans were dividing the spoils, Zealots throughout the city rushed to join those who had taken refuge in the outer Temple where John was trying to organize a counterattack. Although the Idumeans felt confident that they could always defeat the Zealots in straightforward, hand-to-hand combat, what they dreaded was a treacherous assault by night, of the sort that had overthrown Ananus. They were afraid that the Zealots might cut their throats while they slept.

The Idumeans were so discouraged that they assembled the remaining chief priests and asked for advice on how to guard against such an attack. "However, God made them find the worst possible solution to the problem, and they decided on a cure deadlier than the disease."[7] After what must have been an agonizing debate, the chief priests reached the conclusion that the only possible way of getting rid of John was to ask Simon bar Giora to take over, despite his reputation. No doubt, too, they also hoped secretly that he could handle the Idumeans after having so often defeated them. The decision was warmly supported by the surviving notables, who feared for their lives, houses, and property. They seem to have hoped that Simon would turn into a second Ananus. Matthias ben Boethus—a former high priest of impeccable lineage—was sent to Simon's camp outside the walls, where he invited him to come and rule Jerusalem.

Graciously accepting the citizens' invitation, Simon rode in as a man who had come to rescue the city from the Zealots, cheered as a savior. But as soon as he got inside, it quickly became apparent that he too was very much a Zealot. He treated the men who had invited him in as if they were no less his enemies than John's men. At the same time he seized as much treasure as he could from John, who retreated into the outer court of the Temple; Eleazar and his faction continued to occupy the inner court.

"Thus did Simon become ruler of Jerusalem in the third year of the war, Xanthicus (Nisan)," records *The Jewish War*, which means that it was some date in March or April 69.[8]

The term Zealot is derived from Phineas, who in the Book of Numbers was zealous for God in slaying Zimri and his foreign whore.[9] *The Jewish War* uses the term only for those followers of Eleazar ben Simon, but it is likely that all three leaders (John of Gischala, Simon bar Giora, as well as Eleazar ben Simon) and their supporters took the name, because they shared the same ideals. It is certainly the best term for describing the defenders of Jerusalem, which is how it will be used from now on in this book.[10]

Josephus, who tended to see human beings as either wholly bad or wholly good, refuses to credit Simon with a single good quality, apart from brutal courage, ruthless fighting skills, and a deceptive magnetism. Yet the people who invited Simon into Jerusalem cannot have been complete fools; indeed, many of them continued to support him until the end. However murderous he may have been, it is clear that in some ways he was preferable to John of Gischala. He was joined by many Idumeans, led by an ambitious officer, James ben Sosias, and even by a number of patrician Jews such as Ananus ben Bagdatus, who became one of his leading henchmen.

Yet John was far from finished. He, too, had devoted followers. They and Eleazar's men held out stubbornly in the Temple—in the outer and inner courts, respectively—despite being besieged by vastly superior numbers. Aided by the citizens, Simon mounted assault after assault. However, both groups of Zealots in the Temple had the artillery captured from the Romans and had learned how to use it at point-blank range, if not yet at long range. Mounting the ballista and scorpions on four newly built towers, they shot a murderous hail of stones and arrows at the besiegers. At the same time, slingers and bowmen fired steadily down on them from snipers' nests on the colonnades and battlements. Although Simon had slingers and archers, he lacked artillery to counter this sustained bombardment, and many of his men were killed or wounded every day. Their attacks on the Temple gradually petered out, as they grew disheartened by superior firepower. Even so, they went on blockading the Zealots in the Temple until almost the end.

Simon bar Giora's arrival on the scene deprived Jerusalem of any hope of a united command. From the Roman point of view, there could have been no more promising development. Just as Vespasian had foreseen, Jerusalem's defenders were split into hostile Zealot armies, each intent on exterminating the other. For the time being, however, he was forced to postpone the siege that he had been planning. Too much of vital importance was happening in Europe.

15

The Year of the Four Emperors

"When Nero died, everything broke down. The confusion encour-aged several men to try and make themselves Emperor, while the legionaries wanted change as they were all hoping for plunder."

JOSEPHUS, *THE JEWISH WAR*, 1, 5

N EWS OF NERO'S SUICIDE must have reached Vespasian by the au-tumn of 68 CE. This was the start of what is known as the "Year of the Four Emperors." Although he had sent messages of loyalty to the new emperor, Galba, Vespasian never received a reply. More disturbingly, no confirmation of his appointment came, nor did any fresh orders. Reluc-tantly, he called a halt to the Judean campaign and made no further move against the Jews until spring 69.

He stayed permanently at Caesarea Maritima, since the couriers from Rome to Judea landed there first, bringing reports of what had been hap-pening at the capital, together with orders and correspondence, although their information was at least six weeks old by the time it arrived and might have been overtaken by events. (After October couriers took still longer because of the winter storms that made any journey across the Mediterranean extremely hazardous.) While Vespasian waited for orders, Zealot forces took advantage of the lull and recaptured parts of Judea, no-tably Hebron.

Josephus tells us in *The Jewish War* that he has no intention of discussing at any length the death of Nero, "who had wantonly abused his authority," although he notes with approval "that before very long punishment overtook those who had brought about his destruction."[1] This guarded statement hints at the veneration in which he held all emperors, a veneration that was now transferred to Vespasian and profoundly affected their relationship. Although in no way a pagan, Josephus was not immune to the semi-divine aura that surrounded a Caesar.

It very much looks as if, when writing about the civil war in Italy, he had access to a lost and unidentified "common source" that was also used by Tacitus and Suetonius. He has little to say about Galba's harsh and inept reign from June 68 to January 69 and his assassination in the Roman forum or about the brief reign of his still more incapable murderer and successor, Otho, which ended in suicide in April. He tells us rather more, however, about the assumption of power by Vitellius, formerly in command of the legions on the Rhine, whom Vespasian publicly acknowledged as his emperor at Caesarea in May 69. Significantly, when the general did so in front of his men, pledging his loyalty, they listened to him in silence.

Vespasian then embarked on what was to be his last campaign, attacking the few places in Judea that still held out against the Romans. A much less demanding operation than his previous campaigns, it could be swiftly ended if necessary without any loss of face or giving too much encouragement to his opponents. Going up into the hill country, he subdued the areas around Gophna and Acrabatta, after which he captured the small towns of Bethel and Ephraim, installing garrisons. Then he advanced toward Jerusalem, killing or enslaving any Jews that he was able to catch, deliberately spreading terror.

At the same time, Sextus Cerealis, commander of the Fifth Legion, took a small force to lay waste Upper Idumea, burning the large village of Caphethra before besieging the city of Capharabin, whose inhabitants came out carrying olive branches in token of surrender after the Romans' first assault. Cerealis's final exploit was to storm his way into Hebron— already devastated by Simon bar Giora—where he killed old and young alike, leaving the city in flames.

Tacitus comments, "In two summer campaigns, through his determination and usual good luck, and with the help of some outstanding officers,

Masada, where the Zealots committed mass suicide in 73 rather than surrendering. Their story was saved from oblivion and immortalized by Josephus, who must have heard it from Roman officers present at the siege—no other ancient historian mentions it.

First century portrait bust of Josephus <??> found at Rome. If the attribution is correct, it may have been commissioned by the Empress Poppaea, and shows how well Josephus was adapting to life at Nero's court.

A convincing reconstruction of the Second Temple, from J. de Vogüé's *Le Temple de Jérusalem*. Josephus says that from a distance it "looked like a mountain covered in snow since it was so wonderfully white where it was not clad in gold."

The Emperor Nero (54–68) whose choice of inept procurators was largely responsible for the Jewish war. He may have met Josephus, but it is unlikely that he employed him as a spy— as suggested by some historians.

Empress Poppaea Sabina, c. 62, later murdered by Nero with a kick in the stomach. A friend of Jews, she took a fancy to the young Josephus, who says the Empress was a "worshipper of God" and that she gave him "large gifts."

Three Emperors who reigned during 69: Galba, assassinated in January (top); Otho who committed suicide in April; and Vitellius, lynched in December (right). Josephus had prophesied that Nero's immediate successors would not last.

Vespasian, the Roman general (and former mule trader) whom Josephus prophesied would become undisputed Emperor of Rome, which he did at the end of 69. The prophecy saved Josephus's life.

One of the "Seven Wonders" of the ancient world, the Pharos lighthouse opposite the Jewish quarter by the sea at Alexandria where Josephus spent the winter of 69–70. He must have seen it everyday.

The Emperor Titus (79–81), who destroyed Jerusalem and the Temple. Throughout the campaign he employed Josephus as an intelligence officer, while later he ordered the publication of Josephus's *The Jewish War.*

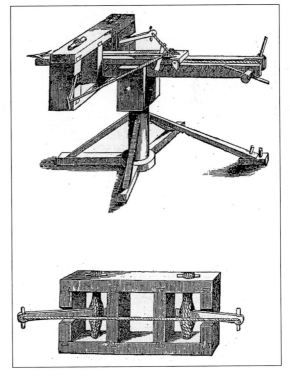

A *catapulta* of the type that formed the bulk of Roman siege artillery, and its firing mechanism. There was a smaller, portable version known as "a *scorpio.*" The defenders of Jerusalem used captured weaponry of this sort against the Romans.

The destruction of the Temple by the Romans under Titus in August 70, based on the description in The Jewish War by Josephus, who had been present. From a painting by Francesco Hayes (1791–1881) in the Galleria dell' Academia, Venice.

A relief from the Arch of Titus at Rome, built in 81, that shows loot from the Temple—including the seven-branched menorah—that Josephus saw being born in procession during the Triumph of Vespasian and Titus.

The Emperor Domitian (81–96), Vespasian's younger son, who became a murderous tyrant and was assassinated. He punished Josephus's "Jewish accusers" and exempted his Judean property from taxation.

Empress Domitia, who "never ceased conferring favors on me," says Josephus—clearly he knew how to please great ladies. She encouraged the assassination of her husband Domitian.

The menacing outline of the Roman headquarters camp below Masada, from where in 73 Lucius Flavius Silva, governor of Judea, directed the building of a wall to prevent the defenders from escaping and then of a siege ramp as tall as the mountain.

A fanciful portrait of Josephus, from William Whiston's famous if inaccurate translation of his Works (1737). In reality, Jewish clothing in Josephus's time was no different from that of their neighbors in the Eastern Empire.

[Vespasian] had overrun the entire country and captured every single city with the exception of Jerusalem."[2] Only the fortresses of Herodium, Machaerus, and Masada remained in Jewish hands. Even if worse would follow, the forebodings of Josephus had been confirmed, although there was a brief respite for the Jews because of the struggle for the imperial throne.

The sixty-year-old Vitellius made himself unpopular in Rome from the start by bringing 60,000 troops from the Rhineland, with a mob of barbarous German camp-followers. Their discipline collapsed, and they and their long-haired, trouser-wearing friends, who smeared their hair with butter, terrorized the capital, robbing and raping its citizens. The Romans deeply resented this unaccustomed occupation by barbarians, and although they were no strangers to gluttony, they were profoundly shocked by the excessive feasting of yet another new emperor and his men. "In the army of Vitellius, all was confusion and drunkenness," says Tacitus.[3] By June he was beginning to run out of ready money, unable to pay his own men, let alone his other soldiers, whom he had already outraged by executing all the centurions of Otho's legions.

The catalyst that spurred the ultra-cautious Vespasian to make a bid for the throne was the ambitious Titus, who talked his father into pursuing it and persuaded other generals to support him. He may have been planning a coup ever since Nero's death. Sent to Rome by his father to pay homage to Galba and to seek orders for the conduct of the Judean war, Titus had set off in a galley in about February 69, accompanied by King Agrippa II. En route, the pair put in at Paphos on Cyprus, where Titus took the opportunity to visit Aphrodite's oracle, supposedly for advice about his journey, but secretly hoping to obtain a favorable omen for his father's future.

As they were continuing their journey, along the coast of Greece, they heard of Galba's assassination. Agrippa decided to go on to Rome, but Titus, "as if by divine inspiration," sailed back to Syria and quickly rejoined his father at Caesarea Maritima.[4] His decision to return to Judea, instead of going on to Rome and paying homage to Vitellius, indicates that he believed the time was right for his father to launch a fight for the supreme power. Never a gambler, Vespasian was reluctant. "It would be a very strange thing if, at the age of sixty and with two sons, I committed myself to a civil war," he muttered.[5] He seems to have thought that he was too humbly born, too obscure, and too old to succeed.

Vespasian was finally persuaded to act, however, after he heard a speech that was delivered in the presence of his senior officers by the legate of Syria, Licinius Mucianus. Although the legate was a fine soldier, he and Vespasian did not have much else in common. Mucianus was a flamboyant homosexual who enjoyed dressing in women's clothes and an intellectual who had written a book on the natural wonders of Syria, *Mirabilia*. It was probably Mucianus who inspired Vespasian's quip remark, "I am content to be a man." Moreover, it seems that they had had some irritating disputes over supplies and jurisdiction. Yet the legate was a shrewd politician, who discerned in Vespasian all the qualities that would make him an excellent emperor.

"Whatever spirit and fire Vitellius's soldiers may once have had for war is being drained away in taverns by drunken brawling and aping their leader's vices," Mucianus told him. "You, by contrast, have complete control of Syria, Judea and Egypt, you have nine good legions unweakened by fighting too many battles and made up of men who don't quarrel among themselves, you have an army toughened by plenty of campaigning that defeats its country's enemies again and again, you have a fine fleet, sound cavalry and auxiliaries, you have local kings who are devoted to you, and finally you have your own unrivalled military experience."[6]

After this peroration Vespasian's officers begged him to save the Roman Empire, citing oracles that had predicted his inevitable success. On 1 July 69, in front of legionaries who roared their applause, he was proclaimed Caesar at Alexandria by the prefect of Egypt, Tiberius Alexander. The troops in Judea began addressing him as "Imperator," while those in Syria showed no less enthusiasm. Local rulers offered to help finance his campaign, including Agrippa II and Berenice, and to lend him their own troops.

A conference was held at Berytus (Beirut) by his supporters to work out how they should topple Vitellius. One of the first decisions was to call off all operations against Jerusalem, so that the legions involved could be transferred to the task force that was about to invade Europe. It was decided, however, that the garrisons in Judea must be kept up to strength and that as soon as Vespasian was on the throne Titus should resume the Judean campaign. A plan to invade Europe and then, in cooperation with forces from other parts of the empire, locate and destroy Vitellius's armies was carefully laid out. They also agreed that Vespasian should stay in the East, coordinating the campaign from Egypt.

It must be remembered that when Vespasian claimed the throne, his victory was by no means a foregone conclusion. Far from being defeated, Vitellius was still very much emperor—in fact, as well as name. No doubt, Vespasian was in every way superior, as a soldier and as a man, and he was supported by some of the best officers in the Roman army. Yet it was crucial not to underestimate Vitellius. Although he was incompetent and uninspiring where civilians were concerned, Vespasian's flabby opponent knew how to make himself popular with soldiers, so that he could rely on many thousands of legionaries who would fight to the death for him—and not merely because they hoped to be rewarded with "donatives" (cash bonuses). Moreover, these legions from the Rhine were generally considered to be the finest troops in the entire Rome army. Furthermore, he, too, had some extremely capable commanders—notably Fabius Valens and Caecina Alienus. Above all, the Emperor Vitellius controlled Rome, whose very name was a talisman.

Josephus tells us that from the beginning Vespasian's first priority was to secure possession of Alexandria, since Egypt, with its vast supplies of grain, was the principal breadbasket of the empire. Once in control of what was the region's only port for grain transports, he would be able to starve Italy and Vitellius into submission, if necessary. He also needed the two legions that were stationed in Egypt.

Before leaving for Alexandria in October, he remembered how Josephus had hailed him as emperor even when Nero was alive. Summoning Mucianus and other senior officers, he spoke warmly of Josephus's bravery at Jotapata, reminding them of his prediction, which had clearly been of divine origin. "'It is shameful,' said Vespasian 'that the man who foresaw I would become Emperor and is a messenger from God should still be a captive and treated as a prisoner.'" He gave orders for Josephus to be brought into his presence and formally set at liberty.

"'It is only fair that any reproach of having been a prisoner should be removed with the fetters, and if we cut them off instead of merely unfastening them it will take away the stigma!'" suggested Titus. This was customary in the case of someone who had been unjustly imprisoned, so that he would not suffer from the despised status of "freedman"—former slave. Vespasian agreed, and he had the chains publicly hacked off with an axe. Josephus, who had long ceased to wear them, put them on again for the ceremony. "After he received his freedom as a reward for his prophecy, people believed what he had to say about the future," is his complacent comment.[7]

In Egypt, Vespasian installed himself and his staff at Alexandria, the capital. Founded by Alexander the Great, this was for all intents and purposes a Greek city, with very few native Egyptians among a population that numbered almost a million. The walls were fifteen miles in circumference, around a metropolis of straight, narrow streets laid out on a grid pattern, and the major thoroughfares were filled with mansions, public buildings, and temples. The biggest temple, the Serapeum, housed not only the cult of the god Serapis but a major part of the largest public library in the world. Because Alexandra lacked a natural harbor, a port had been created by constructing a long mole out to the island of Pharos—on which stood a lighthouse 400 feet tall that was one of the wonders of antiquity.

Josephus went to Egypt with Vespasian. Although he would have made himself available whenever needed, this cannot have been very often, as there was little use for expert advice on Judea when the campaign was in abeyance. It is likely that he spent his time among the local Diaspora, which was the most flourishing Jewish community outside Jerusalem, and by now swollen with refugees from Judea. The majority seem to have been poor, although some of them were very rich indeed. A few had even acquired citizenship, including the brother of the philosopher Philo, Alexander the Alabarch (head of the customs service). There was a high degree of hellenization, which, along with the city's superb libraries, offered enviable opportunities for anyone interested in Greek literature.

Josephus chose a new wife from among the Diaspora, although the marriage turned out to be unhappy. (All he says about the wife that Vespasian had given him is that they had parted.) Presumably they began their life together in the Jewish quarter in the northeastern part of the city, on the seashore—"by universal consent its finest residential quarter," he informs us nostalgically.[8] There could have been no more delightful place to spend a winter. His wife would have three sons, one of whom, perhaps significantly, he named Hyrcanus, after a Maccabee ancestor. This was his hero, King John Hyrcanus, "who was unique in possessing three of the most desirable things in the world: the government of his nation, the high priesthood, and the gift of prophecy. The Deity talked to him, so that he knew about everything that happened afterwards."[9]

He tells us nothing about any other contact he may have had with the local Diaspora, although he gives a certain amount of information about anti-Semitism in Alexandria. Ironically, to some extent this was due to the Alexandrian Jews' support for the Romans. He explains how they were organized into what the Greeks called a *politeuma*, a corporation of aliens ruled by a council of seventy elders—a local Sanhedrin—whose head was an ethnarch. They had an assembly and their own law court and archives. The great problem of the Diaspora's richer and more hellenized members was to acquire citizenship without abandoning their religion. If Josephus ever thought of settling here, a handicap of this sort would have driven the idea from his mind.

He has more to say about Vitellius's overthrow. Understandably, he took keen interest in a campaign that was going to decide his future, even if he does not reveal how worried he must have felt while it was taking place. It is likely that he remembered seeing the appalling figure of Vitellius at Nero's court, a big man with a huge potbelly, a limp, and a face purple from hard drinking. "His parents had been aghast at the horoscope drawn up for him by the astrologers," says Suetonius, who alleges that as a boy, Vitellius was one of Tiberius's "wantons" on Capri and furthered his father's career by serving as the emperor's catamite—being branded with the obscene nickname of "Sphintria" for the rest of his life. Suetonius says that he became stained by every sort of baseness as he grew older, that his besetting sins were gluttony and cruelty; he enjoyed inflicting torture and death on anyone, even on friends.[10]

He had no experience as a soldier, and everybody had been astounded when Galba put him in command of Lower Germany, but by tirelessly currying favor with the troops, granting any request they might make, remitting punishments regardless of discipline, he had become hugely popular. They liked his cheerful hail-fellow-well-met manner and were amused by his gargantuan drinking and feasting, which he regularly shared with them at mass, open-air banquets. It was these Rhineland legionaries who had acclaimed him as emperor, hoping for rich rewards.

Meanwhile, besides those in Judea and Syria, other legions in Spain, Gaul, and Britain, in Illyria, Moesia, and Pannonia came out in support of

Vespasian, as a general who knew how to win battles. His cause was helped by the circulation of a letter from the late Emperor Otho—possibly forged—that begged him to save Rome. In possession of the war chest for the Judean campaign, Vespasian had the funds to finance his bid for the throne. He could also rely on the loyalty of the former officers of that gifted general Domitius Corbulo, who for years had fought the Parthians so successfully, before Nero made him commit suicide. They included Mucianus. Vespasian sent him through the Balkans to Italy with a large army and orders to march on Rome. In the meantime, his allies from northern and western Europe invaded the peninsula across the Alps.

By the time reports of the war in Europe reached Alexandria, they were already out of date, leaving Vespasian's supporters in uneasy suspense. The news that came was of very big battles, with massive casualties. It was some time before a decisive confrontation took place, and no doubt Josephus trembled for the future. But over the next few months Vitellius's position deteriorated and then began to collapse, partly because of his self-indulgence, which resulted in a faltering direction of military affairs apparent to everybody—in marked contrast to the leadership shown by Vespasian. Eventually, Vitellius's armies lost two crucial battles in succession—at Cremona in Cisalpine Gaul in October, where he lost 30,000 men, and at Narnia in southern Italy (near modern Spoleto) early in December, when the bulk of his troops went over to the enemy, led by their commander. These defeats proved to be decisive. Vitellius's best general, Fabius Valens, was captured in Gaul, on a desperate mission to raise reinforcements. He was sent back to Italy where he was beheaded. The emperor's other outstanding commander, Caecina Alienus, had already gone over to Vespasian. Terrified, he offered to abdicate in return for a pension.

There were dramatic scenes at Rome in mid-December when Vespasian's supporters, including some senators, failed in a premature attempt to seize the city. Vitellius's soldiers reacted by storming and burning the capitol, the Temple of Jupiter Optimus Maximus, where they had taken refuge, and Vespasian's younger son, Domitian, escaped from the ensuing massacre on the Capitoline Hill only by dressing in the vestments of a priest of Isis. (Tacitus thought that the burning of the capitol was the most disgraceful event in the entire history of Rome.) For a week longer Vitellius clung to the throne.

Vespasian's army marched into Rome on 20 December 69 CE. "Drunk and gorged to excess with the luxuries of the table, as can happen with men when they are in desperate circumstances, Vitellius came out of the palace and, after being dragged through the crowd and treated with every possible sort of indignity, was put to death in the heart of Rome," is how *The Jewish War* describes the former emperor's fate, omitting the sickening details of his lynching that are recorded by Suetonius—how a dagger was held under his chin to make him hold his head up and how he was tortured with exquisite refinements. "He had ruled for eight months and five days and if his life had lasted longer, I personally am of the opinion that the resources of the entire Empire would not been enough to satisfy his vast appetite for self-indulgence."[11]

Even so, as Tacitus emphasizes, the death of Vitellius was the end of the war rather than the beginning of peace. Eventually, however, Mucianus took control of the capital in Vespasian's name.

Josephus comments, with obvious emotion, "The whole empire was safe once again, and beyond all expectation the Roman state survived."[12] Clearly, he had feared that it was going to disintegrate. This is quite understandable since the struggle for the throne had been a cataclysmic upheaval during which tens of thousands died in the fighting. His hero worship of Titus probably dates from this period, as Josephus had seen just how much his skillful organization behind the scenes had contributed to his father's victory.

Vespasian was still at Alexandria when he received the news that he had won, and he remained there for much of the following year. Embassies from all over the world flocked to congratulate him. So many people came that even though the Egyptian capital was nearly as big as Rome, it seemed too small to contain them all, says Josephus—a comment that contains a hint of relief at his patron's triumph. The new emperor was not to enter Rome until September, or perhaps even October, 70. However, Josephus would not be among his entourage—he was needed elsewhere.

Now that the civil war had at last been won, Vespasian "turned his thoughts to what was left of Judea," which meant Jerusalem and the Zealots.[13] Judging from what followed, he and his staff officers planned the campaign in meticulous detail. We can be sure that Josephus was involved in the planning, since he had access to news of what was happening in the enemy capital through letters that were reaching the Alexandrian Diaspora. Titus was sent with a picked force to besiege and capture Jerusalem, accompanied by the former Jewish general.

The bloody upheaval of 69 CE shook Josephus badly, even if he watched it from the safety of Alexandria. He does not mention his personal reactions, as that would undermine his claims to be a prophet. Yet before the civil war broke out, he had already developed misgivings about the future of the Roman Empire and Roman civilization in general. As he wrote in the preface to *The Jewish War*, "The Jews expected that their kindred beyond the Euphrates would join their revolt while in any case the Romans were having trouble with their neighbors the Gauls and the Celts who were restless and on the move."[14] Nero's death had turned an already dangerous situation into one of extreme peril.

The empire's collapse had been the Zealots' greatest hope, but it did not happen. The crisis transformed Josephus. From now on, he would see himself as both Jewish and Roman, a dual identity that he reveals in his books. In addition, he had come to believe that in many important ways Jews and Romans shared the same ideals.[15]

Above all, Josephus decided that he really was a prophet. If he had foretold Vespasian's rise to the throne as a desperate ruse to save his life, the fact that it was borne out by events confirmed his belief that he could see into the future and predict the fate of the Jews. This explains much of his behavior during the fresh campaign in Judea.

16

Titus Takes Command

"And I will take away from you the voice of mirth and the voice of joy and the voice of the bridegroom and the voice of the bride; and all the land shall be without any footsteps of inhabitants."

PROPHECY OF BARUCH, II, 23

"FROM ALEXANDRIA I WAS SENT with Titus to the siege of Jerusalem," Josephus tells us in the *Vita*. He adds, "There my life was frequently in danger, from the Jews who were eager to get their hands on me so that they could wreak their revenge, and from the Romans who attributed every set-back they suffered to some sort of treachery on my part—they were always noisily demanding that the Emperor should punish me as the man who was secretly betraying them. However, Titus Caesar, well aware of just how much the fortunes of war swing backward and forward, silenced his soldiers' grumbling by taking no notice."[1] As so often, Josephus had reason to be grateful to Titus.

In view of his regard for Titus, the patron whom—judging from what he afterward wrote about him—he all but worshipped, it is worth examining the Roman in some detail. An enigma, he baffled contemporaries because of the pleasant face that he invariably showed to the world. Suetonius claims he was "the delight and darling of the human race, because he knew how to win everybody's affection, by nature, cunning or sheer good

155

fortune." The same source also tells us that he was handsome and dignified, a fine soldier and an accomplished horseman. Well read, possessing
an amazing memory, Titus wrote poetry in Latin and Greek, besides
singing and playing the harp. "I have heard from many people that he was
able to write shorthand very fast and liked to have competitions with his
secretaries to see who was quickest," says Suetonius. "He could imitate any
writing shown to him and would joke that he ought to have been 'the
prince of forgers.'"[2] Above all, he appeared to be a kind man, sensitive to
people's feelings.

Outwardly, at least, Titus really does seem to have possessed an unusually attractive personality. His troops were devoted to him. Yet Suetonius,
while on the whole admiring, has to admit that at times he could display
some very unpleasant qualities, such as ruthlessness and cruelty. He had no
qualms about committing murder. When Titus returned to Rome after the
Jewish War, he took command of the Praetorian guard and then used the
guard to liquidate anybody he distrusted. He had a debilitating weakness
for sexual pleasures, keeping whole troops of catamites and eunuchs, besides indulging in a long and potentially disastrous passion for a great Jewish lady. Despite his charm and talent for diplomacy, he had a flair for
turning distinguished Romans into enemies.

What is beyond dispute is that Titus was a shrewd statesman and a
brave if rash general. He fully appreciated that the Roman public would be
unhappy until he captured Jerusalem and restored the imperial army's reputation. If he succeeded, it would shed much needed luster on the new
Flavian dynasty, of which he was the heir. Never for a moment, least of all
on this vitally important expedition, did he lose sight of his goal, which
was to succeed his father on the throne of the Roman Empire. Writing not
long after Titus's death, Tacitus notes, with his usual acuteness, his solici-
tous determination: "in order that he might one day be thought worthy of
an even higher distinction, Titus always dressed splendidly in magnificent
armour, at the same time demonstrating that he was a determined and resourceful soldier, taking care to earn respect [among all ranks] by his unfailing courtesy and friendliness, and by mixing with his troops in action
or on the march without doing any harm to his dignity as a general."[3]

His most obvious handicap as a soldier was a fondness for taking risks.
Like Vespasian, he led from the front, but unlike his father, he could be

reckless to the point of folly. Sometimes his pugnacious liking for hand-to-hand combat endangered not only his own life but those of his men. Although they admired his dash and courage, his wild, often rash gallantry nearly resulted in his being taken prisoner on more than one occasion. Overconfident, he was one of those dangerous generals who are capable of turning victory into defeat.

We know the route that Titus took on his way from Alexandria to Judea in the spring of 70 CE because Josephus traveled with him and has left us an account of his journey, which involved crossing the Egyptian desert. They were accompanied by the elderly prefect of Egypt, Tiberius Alexander, who first proclaimed Vespasian as emperor and had been a devoted supporter of the Flavians from the beginning. "The most reliable of all Vespasian's friends," is how Josephus describes him. "Because of his age and experience, he had unrivaled knowledge of the art of war."[4] He also possessed exceptionally valuable experience of Jews and Judea.

One reason why Vespasian appointed Tiberius as Titus's second-in-command may have been to discourage his son and heir from embarking on any rash adventures. Always a realist, the emperor had often seen Titus in action on the battlefield and knew of his failings. It is likely that the cautious old general's restraining influence made a substantial contribution to the campaign behind the scenes, an aspect of the war that has not received sufficient recognition.

Slightly sinister, Tiberius was that rare phenomenon in the ancient world: a renegade Jew who had betrayed the faith of his ancestors and sacrificed to the pagan gods of imperial Rome in order to further his career. He came from an impeccably patrician background; his father, Alexander the Alabarch, had belonged to one of the great families of the Greek-speaking Jewish Diaspora in Egypt, his brother had been Queen Berenice's first husband, and his uncle was the philosopher Philo. Twenty years earlier, he had been an unusually effective governor of Judea—"making no alteration in the ancient laws, he kept the nation in tranquillity," says The Jewish War.[5] By this Josephus means that he had done so not just by crucifying 20,000 Zealots but by respecting religious beliefs.

Clearly, Josephus respected and admired Tiberius Alexander in many ways. He may even have liked him. Certainly, the pair had a lot in common. Like White Russians fighting the Bolsheviks, as patricians they did not think they were betraying their fellow countrymen; they simply felt disgust that their beautiful capital should be governed by men whom they regarded as criminals from the gutter. Even so, Josephus must have found Tiberius's self-seeking abandonment of Judaism deeply distasteful; "he did not continue in the religion of his ancestors," is his carefully laconic comment.[6] Built on apostasy, a career such as that of Tiberius contradicted Josephus's own cherished view that one could belong to both nations without disowning the Jewish faith.

From Alexandria the Romans marched to Nicopolis, where the troops boarded big galleys and sailed along the Nile through the district of Mendes until they reached the city of Thmuis. Here they disembarked and continued their journey by land, spending a night at the small town of Tanis, where they built their usual fortified camps. The second night was spent at Heracleopolis and the third at Pelusium, where they rested for two days before fording the Pelusian estuary. After a day's march through the desert, they camped at the temple of the Casian Jupiter, and after another day's march, at Ostrakine, suffering from a severe shortage of water since the place had no proper wells. Next, they halted at Rhinocorora, from where they marched to Raphia, which marked the Judean border. Their fifth major camp was at Gaza, after which, continuing along the coast by way of Ashkelon, Jamna, and Joppa, they went on to Caesarea. Here, Titus intended to concentrate his entire army, including local auxiliaries and allies.

The army that assembled at Caesarea was bigger than Vespasian's. Titus had four legions, the best soldiers in the world, supplemented by other forces. The legions included the Fifth Legion commanded by Sextus Cerealis, the Tenth Legion commanded by Larcius Lepidus, the Fifteenth Legion commanded by Titus Frigius, and the Twelfth Legion ("Fulminata") whose commander Josephus does not name—the last understandably keen to avenge its disgraceful rout by the Jews in 66. The Syrian auxiliaries included twenty cohorts of infantry with eight squadrons of cavalry. In addition, there were some substantial detachments of local troops that had been provided by the region's client rulers. These were led in person by King Agrippa II and King Sohaemus of Emeas.

In all, Titus's army numbered between 50,000 and 60,000 men. The sheer size of this force shows just how much respect the Romans must have felt for the fighting quality of the Jews, untrained soldiers though they might be. In retrospect it seems astonishing that Rome would have sent such a big army instead of a small expeditionary force.

Meanwhile, the men who were occupying Jerusalem had now split into three mutually hostile groups. Josephus attributes the development to divine retribution and compares the "sedition" to a wild beast devouring its own flesh. Even those who sympathize with the patriots find it difficult to defend their insane disunity. Throughout *The Jewish War* Josephus makes the claim, directly or implicitly, that if only men of his own class had been left in charge, such as Ananus, then the city might have put up a much better fight and obtained reasonable—although no doubt harsh—terms from the Romans. In fairness to his opinion, it has to be said that nothing could have been worse than what was happening under the Zealot leaders.

The garrison was already divided between John of Gischala's supporters in the Temple and those of Simon bar Giora in the Upper City—and much of the Lower City, when Eleazar ben Simon, who was no less determined to be supreme ruler, fell out with John. Although equally blood-stained, he pretended to be horrified by his atrocities. Eleazar's following included Judas ben Chelcias and Simon ben Ezron, "men of power," and Hezekiah ben Chobari, whom *The Jewish War* calls "a man of some distinction"—fellow members of the old upper class. Josephus adds that each of these men commanded a large personal following, which implies that the defense was fragmented even at grassroots level.[7]

Suddenly, Eleazar and his friends seized the inner court of the Temple, fortifying the gates that led to the Sanctuary. Well armed, they had plenty of food since they felt no guilt about eating the animals brought in for sacrifice, but as there were comparatively few of them, they did not feel strong enough to evict John from the outer Temple. Although John's men outnumbered them, Eleazar's men were higher up in the great complex of buildings and were able to shoot down on their opponents. John nonetheless launched attack after attack, and there were frequent sallies by both sides, with a constant exchange of missiles. Despite suffering more casualties than he inflicted, John would not give up, so that in consequence the Temple was covered in blood.

Seeing John being attacked with such ferocity by Eleazar from above, Simon bar Giora renewed his own onslaught against him. However, John beat off the attacks from below without too much difficulty, by using close-combat weapons such as bows or javelins, while he kept Eleazar's men safely at bay with scorpions and stone-firing ballistae, though his men were not yet very skilled at using them. Unfortunately, the artillery killed not only his enemies but worshippers in the Temple. For the Zealots, until nearly the end, ensured that the sacrifices were continued, and Eleazar's men admitted any Jews who wished to make them, after a careful search—locals from top to toe, strangers less strictly—although having gained admission they sometimes regretted it. There were days when the bodies of natives and foreigners, of priests and pilgrims, lay beside those of sheep, goats, and oxen that had also been caught in the bombardment, and pools of mingled animal and human blood covered the courts of the Lord. Josephus comments that civil war had turned the Temple into a charnel house.

Huge quantities of the wine among the tithes and firstfruits in the Temple storerooms were consumed by Eleazar's party, and in their frenzy of drunken aggression they redoubled their attacks on John's men. However, John's main quarrel was with Simon. Whenever pressure from above slackened—as happened a good deal on account of Eleazar's people being too drunk to fight—he took the opportunity to launch sallies against Simon's troops, frequently driving them back through the streets, before his soldiers were forced to retreat by counterattacks.

During these skirmishes John's men set fire to the storehouses containing the provisions on which Simon's army depended, and then Simon's troops retaliated by setting fire to John's supplies. Their leaders were unable to stop them. As a result, grain that might have fed the defenders for a decade was destroyed during a Sabbatical "seventh year," when the Jews were required to let the land rest and therefore had no harvest to replenish their stores.[8] This burning of irreplaceable supplies underlines the Zealots' two crippling weaknesses—lack of discipline and lack of a proper command structure.

Between them, the three groups of Zealots were tearing the people of Jerusalem to pieces. Ordinary citizens were in utter despair. They could see not the slightest likelihood of the three factions reaching an agreement with each other, and they had very little chance to escape, since there were guards everywhere. If they agreed on nothing else, the Zealot chieftains concurred in murdering anyone who suggested making peace with the Romans or anyone whom they suspected of planning to escape. While the noise made by rival groups fighting each other day and night was deafening, so was the moaning of people who lost friends or relatives but dared not wail. Nobody bothered to bury the dead. Those who did not belong to one of the Zealot groups could see no point in it since they regarded themselves as already condemned to death. On the other hand, patriots fought each other mercilessly, trampling on the corpses beneath their feet.

John appropriated a consignment of huge beams of timber, intended as supports for the Sanctuary, that had been brought down from Mount Lebanon at vast labor and expense by King Agrippa. Instead, John used them to build defense towers for protection against his Zealot enemies. The towers never saw action, however, since events developed too quickly. Shortly after the arrival of large numbers of Jews from all over the East as well as from Judea, pilgrims who had come to celebrate the Passover, Titus appeared in front of the city walls.

Josephus had ridden all the way to Jerusalem with Titus's staff, and he gives us a graphic snapshot of the Romans' advance into enemy territory, something that he had actually seen with his own eyes:

> The allied kings' forces and auxiliary troops went first, and after them pioneers and camp-builders. Next came the generals' baggage with its escort. Then, Titus himself with spearmen and other picked troops, and behind him the legions' cavalry. They rode in front of the army's artillery, which was followed by the tribunes and commanders of cohorts escorted by a crack corps. Then, preceded by trumpeters, came the Eagles, borne by standard-bearers. After them marched the main body of the army, legionaries six abreast, who were followed by their camp-servants and their baggage. Finally came the mercenaries, carefully supervised by a rearguard [of legionaries].[9]

Titus had marched through Samaria to Gophna, and thence, after a long day's march, camped in a valley that the Jews called the "Valley of Thorns" in Aramaic. It was about three and a half miles distance from Jerusalem, although well out of sight of the defenders. From here, with a squadron of 600 picked cavalrymen, he had ridden ahead to reconnoiter the city and find out what he could do to weaken the Jews' morale—and to see if there was any chance of terrifying them into surrender without any fighting. He had the impression, only too well justified, that ordinary folk wanted peace, but that none of them dared say so for fear of the Zealots.

As he rode along the main approach road to Jerusalem a few days before Passover, he could see no sign of life on the walls, but when he left the road to go down the path toward the Psephinus Tower at the northwest corner, leading his troops in single file, a large force of Jews suddenly charged out from the North Gate next to the Towers of the Women from where they had been watching him. They broke through the Romans in such a cunning way that he found himself cut off with only a handful of men.

Since he could not gallop onward because the ground in front of him was a maze of allotments divided by ditches and dry-stone walls, he wheeled his horse around, forcing his way back to the main body of his force through a whole host of enemies, killing several with his sword. Without a helmet or a breastplate, he was lucky not to be hit by the hail of javelins that slew one of his comrades or hacked to death like another companion. The incident was a tonic for the defenders; they had only just failed to catch him, and his death might have prevented the siege from taking place at all.

The Jewish War gives considerable space to this incident, attributing Titus's survival to divine protection. Josephus's horror in the description of Titus's peril and relief at his escape is almost palpable. He knew only too well that had his patron been killed, the Roman officers would have put him to death in the shortest possible space of time.

During the night, the Fifth Legion arrived from Emmaus, and the next morning Titus moved his army up onto the hill called Mount Scopus (Lookout Hill). A low hill to the north of Jerusalem, this was a famous vantage point from where pilgrims caught their first sight of the great city and the gleaming white and gold Sanctuary. He gave orders to build and fortify a joint camp for the Twelfth Legion and the Fifteenth Legion at a spot that was about three-quarters of a mile from the walls, with another camp 600 yards farther back for the Fifth Legion. Realizing his men must be exhausted after a night march, he wanted them to be out of range of the enemy so that they could get some rest before they began to dig entrenchments. They had scarcely started work when the Tenth Legion arrived and was ordered to camp east of the city, three-quarters of a mile away, on the Mount of Olives.

The legionary camp played a vital role in Roman tactics and strategy. Built with amazing speed—the legions had a tradition of teamwork worthy of today's modern armies—it was as much a fortified town as a camping ground. If possible, it was sited near a stream on a dry, well-drained site that was free of undergrowth or could easily be cleared. It always had two broad main streets fifty feet wide, which were joined at right angles by lesser streets. Specific areas for sleeping (under leather tents), eating, washing, and drilling were carefully marked out, and there were ovens, storage depots, drains, rubbish pits, and latrines. An annex contained a wagon park, horse lines, and a smithy. Each camp was protected by ditches and stockades; wooden towers and sometimes dry-stone walls were added if it was to be occupied for any length of time. (A "marching" or overnight camp was much simpler.) A safeguard against surprise attacks, the fortified camp provided a stronghold should things go wrong. Time and again, such a structure averted defeat. On departure, it was burned down so that an enemy could not use it.

During the Judean campaign Josephus was accustomed to living for months on end in camps of this sort, when he was attached to the staff of Vespasian or Titus. Thus, he was able to provide an eyewitness description of what the legionaries were building for a long stay outside Jerusalem:

> The inner part of the camp is for tents, while outside it looks just like a wall with its neatly spaced towers in which scorpions, catapults, stone-projectors and other missile-firers are mounted, always ready to shoot. Four gates are provided, one in each section of the wall, big enough for pack-animals to enter and wide enough for sorties in strength in case of emergency. Inside, the camp is marked out into streets, the officers' tents being in the middle, in the centre of which is the commander-in-chief's tent, looking a bit like a temple. Suddenly you see a city spring up before you, complete with market place and workshops, with offices for the centurions and divisional commanders where they meet or hold court-martials. The outer wall and the buildings inside go up with astonishing speed because so many men are at work. If advisable, a ditch is built around it, six feet wide and six deep.[10]

Watching from the ramparts of Jerusalem, the defenders were horrified when they saw the besiegers starting to erect what looked like three small cities. Seizing their weapons, they made a sudden sortie in force, charging across the Kedron ravine and up the Mount of Olives to attack the enemy. Having taken off their armor and swords in order to dig, the legionaries were caught by surprise and were cut down in droves. Encouraged by the sortie's success, reinforcements rushed out from the city and in a short space of time threw the Romans out of their uncompleted camp.

The entire Tenth Legion might have easily been wiped out if Titus had not arrived with his bodyguard in the nick of time. Cursing his men for being cowards, he rallied them and counterattacked the Jews from the flank, killing many of them and driving the rest into the ravine. They quickly regrouped on the far side, stubbornly continuing the battle. A little after noon, Titus decided that the situation had cooled down enough and, placing reinforcements on the edge of the ravine, sent the battered Tenth Legion up to the Mount of Olives to start a new camp at the top.

Mistaking their ascent for a retreat, the Jews charged once again, "hurling themselves [at the Romans] like ferocious wild beasts," says Josephus.[11] The Romans fled to the very top of the mount, leaving behind Titus and a few troops on the lower slopes hemmed in by the enemy. His men shouted at him to break through immediately and to run for his life. Instead, he tried to beat back the Jews, who were attacking uphill in increasing numbers, attempting to drive them down into the ravine. Daunted by his extraordinary ferocity, the enemy gave Titus a wide berth but went on pursuing panic-stricken Romans up the mount. Finally, after realizing that Titus had not run away with them but that he was still fighting and ashamed at having abandoned their general, the legionaries on top of the mount regrouped and countercharged downhill, pushing the Jews into the ravine. Titus went on fighting until the Jews had been evicted from the Mount of Olives. Even before the enemy retreated, he once again gave orders for the Fifth Legion to build their camp on top.

"Without the slightest flattery or without in any way being prejudiced in his favor, I want to emphasize as strongly as I can," writes Josephus, "that it was [Titus] Caesar himself who personally rescued the entire legion from annihilation and then gave it a chance to build its camp in safety."[12] Nevertheless, while Titus may no doubt have given a superlative display of combat skills and showed dazzling leadership in action at close quarters, this was the second day on which the Roman army's supreme commander had risked and nearly lost his life. Yet again, Josephus must have reflected on the imminent likelihood of a painful death.

Fortunately for the Romans, these discouraging preliminaries to the siege failed to unite Jerusalem's defenders, and there was yet another outbreak of bitter, self-destructive infighting within the city walls. With the start of Passover on 1 May, Eleazar unwisely opened the gates of the inner Temple to let in anyone who wanted to worship. John sent in some of his less-well-known followers, heavily cloaked in order to avoid being recognized. Once inside, they gathered together, drew their weapons from under their cloaks, and attacked everybody in sight. It appears that Eleazar was killed in the fighting, and his men fled from the ramparts to hide in the huge vaults beneath the Temple, while the terrified worshipers who huddled around the altar or in front of the Sanctuary were clubbed or cut down. Many harmless people died as the victims of some private hatred, murdered on the pretense that they belonged to the other side.

Although John's men went on killing and torturing innocent worshipers caught up in the fighting, his lieutenants did reach an understanding with the Zealots hiding in the vaults, who were allowed to come up and join them. Now he had gained possession of the Temple's inner court and all its stores, and Eleazar had been eliminated. A conflict between three factions had been reduced to a conflict between two.

In the meantime, undismayed by his experience on Mount Scopus, Titus decided to establish a camp nearer Jerusalem. He stationed a force of infantry and cavalry, all of whom were picked men, in sufficient strength to deal with any sallies by the defenders, and then used the rest of his troops to level the ground for 400 yards in front of the walls. This was a lengthy business since fences around the gardens, vineyards, and olive groves had to be pulled up, trees cut down, hollows filled in, and hillocks leveled, and every big rock needed digging up with iron crowbars. He intended to flatten the entire area from Mount Scopus to Herod's monuments near the Serpent's Pool.

While this work was in progress, a group of Jews emerged in front of the walls from the Women's Towers, as if driven out by people inside who were insisting that Jerusalem must surrender at once, and began to cower dramatically under the ramparts. Other Jews on top of the walls shouted offers to the Romans to make peace, throwing stones at the supposed fugitives below and promising that they would open the gates. Delighted, the legionaries moved forward, thinking that they were being given an opportunity to rush the defenses and charge into the city.

Titus quickly smelled a rat—only the day before, using Josephus as an intermediary, he had offered terms of surrender, but the Jews had demanded impossible conditions—so he shouted to his men to stay where they were. However, some of the Roman troops who were too far out in front to hear him continued to run forward. As soon as they reached the walls, the Jewish "fugitives" produced swords from beneath their clothes and attacked them, and they were showered with stones and javelins from the ramparts. Those who survived the ambush turned and ran, as the Jews continued their attack. The defenders on the ramparts cheered and brandished their weapons in triumph, jeering at the Romans.

Titus was furious. "Although they may be driven by sheer desperation instead of real leadership, so far everything the Jews have done has been properly worked out well beforehand and very carefully calculated, with nicely planned tactics and ambushes—they are having all the good luck because they obey orders, they help each other, and they know how to be loyal," he told his officers angrily. "Yet Roman soldiers, who've always won because of discipline and strict obedience to their officers, have started doing the exact opposite and are now being beaten on account of their wretched impetuosity. What makes it even more disgraceful is that they have let themselves fight without a leader although a Caesar was present. This sort of behavior is an insult to the Roman army, and an insult to my father."[13]

Everybody who heard Titus was convinced he was going to punish the humiliated legionaries by decimation, which meant executing every tenth man involved in the route. If he had intended to do so in the heat of the moment, he was persuaded to change his mind. Josephus, who must have been present as a member of the staff, explains that although Titus believed in individual executions for the sake of discipline, he thought that mass punishments were extremely bad for morale. In any case, he had made his point and frightened his troops into a more alert frame of mind.

Determined to forestall any further surprises by the Jews and to ensure that baggage and provisions could reach his men in safety, he completed the leveling of the ground between his headquarters and the city within a mere four days. He then stationed his best troops seven ranks deep, in strongly fortified positions that were sited opposite the city's northern and western quarters, but just out of range of the defenders' bowmen. Three ranks of legionaries were in front, a rank of archers was in the middle, and three ranks of cavalry were at the rear. Supplies could now be brought up to the Romans on muleback from the depots without risk of being shot at. Moreover, from this point on, the defenders did not dare to make sorties outside the walls. Titus moved his headquarters camp to a spot that was also only about 400 yards from the ramparts. It was opposite the great tower called Psephinus, which was where the walls bent around from north to west. Another group of troops was entrenched opposite the tower named Hippicus—the tower of the Upper Palace—and similarly about 400 yards from the city. The Tenth Legion continued to occupy its position on the Mount of Olives.

Titus finally started his siege on 1 May, the day that John of Gischala stormed the inner Temple. From the Roman point of view, it had scarcely been an auspicious beginning. Inside Jerusalem, the Zealots, having experienced a measure of success in their skirmishes with the Romans, were feeling rather confident.

17

The Siege Begins

"Gird yourselves and be valiant men and be ready against the morning, that you may fight with these nations that are assembled against us to destroy us and our Sanctuary. For it is better for us to die in battle than to see the evils of our nation and of the [Holy] of Holies."

FIRST BOOK OF THE MACCABEES, III, 58–59

TACITUS IMPLIES THAT for Titus the siege of Jerusalem was just another step in his career, a means of showing the world that he was a gifted soldier and of demonstrating that sheer ability justified the Flavians' occupation of the imperial throne. Yet at the time it must have seemed all too obvious that if Titus should fail to capture the city, then a humiliation on such a scale would be so shattering that it might easily topple his father, the new Emperor Vespasian.

On the other hand, for the Jewish people—however low may have been Josephus's opinion of their capital's defenders—it was a vital struggle to preserve the faith, the nation, and the land. More than life or death was at stake, on both sides.

It is important to remember that at no time in their history had the Romans ever besieged such a big city before, nor such a strong one. (Carthage was far smaller.) Shocked by Pompey's humiliating occupation, the Jews had been preparing since King Herod's time for a siege against Jerusalem, methodically bribing Roman officials to let them fortify the place as strongly as possible. Survivors who saw the capital in all its glory gave Tacitus the benefit of their recollections, and he describes how daunting it must have looked to the Romans:

> Standing on a height which is naturally difficult of access, Jerusalem was rendered even more impregnable by ramparts and bastions that would have made even places on a flat plain more than adequately fortified. Two very high hills were surrounded by walls that in some places jutted out but in others curved in, so that the flanks of any besiegers were exposed to enemy fire. Moreover, the hills were bordered by crags and ravines. Since the towers on the hills stood sixty feet high and those on level ground a hundred and twenty, they made an astonishing impression on anyone seeing them for the first time—from far away they seemed to be the same height. Inside the city there were further fortifications defending the royal palace, together with the fortress of the Antonia with its awesome turrets—named by Herod in honor of Mark Antony. The Temple was designed like a citadel, enclosed by walls that were thicker and more elaborate than anywhere else.[1]

Even the Temple's colonnades were defense works in their own right. A spring down in Siloam supplied it with drinking water, but in case it should run dry, huge cisterns stored the rain. As for food, further supplies could supposedly be brought in through secret tunnels under the walls, although this was not borne out by events.

According to Tacitus—Josephus gives us a much bigger figure—Jerusalem contained at least 600,000 men, women, and children, who preferred to die rather than leave the holy city. Many were refugees, including, in the words of Tacitus, "the most indomitable spirits." Among these fanatical hard-liners were 2,000 Tiberians, burning for revenge. In theory, it possessed a more-than-adequate garrison. Simon bar Giora had 10,000 followers under fifty officers, and he had been joined by 5,000 Idumeans with ten officers, of whom the senior were James ben Sosias and Simon ben Cathlas. In the Temple, John of Gischala had about 6,000 men and twenty officers, supplemented by the 2,400 Zealots who had gone over to him after Eleazar's death and were led by Simon ben Ari.

At a conservative estimate, the garrison of Jerusalem therefore amounted to over 20,000 well-armed troops, who still possessed the artillery they had captured from the Romans. Unfortunately, they were divided into two mutually hostile factions. This lack of unity was made even more serious by an obsession with exterminating the remaining members of the ruling class who had not become Zealots.

Simon bar Giora occupied the Upper City and the Great Wall, as far as the Kedron, along with a large part of the Old Wall, where it curved around east from Siloam and went downward to the palace of King Monabazus (of Adiabene). He also occupied the fountain together with a good deal of the Lower City, extending right up to the palace of Queen Helena, Monabazus's mother. John of Gischala held the Temple and much of the surrounding neighborhood, with Ophel and the Kedron Valley. The two leaders had already wrecked the area in between, demolishing houses to get a clearer field of fire at each other. At this stage, apart from the brief moment of reality when they made their first sortie, they never stopped fighting, despite the Romans being just outside the walls.

"They did more harm to each other than anything the Romans did so that nothing worse could happen to the city," comments Josephus in *The Jewish War*. "No horrors more dreadful can possibly be imagined."[2] As Josephus puts it, their ceaseless, fratricidal combat undermined the defense, until the Romans finally put an end to the feuding—"even harder than destroying the walls."

Titus, this time with an adequate escort, rode around the imposing walls of Jerusalem, searching for the best place to attack. It was not an easy decision, since on the south and on the east the city was protected by the steep ravines of Hinnom and the Kedron, which would make it impossible for the besiegers to use battering rams and siege towers. The northern side was a bit more feasible, without any precipices or valleys in front of its ramparts. Although the Old Wall here had recently been supplemented by two additional walls, they were still a considerable way from completion, especially the outermost, Agrippa's Wall.

Titus decided to launch his main assault on this side, the weakest spot in the defenses, from a position that lay northwest of the Jaffa Gate and more or less opposite the tomb of John the High Priest. The ramparts were still unfinished; Agrippa's Wall was not yet high enough, and there was a big gap in the Second Wall. His plan was to smash through the first two walls, and then through the Old Wall, so that he would be able to push on into the Upper City and capture the Antonia Fortress, and finally the Temple.

Almost certainly Titus consulted his tame Jewish general, who, as a native of Jerusalem, had been familiar with the city since boyhood. Josephus may even have suggested the exact spot where the main assault should be launched. He had become an indispensable member of the Roman staff. Even so, he was distrusted by most officers, and throughout the campaign he had to keep as close to Titus as possible. However, it looks as though one or two had confidence in him. He tells us that he accompanied Titus during his ride of inspection around the walls and that his old friend, the tribune Nicanor, was wounded by an arrow in the shoulder when he himself was shouting up at the ramparts and advising the defenders to make peace.[3]

Titus ordered the construction of three siege ramps. To create these huge mounds of earth and timber, the legionaries demolished the suburbs and cut down trees for miles around to provide the building materials. As soon as the mounds began to rise and could give enough shelter, Titus positioned archers and javelin men between them and placed scorpions, catapults, and stone-projectors in front—their job being to fend off Jewish sorties and pick off defenders who were shooting from the ramparts in an attempt to slow up the work

According to *The Jewish War*, many in Jerusalem were delighted to see the siege making such rapid progress, hoping they might be left alone while their persecutors were distracted. They even looked forward to the Zealots getting their due when the Romans succeeded in capturing the city.[4] When he wrote this, however, Josephus must have meant survivors of the ruling class rather than the population as a whole.

For the moment, John of Gischala was too nervous about an attack by Simon Bar Giora to make any useful contribution to the defense, and so Simon's followers had to do most of the fighting, since they controlled the area where the main assault was expected and were in the front line. Simon mounted captured artillery on the ramparts, but his men proved incapable of operating them at long range, save for a few who had learned from deserters. Instead, they only had bows and slings to shoot at the legionaries who were building the ramps, sometimes sallying out to attack them.

The legionaries were amply protected, however, by wooden hurdles stretched across palisades, while their own artillery coped with raiding parties. The engines of the Tenth Legion proved especially lethal; in addition to utilizing exceptionally large stone-projectors, they employed unusually powerful, quick-firing scorpions that fired volley after volley of iron bolts. These machines kept the Jewish sorties at bay besides killing many defenders on the ramparts. The stone-projectors had a range of about 400 yards and hurled rocks as big as a cow that weighed over half a hundredweight (38 kilos) and had a devastating impact. The Jews knew immediately when they were fired—not only from the noise made by the missiles as they whizzed through the air but also from their light color—having posted lookouts on the wall towers to monitor the loading of the projectors and to give warning—until the Romans painted the rocks black. Despite heavy casualties, the defenders managed to delay the ramps' construction by harrying the builders day and night.[5]

After measuring the distance to Agrippa's Wall by means of lead and lines thrown from the mounds—bowmen shooting from the ramparts made it impossible to measure across open ground—the engineers reported that the ditch below the wall had been filled in and the ground in front was completely flat. Everything was now ready for the Roman battering rams to go into action. Titus gave orders for his artillery to bombard the ramparts and make the defenders keep their heads down, so that the three monstrous machines could be moved up from the shelter of the mounds.

Suddenly, the tremendous thudding of the rams against the walls echoed throughout the city, terrifying everybody within. The feuding forces of Simon and John started yelling accusations at each other that they were helping the enemy but then became sufficiently frightened by the relentless hammering to man the walls together, shooting flaming arrows and throwing firebrands at the rams and their crews. A party of Jews dashed out to attack them, trying to pull off the protective hurdles, but it was driven back by cavalry and archers that Titus had placed here in readiness and commanded in person. For the moment, however, Agrippa's Wall remained firm despite the unremitting hammer blows it was receiving, except for a corner of a wall tower that was knocked down by the ram manned by the Fifteenth Legion.

The defenders began to think the Romans had lost heart. Emerging from a postern door in the wall next to the tower Hippicus, a large detachment of Jews charged the siege works to set fire to the rams. A savage struggle began, with many casualties on both sides until, fighting with desperate courage, the Jews seemed to be getting the upper hand. The fire had already taken hold of the rams, which would certainly have been destroyed if some crack troops from Alexandria had not put up an unusually stubborn fight. Then Titus appeared at the head of a troop of cavalry, personally cutting down a dozen of his opponents and driving the rest back to the city. One of the raiding party was taken prisoner, and Titus had him crucified in full view of the ramparts, trying to frighten the defenders into surrender.

The Jews suffered another loss with the death of James, the general who commanded the Idumeans in the city. He had been talking to a soldier on the walls when he was hit in the chest by an arrow shot by an Arabian archer and dropped dead. The defenders were shocked since he had been a particularly tough and effective soldier.

On the following night, Titus gave orders for three siege towers, known by legionaries as *helepoles* ("city-takers"), to be erected on top of the ramps. These menacing structures were seventy-five feet tall, with five wooden platforms or more on top of each other, guarded against arrow-fire by a carapace of iron plates. One had been badly constructed and collapsed, creating a frightening clamor in the dark of night, spreading panic among the Romans, until Titus made sure everybody was told what had happened. It was only a brief setback. Soon archers, javelin men, and slingers were shooting down from the two other towers, making it impossible for Jews on the ramparts to harass the ram crews.

Finally, Agrippa's Wall began to crumble under ceaseless blows from the biggest ram, which was wryly called Nikon or "Victor" by the Jews because it always succeeded in bulldozing everything in its path. As soon as the Romans stormed in through a breach made by the ram, the defenders fled to the Second Wall without striking a blow, after which the attackers opened the gates to let in their comrades. Josephus comments that the Jews must have been either too worn out or too lazy to defend Agrippa's Wall properly, or perhaps even too confident—there were still another two walls behind. This took place on the fifteenth day of the siege.[6]

Titus now moved his camp inside Agrippa's Wall to a place known as the Camp of the Assyrians, after an earlier siege. It covered a large area of ground down to the Kedron but was far enough away from the Second Wall to be out of range of missiles. The Jews went on fighting with the utmost courage. John of Gischala's Zealots directed their defense from command points on the Antonia, the northern colonnade of the Temple, and King Alexander's tomb, while Simon bar Giora's men concentrated on defending the areas around the monument to John the High Priest and the watergate of the Hippicus Tower. Protecting Bezetha, the "New City," the Second Wall was much stronger than Agrippa's, with a tower at each end and a larger tower in the center, and in every way easier to defend since, as Tacitus notes, it zigzagged in and out, making it easy for defenders to shoot at the besiegers' flanks.

After the battering rams recommenced their work, shaking not just the Second Wall but buildings that stood some distance behind it, John of Gischala recognized Simon bar Giora as the leader of the city's defense, allowing his followers into the Temple. Even he had been frightened into acknowledging that the city would be lost unless some sort of cooperation existed between their two forces.

The Romans' main point of attack was the central tower, which stood over a gate from where a path led out to Golgotha. There were a number of concealed posterns in the curving wall, so that the Jews were able to make sorties. However, they were always beaten back by their opponents' superior weaponry.

"A spirit of daring, strengthened by fear, and supported by the natural fortitude of their race in the face of misfortune, gave heart to the Jews," comments Josephus, who could not help admiring the indomitable courage of his fellow countrymen.[7] They fought the Romans from dawn to dusk but found the hours of darkness harder to bear. "For both sides the nights were a time without sleep that was more oppressive than daytime, since one lot dreaded that the wall might be captured at any moment while the other was afraid the enemy might suddenly attack their camp. The two armies spent the hours of darkness under arms, ready for battle at dawn."[8]

The Jewish War says that the Jews were always prepared to risk their lives to please their officers, especially Simon who had such magnetism that his followers were ready to die for him, and even commit suicide should he order it. In Josephus's opinion, what gave the Romans courage was the habit of winning and never being defeated, pride in their empire's grandeur, and above all, the presence of Titus, who seemed everywhere at the same time, standing by each soldier. If he congratulated a man on his bravery, it was considered to be a good enough reward; many troops found courage that until then they had never known they possessed. This sometimes resulted in Homeric duels before the walls, although these were frowned on by Titus.

On one occasion, when a force of Jews emerged from the walls and began throwing javelins from a distance, a cavalry trooper named Longinus suddenly charged them single-handedly, killing two of the toughest; he stabbed the first Jew through the face, wrenched the spear out, and plunged it into the side of the next, and then safely rejoined his comrades. Several other Roman soldiers tried to copy him. Some of the Jews had the same contempt for danger and worried only about savaging their opponents, unconcerned about dying so long as they took an enemy with them. However, Titus seemed more concerned for his men's safety than winning, and he discouraged them from heroics of this sort. He issued orders that Roman troops were not to show off by risking their lives.

While Josephus relished the epic dimension, there were incidents that appealed to his keen if savage sense of comedy, such as the story of Castor. *The Jewish War* tells us that after Titus had concentrated his bombardment against the second wall's big central tower and the great ram Nikon had been hammering away at its masonry for a few days, it began to show signs of collapsing. A sustained hail of bolts from scorpions, which was supplemented by archery fire, forced most of the defenders to abandon it. However, "a certain crafty Jew called Castor," with ten resourceful companions, refused to quit, crouching down behind the ramparts.

As the tower began to crumble beneath them, Castor stood up and, in a piteous voice, begged Titus to forgive him. Thinking that the man was sincere and that the defenders were starting to lose heart, Titus immediately stopped the battering ram's hammering and the bombardment and shouted back, asking Castor what he wanted. The Jew answered that he would like to come down under a safe conduct. In reply, Titus said how delighted he was that Castor was being so sensible and that he would be even more pleased if everybody else had the same idea, promising to guarantee the safety of the entire city. Five of Castor's comrades joined in this fake plea for mercy, while the other five made them seem sincere by yelling they would never be Roman slaves and were going to die as free men. The parley went on for some time, as did the halt to the bombardment.

As the parley continued, Castor sent to Simon bar Giora for instructions, saying that he could go on fooling the Roman general for some time. Meanwhile, he ostentatiously tried to force the five "patriots" to accept Titus's terms. In response, they brandished their swords and then fell down as if the other five had killed them. Unable to see from below what was happening on the ramparts, Titus and his staff could not help admiring their loyalty. Meanwhile, Castor was wounded in the nose by an arrow and complained that he had been betrayed, whereupon Titus reprimanded the archer responsible. Then he asked Josephus to go up to the walls and bring Castor back. Josephus had already smelled treachery and refused, besides restraining his friends from going. However, a Jewish deserter named Aeneas ran forward when Castor promised to throw money down to anyone who showed sympathy. As soon as he reached the tower and was within range, Castor hurled a huge rock at Aeneas, who managed to dodge it, although it wounded a soldier who had followed him.

Furious, Titus ordered the recommencement of the bombardment and the battering. The tower soon gave way, the honey-tongued Castor and his comrades setting fire to the ruins as it was collapsing, before jumping down through the flames. They landed in the cellars below and escaped through a cave, but the Romans thought they had chosen to die in the flames rather than surrender and were deeply impressed by such heroism. One cannot help suspecting that, for a moment at least, the author of *The Jewish War* was on the defenders' side.[9]

The destruction of the tower opened a breach that was wide enough to enable the Romans to storm the Second Wall a mere four days after the fall of Agrippa's Wall. The Jews fled, and Titus, escorted by his bodyguard, charged in at the head of a thousand men, into a part of the New City that contained the clothes market and the metal workers' shops. Always too inclined to optimism, he had become overconfident and received a nasty surprise.

"If he only had immediately knocked down a bigger section of the second wall or demolished every house inside the area captured, as he was entitled to do by the rules of war, he would have suffered no further casualties," comments Josephus in *The Jewish War*. "But he thought that if he showed himself reluctant to do the Jews any more harm when it was so obviously in his power, then they would be impressed [by his magnanimity]. So he did not bother to widen the breach in a way that would allow his men to withdraw swiftly. He was under the illusion that people were going to repay him with equally decent behavior if he treated them kindly."[10]

On entering the New City, Titus gave orders that prisoners must not be killed or houses torched. Any Jew who wished to go on fighting could join his comrades on the Old Wall, while any citizen who wanted peace would be given back his property. Titus still hoped to capture Jerusalem intact and save the Temple. But while he was right in assuming that ordinary citizens were ready to accept whatever conditions he offered, his surprisingly generous terms convinced the Zealots that he had given up hope of defeating them and was acting from weakness.

Threatening to kill anybody who mentioned the word surrender, executing anyone who suggested making peace, the Zealots regrouped and attacked the Romans inside the New City, ambushing them in the streets and alleys or from houses, or jumping down on them from the ramparts. The Roman guards on the captured wall were so badly shaken that they abandoned their posts and ran back to the safety of their camps. Shouts for help came from legionaries trapped inside the New City, who were hemmed in on all sides. Growing in numbers and strength, the Jews drove them by sword or spear back through the streets toward the breach. However, since it was so narrow, only a few men at a time could pass through, and the rest had to stand and fight against overwhelming odds.

If Titus had not brought up reinforcements in the nick of time, every single Roman soldier who was still inside would certainly have been slaughtered. Stationing archers at the end of each street with orders to shoot toward where the enemy was thickest, he kept the Jews at bay by the sheer force of firepower, holding them off until the last of his troops had got out. However, he had lost possession of the Second Wall, a humiliating although very minor defeat.

In *The Jewish War*, Josephus describes the determination of the Zealots:

Intoxicated by their success, the spirits of the war party rose to fever pitch. They were convinced the Romans would never dare set foot in the New City again, and that they themselves would be unbeatable when they next marched out to battle. Yet because of their sinful deeds God made them blind to the real situation—they ignored the number of Roman troops outside, far more than those they had driven out, and the famine that was almost upon them. Until now they had been able to batten on the misery of the general public and drink the city's blood. But decent people had been starving for some time, and already many were dying from lack of food. However, the death of such folk encouraged the patriots, since it left more to eat. They only cared about the lives of those who were against peace at all costs and lived only to fight Romans. They were delighted by the way moderates were dropping dead from hunger at the roadside, men whom they regarded as encumbrances—that is how they felt about fellow citizens. Meanwhile, having manned the breach and blocked it with their bodies, they beat back the Romans who were trying to storm in once again.[11]

For three days they held off the besiegers, fighting with extraordinary ferocity, but on the fourth day they gave way before Titus's repeated assaults. Once he had regained possession of the Second Wall, he immediately demolished its northern section, placing garrisons in the surviving towers. Then he called off the offensive for a brief interval, to see if the loss of the Second Wall or fear of famine might persuade the Jews to open negotiations. He believed, mistakenly, that they could not feed themselves for much longer solely by robbing their neighbors.

He decided to impress them by holding a carefully staged pay parade in front of the wells but just out of range. Behind the menacing eagles, legionaries and auxiliaries marched at a strictly regulated pace onto a neatly marked out parade ground, having polished their weapons, helmets, accoutrements, and horse furniture. The cavalry led the parade, with dazzling horse trappings. Everywhere there were gleams of gold and silver.

The focus of attention was, of course, the glittering figure of the commanding general, Titus, who was accompanied by his staff, every one of them in fine cuirasses or jerkins scaled in burnished steel or bronze, helmets with stiff crests of red horsehair and cloaks colored according to rank, shining metal greaves on their legs. Titus and some of the staff may have worn ceremonial masks of gilded metal over their faces. All officers, including centurions, put up full decorations—gold and silver torques, armbands, and neck chains, together with the regulation sets of nine medallions of gold or silver on their chests. Even their splendidly caparisoned horses' harnesses and their saddles were adorned with gilded bronze plates.[12]

The city's entire population watched from the Old Wall or the Temple. The spectacle must have put many in mind of the description in the first book of the Maccabees of the Seleucid host that confronted Judas Maccabaeus. "Now when the sun shone upon the shields of gold and of brass: the mountains glittered therewith and they shone like lamps of fire."[13] The watchers might also have remembered how on another occasion the intrepid Judas had told his outnumbered followers, "Fear ye not their multitude, neither be ye afraid of their assault," and gone on to triumph over his enemies.[14]

On this occasion, however, the people of Jerusalem were not feeling quite so optimistic. "When they saw the entire Roman army assembled on one piece of ground, the quality of their equipment and their discipline, even the bravest defender was horribly dismayed," *The Jewish War* tells us. "I am convinced that the rebels might have changed their minds if they [had] not given up hope of obtaining mercy from the Romans after the awful way in which they had treated the people [of Jerusalem]. Since laying down their arms [and surrendering] would mean inevitable punishment and death, they thought it preferable to die in battle."[15] But Josephus never does justice to the Zealots' belief in their cause.

After four days, all the soldiers had received their pay and the parade came to an end, but the defenders remained uncowed. Receiving no offers of peace from them, on the fifth day, Titus formed his four legions into two army groups and began building more ramps, this time opposite the Antonia and the tomb of John the High Priest—the Antonia being an especially difficult nut to crack as it was defended by a huge ditch, which in places was fifty feet deep and would have to be filled. Basically, his plan was to break into the Upper City from the Antonia and into the Temple from John's tomb; unless he gained possession of the Temple, his occupation of the city was always going be at risk.

In repeated sorties Simon's troops and their Idumean allies had considerable success in slowing up the besiegers' work at the tomb of John the High Priest, while those at the Antonia were seriously hindered by John's Zealots. Everywhere, the Jews did serious harm to the besiegers, not merely in hand-to-hand combat, in which they had the advantage of fighting from higher ground, but also by undermining the ramps. They also had learned to use the captured artillery to lethal effect, practicing every day to improve their accuracy. They had 300 quick-loading, bolt-firing scorpions and 40 stone-projectors that made life extremely unpleasant for the Romans who were trying to build the ramps.

It was probably now that Titus was hit on the shoulder by a stone from one of the Jews' projectors. It was a serious injury that left him with a weak left arm for the rest of his life. Josephus does not mention the incident, which we only know from a third-century Roman historian, Dio Cassius.[16] However, it does not seem to have noticeably reduced Titus's energy or lessened his determination.

Still eager to capture Jerusalem intact, Titus never abandoned his hopes of persuading the Jews to surrender. He constantly shouted up at the walls that good terms remained on offer for those who would accept them. He used Josephus to try and talk the defenders into a more sensible frame of mind, under the illusion that they might be more likely to listen to a fellow countryman. Josephus had to go all around the wall before he could find a spot from where he could be heard without too much danger of being shot at. Anticipating the role of a Jewish "Lord Haw-Haw"— the sardonic Nazi propagandist—he then begged the defenders at considerable length to spare themselves and the Jewish people, above all to spare their country and the Temple, and show more concern for them than defeating foreigners.

To a large extent his speech can be reconstructed from *The Jewish War*. Even if polished up several years later, and no doubt including what he would like to have said, extracts are worth quoting, since they give a useful insight into his mind and how he saw relations between Jews and Romans. It is almost as if he had been talking to himself.

Although they do not share your beliefs, the Romans genuinely respect your holy places and have so far avoided doing any damage to them—in contrast, some of the people whom you've brought into this city seem bent on wrecking them. You can see how your strongest walls came tumbling down, and that the only remaining one is the weakest of the lot, while you know perfectly well that nothing can stand up to Roman power. You also know that the Jews are used to being governed by them. If fighting for the sake of freedom is so honorable, then you ought to have started fighting years ago, but after giving in and letting yourselves be ruled for such a long time, a war like this can only be the work of men who are in love with death, not of men who love liberty.

It is all very well despising rulers who are inferior to one, but these people happen to rule the world. The only places which don't belong to the Romans are not worth having, because they are either too hot or too cold. Everywhere, Romans have had a monopoly of good luck, and God who gives sovereignty to nations has taken up his residence in Italy. It is a well known law of nature, even among wild beasts as well as us men, that the strongest are always going to win and that being on top belongs to those who fight best. That is why your ancestors who, body and soul, were infinitely better people than you are in every other way, gave in to the Romans—something they would never have done if they had thought God was on their side.

Just why are you so confident about being able to hold out when most of your city has already been captured and when those inside what is still left of it are suffering far worse than being taken prisoner? The Romans know perfectly well that famine is raging in this city, that it is already killing citizens and that soon it is going to kill plenty of those under arms as well. Even if the Romans decide to call off the siege and not to storm the place at the edge of the sword after all, a new and very different sort of war is coming nearer every hour. But perhaps you will put away your weapons and fight the famine, and somehow contrive to show us you are the only men who are able to conquer nature?

You would be wise to change the way you have chosen to behave before total disaster becomes unavoidable and to take some helpful advice while there is still a chance of doing so. The Romans are not going to bear a grudge against you because of what has happened, so long as you stop being stupid. They like to be merciful when they win and they always prefer to do something positive instead of taking revenge—something that does not mean exterminating the city's entire population and reducing the whole country to a desert. That is why our Caesar is still ready to take you under his protection, even now. But if he has to take the city by storm, then he will slaughter every single one of you, for turning down his offer when you were very nearly beaten. You can tell how quickly the Old Wall is going to be captured from the way the other two were taken. And even if that particular job turns out to be difficult, remember that famine is fighting for the Romans.[17]

Josephus must have had lungs of leather if he said all this at the top of his voice. The Jews' reaction was disappointing. They felt he was talking down to them, sensing his anger and contempt. In his account he makes no attempt to conceal the fact that he was jeered from the ramparts, with many defenders yelling insults and others throwing stones or javelins at him. Luckily, they missed and he went on shouting.

You miserable crew! Don't you know who your real friends are? How can you explain why you're fighting the Romans with nothing more than weapons and human hands? Have we ever succeeded in defeating another nation like this? When did the God who created us ever fail to avenge genuine wrongs done to the Jews? Why can't you turn round and look behind you [at the Temple], then remember the holy place from where you go out to battle and realize how omnipotent is the Ally you have polluted? Surely you remember the numberless superhuman victories that were won by our fathers and the countless terrifying enemies they destroyed in times gone by, all through His help for our sake? I am horrified at having to remind such worthless hearers of what God did for them. All the same, you can listen to me, so that you will understand that you are not just fighting Romans but God.

Wars had always been disastrous for Jews who were meant to rely on divine and not human power, Josephus explained. "Do you really think that what you've done has been blessed by the Lawmaker?" he asked the defenders. "You have not exactly avoided secret sins, have you—thieving and adultery—while you compete with each other at murder and rape, inventing new forms of evil. The Temple, which even Romans respect despite their own customs, is open to anybody and polluted by our own countrymen." The Romans were simply demanding the normal tribute that had always been paid, in return for which they guaranteed family, property, and the Law. It was madness for the Jews to expect help from God in such a war. Instead of blessing them, so far he had blessed Vespasian, who had become emperor, and Titus, for whom fresh springs of water had flowed miraculously during his campaign

He made a final, tearful appeal. "Men with iron hearts! Why don't you drop your weapons and take pity on a country already on the brink of destruction? Turn round and look at the beauty you are betraying—what a city, what a temple!" He ended by expressing a personal wish to save Jerusalem, however much it cost him. "I am fully aware that I have a mother, a wife and a fine family, and belong to an ancient and illustrious clan, and that every one of them is in danger. Perhaps you think I'm giving you advice only to save their lives? Well, kill them, if you want. Shed the blood of my kindred, so long as you think that it's going to save you. I am ready to die myself, provided you learn some sense after my death."[18]

There can be no doubt that Josephus regarded his harangues as more than psychological warfare and that, standing below the walls and bellowing up at the Zealots, he had begun to see himself as a prophet in the full sense. He took very seriously indeed the prophecies in the Torah and in other sacred writings that foretold terrible disasters for Jerusalem—warnings that had come true—and he applied them to the circumstances of 70 CE. After all, as he saw it, he was doing his best to save the Holy Places of Israel.

From a careful reading of his writings it is clear that he was fascinated by prophets because they saw into the future. "Nothing is more valuable than the gift of prophecy," he wrote in his *Antiquities*.[19] He regarded Daniel as a particularly great prophet, "a man who could discover what was impossible for anyone else to find out," somebody who really must have spoken with God, because he had been so specific about what was going to happen.[20] He also admired the Hasmonean King of Judea, John

Hyrcanus, to whom he unhesitatingly attributes the gift of prophecy. "For the Deity conversed with him, and he was not ignorant of anything that was to come afterwards," he wrote in the early part of *The Jewish War*.[21] As has already been said, the gratifying accuracy of his own prediction about Vespasian becoming Emperor of Rome can only have added to his confidence in this field. Presumably, as at Jotapata, he was having nightly dreams during the siege of Jerusalem—this time about the ghastly fate in store for the Jewish people—while no doubt he was poring over the scriptures as well, in the best Essene style.

Reminding his listeners of how the King of Babylon had overthrown King Zedekiah and demolished the city and the Temple, Josephus went so far on one occasion as to compare himself with Jeremiah. "Neither king nor people tried to kill him. You, in contrast—I ignore what goes on behind your walls since I'm incapable of describing all the horrors you omit—howl abuse at me for begging you to save yourselves, and throw javelins." It has to be admitted that few prophets were more justified in their warnings.[22]

18

Inside Jerusalem

"They that did feed delicately are desolate in the streets; they that were brought up in scarlet embrace dunghills."

LAMENTATIONS OF JEREMIAH, IV, 5

WHEREAS THE ZEALOTS PROVED deaf to the appeals that Josephus constantly roared up at them, his words had a very different effect upon ordinary folk, more of whom tried to escape from the horrors of life in besieged Jerusalem. Many began selling houses or precious possessions for gold pieces, which they swallowed so that their rulers could not steal it, and then fled to the Roman lines where they emptied their bowels and recovered the coins, which they used to buy food. After questioning them, Titus generally let humbler refugees of this sort leave the area and go anywhere they liked, which was an added incentive to desert the city. Those who belonged to the nobility were told that he meant to give them back their estates after the war was over, when they would have a role in the new, restored Judea, but in the meantime they were sent to Gophna to be interned in a kind of open prison. Too many of their class had joined the Zealots for the Romans to feel entirely confident of their loyalty.

"I kept a very careful record of everything that went on before my eyes in the Roman camp, being the only man there who knew how to extract worthwhile information from deserters," says Josephus in his *Contra Api-onem*.[1] This was written toward the end of his life, when he had dropped his guard a little. Nowhere in the *Vita* or *The Jewish War* does he admit that interrogating refugees and prisoners was among his responsibilities. Being a Jew, he was better than any Roman at detecting those who were spies or messengers instead of genuine deserters, and at finding out from them exactly what was going on in Jerusalem. It is likely that he ran his own network of spies inside the city, but naturally he preferred not to give details in his account of the siege of these activities.[2]

His "record" was probably some sort of journal, written from notes that had been taken down in shorthand in the usual Roman way, with a bone stylus on wax-coated wooden tablets and then transferred on to papyrus rolls with reed pens. He may have been given a secretary to help him. Each legion seems to have compiled a daily record, not unlike a modern army unit's war diary. Following Julius Caesar's lapidary example, Vespasian kept campaign notes of his own—presumably dictated to a secretary—which he later lent to Josephus.

By now, however, it was even harder to get out of the beleaguered cap-ital, since John and Simon seemed almost more concerned with stopping people from leaving than with preventing the Romans from entering. Any-one suspected of trying to flee was killed on the spot. Yet staying was no less dangerous for the rich, who were always being falsely accused of plan-ning to escape and then put to death in order to lay hands on their wealth.

By now, too, the famine was beginning to bite inside the city so that starvation was becoming widespread among noncombatants, some of whom were selling everything they had for just a single measure of grain— wheat if they were rich, barley if they were poor. People would devour it uncooked in a dark corner, or pull it out of the fire and swallow it half-baked. Wives started snatching food from their husbands, children from their parents, and still more pitiable, mothers from their babies, even when it was obvious that they were dying from lack of nourishment.

The defenders had to eat if they were to fight. After the shops ran out of grain, they broke into houses which they ransacked; when any flour was found, they tortured the owner for having hidden it. If they saw a dwelling that was locked, they at once suspected those inside of having a meal and rushed inside, almost pulling morsels out of the diners' throats. Old men were beaten to make them disgorge food, and women were dragged around by the hair of their head. According to *The Jewish War,* they sometimes tortured people to make them reveal where just a single loaf of bread or a handful of barley was concealed; they would block a victim's genital passage with bitter vetch or drive a stake up his anus. Those who looked well fed could expect such treatment, but the emaciated were left alone, although the rebels robbed the pitiful creatures who had crept through the Roman sentries to gather wild plants and herbs.[3]

Wealthy men were methodically marked down and killed. Hauled in front of one of the two leaders, some were falsely accused of scheming and then executed, while others were slaughtered after being charged with conspiring to surrender the city to the Romans. Whatever Josephus may imply, the motive for their destruction was not so much leveling as a straightforward desire to get hold of their money. The easiest way of liquidating them was of course to pretend that they were plotting to escape from Jerusalem. Anyone who managed to survive an accusation in front of Simon was handed over to John, who soon finished him off; similarly, John gave unwilling victims to Simon. The pair "drank the blood of their fellow countrymen and divided their carcasses between them."[4]

> No other city has ever had to endure horrors like this, no generation has ever existed that was more stained by crime. Towards the end, these creatures even pretended to despise the Hebrew race, in order to conceal their lack of respect for other human beings. Yet in their everyday behavior they revealed themselves to be what they really were, the dregs of society, the bastard scum and abortive refuse of our nation. These were the people who destroyed our city, even though the Romans had to take all the blame after winning a melancholy victory, these men who seemed to think that the Temple was burning too slowly. When they were to watch it burning from the Upper City they were not going to shed a single tear, although even the Romans would be overwhelmed by sadness at the sight.[5]

Josephus's tirade sounds suspiciously like the outpourings of a patrician quivering with fury at the injuries done to his own class. He was incapable of feeling sympathy for the "brigands" among the defenders [*lestai*], whom he regarded as subhuman. They seem to have formed the largest part of the garrison, most of them peasant refugees from the Judean countryside, young men who were brutalized by years of want and ill treatment. They had never fed or drunk so well before their arrival in Jerusalem, never lived better. Naturally, they could see no overriding reason for making peace with the Romans, if peace meant going back to the soil or beggary, while it was understandable that they should dislike magnates.

"From one point of view, at least, the Zealots certainly earned their name, and that was the way in which they behaved," Josephus writes at his most bitter in *The Jewish War.*[6] "They did their very best to copy every evil deed that had been committed throughout history, leaving no single crime from the past unrepeated. They appropriated the name [of Zealot] for themselves to demonstrate that they were 'zealous' in practicing virtue while all the time, animals that they were, they were jeering at those whom they ill-treated and pretending that their worst cruelties were acts of kindness."

Carefully highlighting any atrocities committed by the defenders, *The Jewish War* tries to obscure the genuine patriotism of those who were neither bandits nor *'am ha-arez* and who really deserved the name of Zealot. Even Simon bar Giora and John of Gischala had their ideals. Significantly, they were supported by the lower clergy, who continued to offer the sacrifices at the Temple for as long as possible. Any proper analysis of the Zealots—who they were, what they thought—is impossible, however, because we have no source of information apart from Josephus. Although he deliberately calls them "brigands" or "rebels" instead of Zealots, he nonetheless admired their courage, and he mentions several whom he obviously accepts as his social equals.

For all their conviction that God would save them from the Romans, there was nothing messianic about the Zealots' inspiration or their beliefs. On the contrary, we can assume with some certainty that they read the two books of the Maccabees over and over again, and that Simon and John were each hoping to establish a new Judean monarchy with himself as king. It is a tragedy that the Zealots did not produce a chronicler to record their particular point of view, although we will catch a hint of it in the two speeches made by Eleazar ben Yair at Masada. Whatever Josephus may say, there must have been some fine men among them.

In the meantime, Titus's assault ramps were nearly ready, although the defenders' artillery—now that they had learned how to fire it—was inflicting heavy casualties on the legionaries who were building them. Irritated by this ferocious resistance, Titus sent a detachment of horse to lie in wait for Jews searching the ravines for food. The majority of these seem to have been poor citizens driven by acute starvation, men who did not dare to try and escape because of what might be done to their wives and children, since it was far from unknown for the families of deserters to be butchered in reprisal. They fought desperately to evade capture so that when finally overpowered there was little point in their begging for mercy. After being scourged and tortured, they were crucified in front of the Old Wall.

Five hundred or more people like this were caught and crucified every day. Titus felt a twinge of pity—or at least Josephus claims that he did—but he was not going to risk freeing a large number of men who might turn out to be soldiers in disguise, and his army could not afford to waste time standing guard over several thousand prisoners. What really counted with Titus was the possibility that the sheer number of crucifixions might terrify the Jews into surrendering, out of fear that they themselves might die the same way. Angry at the high casualties they were suffering, the legionaries amused themselves by nailing up the captives in grotesque attitudes. So many were crucified that eventually there was no more wood left to make crosses.

The daily spectacle of these atrocities had no perceptible effect on the defenders' morale. They dragged deserters' kindred onto the ramparts, with any other citizens who were under suspicion, and pretended that the men hanging from the crosses had tried to desert to the Romans. Titus's response to this was to cut off the hands of several of his captives and send them back into the city with a message for Simon and John. "Stop [your madness] and don't force me to destroy the city. However late in the day it may be, even now you can still change your minds at the last moment, and save your lives and your famous city and preserve its marvelous Temple."[7] Then he visited his ramps, telling the legionaries to hurry up, to show the Jews that he was going to launch an assault if they did not respond to his appeal.

After yelling insults at Titus and his father, the Jews on the Old Wall shouted back that they didn't mind dying, as it was better than slavery, and that while they stayed alive they would do all the harm they could to the Romans. They added that since they were going to die so soon, they did not care what happened to their city. The world itself would make a better Temple than their own. Even so, they insisted that the Temple of Jerusalem was going to be saved by the God who inhabited it, and because they had him for their ally they could laugh at any threats from Titus.

An interlude was provided by the arrival of Antiochus Epiphanes, the king of Commagene, who had brought his heavy infantry. They were fine-looking young men, armed and trained in the Macedonian way—carrying the long *sarissa*, or two-handed pike, and operating in a massive phalanx sixteen ranks deep. These were the troops with which Alexander the Great had overthrown the Persian Empire. Athletic and arrogant, the king asked Titus's permission to attack at once. He agreed, commenting with a wry grin, "Well, you've got as much chance as anybody else." Antiochus immediately led his men in an attack on the Old Wall, but his soldiers were Macedonians in name only, while the ponderous phalanx and the clumsy *sarissa* were things of the past. Alexander's troops had never had to face scorpions or stone-projectors, and their would-be heirs soon had to withdraw after being shot to pieces by the Jews. Josephus observes sardonically that if Macedonians were expecting to win victories in the way that Alexander did, then they needed some of his good luck.[8]

The legionaries made heroic efforts to make their ramps tall enough, laboring day and night. They had begun work on 12 May but only finished on 29 May, after seventeen days of exhausting toil that involved filling in the great ditch in front of the Antonia, which in places was fifty feet deep. All four ramps were huge. One of those at the Antonia had been constructed by the Fifth Legion in the middle of the reservoir known as the Quince Pool, while another, thrown up by the Twelfth Legion, was ten yards away from it. The Tenth Legion's ramp, farther off, was near the reservoir called the Almond Pool, and the Fifteenth Legion had erected another, forty-five feet away, that stood next to the tomb of John the High Priest. Titus gave orders for the troops to bring up the battering rams and the siege towers, in preparation for an all-out assault on the Old Wall.

In the meantime, however, the Jews had been taught how to mine by a contingent of Jewish soldiers from Adiabene who were skillful sappers.

John's men tunneled beneath the ground between the Old Wall and the siege lines, undermining the ramps to such an extent that—unknown to the Romans—they were resting only on pit props. The Jews filled the space with fagots covered in pitch and bitumen—obtainable in large quantities from the Red Sea. Then they set light to the props. Suddenly, the ramps in the Antonia area collapsed with a deafening roar into the chasms that opened up below, taking the siege towers with them. Dense clouds of smoke billowed from the debris as the fire below was smothered for a moment, until flames burst up from the bitumen and burned steadily.

The Romans were aghast at this unexpected blow and their enemies' ingenuity. Having thought that victory was within their grasp, they became badly discouraged. There was no point in trying to put out the flames after the destruction of the ramps.

Two days later, a band of Simon's followers made a sortie during the night to destroy the remaining ramps, from where the Roman battering rams had started to pound the Old Wall, which was beginning to shake alarmingly. The leaders were a Galilean called Tephthaeus and a former bodyguard of Queen Mariamne named Megassarus, along with a half-crippled Adiabenian nicknamed Ceagiras ("The Lame"). Running through the astonished Romans as if they were friends instead of foes, they snatched up flaming torches and hurled them at the siege machines. *The Jewish War* informs us that these three Jews were among the toughest and most feared rebels in Jerusalem, renowned as hard men who were frightened of nothing. (The fact that Josephus knew such a lot about them shows the extent of his intelligence network.) Somehow surviving the javelins and sword thrusts aimed at them from all sides, they stayed there until they had succeeded in setting the rams and the towers on fire while their comrades beat off the enemy.[9]

Rushing out from their camps when they saw the flames roaring skyward in the dark, the legionaries tried desperately to save the rams, attempting to drag them out of the fire since the hurdles covering them were already ablaze. They were prevented by a host of Jews, who poured out from the postern gates in the Old Wall and started a pitched battle, pulling the rams back by their iron covering, although by now it was red-hot. The rams caught fire, and surrounded by a circle of flames, the demoralized legionaries gave up in despair, retreating to the safety of their camps.

The Jews, more of whom now ran out from the city to join in the fighting, became so encouraged that they chased the Romans back to their camps, setting fire to the stockades and attacking the astonished sentries. The author of *The Jewish War* is of course too tactful to admit to his readers that such a humiliating possibility had ever existed, but for a few moments, it really must have seemed that the outcome of the siege of Jerusalem lay in the balance.

Fortunately for the Romans, their strict military procedure came to their rescue. To deal with unexpected crises an armed guard was always stationed in front of every legionary camp, who was relieved at regular intervals. Any member of the guard who left his post was executed immediately, however good his excuse might be. Preferring to die with honor in battle rather than branded as cowards and hanged, these men stood firm. Soon, many of the troops who had run away rallied, mounting scorpions on the remnants of the Second Wall and firing at close range into the attackers. Even so, the Jews still came on, oblivious of the hail of bolts, and were soon on the point of driving the Romans back. "They gave ground more because of Jewish gallantry rather than from the casualties they were suffering," comments Josephus, not without a hint of pride.[10]

At last, Titus galloped over from the Antonia, where he had been choosing sites for the new ramps. He gave his soldiers a short but furious dressing-down. "After taking two of the enemy's walls, you've managed to put your own defenses at risk and are now being besieged yourselves, all because you've let those Jews out of their cage!"[11] Then he led his mounted bodyguard in a fierce charge against the attackers' flank. Despite having to fight on two fronts, the Jews battled on, both sides cutting and thrusting at close quarters, so closely engaged that, blinded by the dust and deafened by the shouting, it was impossible amid the confusion to make out who was friend or foe. Even so, the Jews kept on fighting—not to win but to stay alive. Having regained their nerve, the humiliated legionaries fought to regain their self-respect. Finally, realizing that the battle was lost, the Jews retreated into the city.

The Romans had won, but they saw very little reason for triumph. They prided themselves on being the best soldiers in the world, and yet they had nearly been routed by what they regarded as a bandit rabble. Not surprisingly, they were thoroughly dejected. The success of the enemy's sorties must have intensified their suspicion of Josephus—had he told his former comrades where and when to attack?

The destruction of the ramps meant that the legionaries had lost the product of weeks of back-breaking work. It was already midsummer, the hottest season of the Palestinian year, when the sun beat down mercilessly, a time (as Benjamin Disraeli described it long afterward) when Jerusalem becomes "a city of stone in a land of iron, with a sky of brass."[12] Water was in short supply, since it had to be fetched on muleback from many miles away, as did the other supplies. The besiegers' morale began to show signs of collapse; some of them deserted and went over to the Jews. By now, an increasing number of Romans were beginning to lose hope in their ability to capture Jerusalem.

19

The Wooden Wall

"A wonderful and horrible thing is committed in the land."

JEREMIAH, V, 30

T HE SITUATION WAS so discouraging for the Romans that Titus summoned a council of war. Some of his officers were in favor of an all-out assault on the Old Wall by every soldier who was available, backed by a massive bombardment, arguing that so far the Jews had only been engaged by a small part of the imperial army. Others proposed rebuilding the ramps. A third group at the council suggested blockading the city and letting starvation do its work; too many casualties were bound to result from fighting men who so obviously preferred death in battle to crucifixion.

For the first time Titus showed that he was beginning to understand the value of caution. While he rejected the idea of a general assault as suicidal, and while for the moment he could see no point in rebuilding the ramps, he did not want to remain inactive. There was always a danger of the Jews launching further sorties, and they might bring in enough food for their soldiers through secret tunnels. In his view, the best solution was to build a wooden wall around the city, a *circumvallatio*, a method that had been used by Julius Caesar in Gaul a hundred years earlier, although never against such a big city. The idea, which may have come from Titus's chief of staff, Tiberius Alexander, was applauded by his officers.

According to *The Jewish War*, the entire Roman army, who by now hated Jews with an obsessive hatred, was no less delighted by the plan. All the troops showed extraordinary keenness, legion competing with legion, cohort with cohort. Titus personally inspected progress several times a day. When completed, the wall ran from his headquarters at the Camp of the Assyrians to the New City below and then through the Kedron to the Mount of Olives. Then it bent to the south, around the rock called the Dovecote and the nearby hill that overlooks the valley next to Siloam. To the west it went down into the valley of the fountain, after which it went up past the tomb of Ananus the High Priest, taking in the hill where Pompey had camped. Going north it reached the village known as the House of Peas and then went around Herod's mausoleum until it reached Titus's camp, the point from where it started. Nearly five miles long, the wall was strengthened by thirteen forts, each of which was 200 feet in circumference. Thanks to the legionaries' unflagging enthusiasm, the whole structure was finished in three days, astounding even the Romans.

Now that he had enclosed Jerusalem inside a wall and garrisoned the forts, Titus showed his appreciation of the army's remarkable achievement by taking the first night's watch himself, personally making the rounds of inspection. Tiberius Alexander took the second, and the third watch was shared out among the legates commanding the legions.

Josephus's frightful description of what went on inside the city at this period deserves quoting. It carries conviction and must be based on reports given to him by spies or by inhabitants who lived through it:

> All chance of leaving Jerusalem came to an abrupt end and the Jews inside suddenly found themselves deprived of any hope of survival. Famine was raging more terribly than ever, devouring entire houses and families. The upper rooms were full of dying women with their infants, and the lanes were filled by old men who had already died. Bloated with hunger, youths and children wandered like shadows around the market places, remaining on the ground wherever they dropped dead. Famished men were too weak to bury their kindred, while anyone who was still strong enough did not bother because there were so many corpses and because they themselves expected to die soon. The few people who made some

sort of effort to inter the dead expired while doing so, while others got
into their shrouds to await death.

Amidst all this misery there was little weeping or wailing. Starvation
had killed all sense of affection, so that the slowly dying gazed with dry
eyes and open mouths at anyone who had passed away before them. A
deep silence resembling darkness reigned throughout the city, as though
to proclaim the presence of death. Still more dreadful were the robbers,
who broke into houses that had become tombs, plundering the dead
bodies, laughing as they stole the clothes off them. They tried out their
swords on corpses, and to test their blades' sharpness ran through dying
men who were still breathing—but refused to kill anyone who begged
them to finish him off. All these citizens [who died from the famine]
drew their last breath with eyes firmly fixed on the Temple, trying to
ignore the rebels. Finding the stench that arose from so many dead bodies all over the city almost unbearable, at first the rebel leaders gave orders for them to be buried at the public expense, but when the sheer
number made it impossible they had them thrown over the walls into
the ravines below.[1]

The Jewish War contains a flattering vignette of the Roman general's
compassion, no doubt intended for imperial eyes. "Going the rounds [on
his new wall], when Titus saw the ravines filled with corpses and the great
stream of rotting matter that flowed from them, he groaned and called on
God to bear witness that it was not his doing."[2] However, one may feel
that Josephus goes a little too far in claiming that Titus's wish to rescue the
survivors was the reason why he issued orders to start building new ramps
at four sites opposite the Antonia. This was difficult, since all the trees
round the city had been cut down for the wall, and the legionaries had to
fetch timber from ten miles away.

Within Jerusalem, the rebels appeared to remain completely unshaken
by the wall that cut them off so finally and completely from the world outside. Nor were they moved by the sufferings of the civilian population.
They felt no pity for those who were starving and "continued like dogs to
maul the very carcass of the people, packing the prisons with the feeble,"
says Josephus.[3] Yet to some extent his obvious anger may be due to his feelings of outrage at further attacks on rich magnates.

Not even Matthias ben Boethus escaped, although it was he who had persuaded the citizens to ask Simon bar Giora to take over the city. Wealthy and a well-known member of a high priestly family, he was an obvious target. He was summoned before Simon, accused of being a supporter of the Romans, and condemned to death with three of his sons. A fourth had fled. Reminding Simon that it was he who had invited him into Jerusalem, Matthias begged to be executed before his sons, but his request was refused. He was killed on top of his sons' corpses, on the Old Wall where they had been led out to die in view of the Romans and butchered in front of their father's eyes. Nor would Simon allow any of them burial. Among others executed were Ananias ben Masambalus, who was a distinguished priest, and Aristeus, a former secretary of the Sanhedrin, with over a dozen equally eminent men.

But has Josephus given us the whole story? All these unlucky nobles who perished, including Matthias and his sons, may conceivably have been supplying Titus with information or guilty of defeatist talk. They may even have been conspiring to let the Romans into the city.

In contrast, Josephus's father, Mattathias, and his mother were merely sent to prison by Simon, although it was proclaimed that on pain of death no one should speak to Mattathias or express regret at his arrest. It seems extraordinary that the couple escaped being executed out of hand, as parents of an arch-traitor. Again, we can only speculate on the possibility that Josephus might have retained some sort of influence within the city. It certainly looks as though he had some important contacts inside the walls. Did he negotiate a secret deal with Simon?

Not all Simon's followers obeyed him blindly. Judas ben Judas, a junior officer in command of a tower on the Old Wall, was outraged by the executions. "How much longer must we put up with such crimes?" he asked ten trusted subordinates. "What chance of survival can we possibly have if we stay loyal to this evil man? Aren't we suffering from famine and aren't the Romans practically inside the city? Simon likes to betray even the people who have done him a good turn and he might easily decide to get rid of us too, while at least we can trust the Romans. We ought to hand over our part of the wall to them, and make sure of saving ourselves and the city. Simon won't suffer all that much more if he gets what's coming to him just a little bit sooner—in any case, he's already given up hope."

Early next morning, Judas and his ten companions tricked the rest of the tower's garrison into leaving and then shouted to the Romans that they wanted to surrender, but it was a long time before they were taken seriously. The legionaries did not trust them, fearing a trap, and only jeered in response to the offer, until Titus came up to the wall with his bodyguard. However, by now Simon had been warned. He got there first. Quickly, he stormed the tower, killing Judas and his friends and throwing their mutilated bodies down from the wall. Josephus observes with his usual cynicism that while to some extent Judas may possibly have been driven to rebel by pity, his real motive must have had more to do with providing for his own safety.[4]

Meanwhile, Josephus was still indefatigable in shouting up at the wall, daily telling the defenders how crazy they were not to surrender. On one occasion he was knocked senseless by a well-aimed stone thrown from the ramparts. The Jews rushed out to drag him into the city, but luckily Titus saw the incident and sent troops to rescue him. Barely conscious of what was happening, Josephus was pulled to safety. The rebels thought they had killed him and yelled with delight.

Inside the city many of the Romans' secret supporters were depressed by the supposed death of the man who was always encouraging them to desert. In prison, his mother coldly told the guards, "That is what I've been expecting this since Jotapata—I never saw much of him when he was alive." In private, she was grief-stricken, telling her maids—it seems to have been an unusually comfortable prison—that "This is all one gets from bringing children into the world, not even being able to bury a son whom I had expected would one day bury me." But Josephus made a speedy recovery and reappeared before the ramparts, shouting that before long he would be taking his revenge on whoever had thrown the stone at him. He also shouted that deserters would still find protection.[5]

This was not quite true. Most of the deserters who jumped down from the walls or ran toward the Roman lines, pretending they meant to throw stones at the enemy, were bloated by starvation and looked as if they suffered from dropsy. However, when they arrived, they were given as much food as they wanted, so that many stuffed themselves until they literally burst their bellies.

There was an even more lethal form of welcome. A group of Syrian auxiliaries spotted a deserter sifting through his excrement to pick out gold coins he had swallowed before escaping. (Because of the collapse of trade, the value of gold circulating in Jerusalem, mainly Attic drachma, had fallen by half.) Instantly, a rumor spread among the besiegers that Jewish deserters were stuffed with gold, and Arab and Syrian troops immediately started cutting them open in order to search their intestines. "In my opinion, nothing more dreadful has ever happened to Jews," says Josephus. "Two thousand were ripped up during one night alone." Many of the victims had deserted after listening to Josephus's reassurances about good treatment.[6]

When he heard about these atrocities, Titus was so angry that for a moment he thought of encircling the perpetrators with his cavalry and riding them down, but too many in the army were implicated. What made him angrier still was that Roman legionaries as well as auxiliaries had been carving up the refugees. Summoning the commanders of all units, he told them they ought to be ashamed of their men, giving strict orders that any legionary involved must be brought to him for punishment, and the auxiliaries were warned that in the future the crime would incur the death penalty. Even so, local troops continued to disembowel deserters discreetly, despite finding gold in only a few cases. The refugees grew so terrified that many fled back to Jerusalem.

Inside, the citizens had been so savagely plundered that most of them had nothing left worth stealing, so John of Gischala turned his attention to the Temple treasury, melting down all gifts of precious metal, together with ceremonial vessels such as bowls, dishes, and tables—many made from gold or silver. Josephus was particularly horrified at his appropriating some wine flagons that had been presented by the late Emperor Augustus and the Empress Livia.

"This so-called Jew . . . told his fellow thugs that they could make use of God's property without being afraid in the slightest since it was all for God's benefit, and that as men who were fighting for the Temple they had every right to consume it," *The Jewish War* informs us.[7] John then seized the sacred wine and oil, which were stored in a chamber at the southwest corner of the Women's Court. Although these were reserved for the ritual burnt offerings, he shared them among his followers, some of whom often drank over a hin of wine, which was more than five liters.[8]

"In this instance, I cannot restrain myself from expressing my inmost thoughts," says Josephus bitterly. "In my considered opinion, had the

Romans put off punishing such animals as these were, then the earth would have opened and swallowed up the city, or else it would have been swept away by a flood or struck by lightning like Sodom, because it had spawned a far more godless people. The madness of these men was dragging the whole of the nation down with them in their ruin."[9]

Mannaeus ben Lazarus was a deserter who managed to escape to Titus without having his belly ripped open. He told the Romans that between 14 April, the date when they first set up camp, and 1 July, he had counted 115,800 corpses, all paupers, carried out through a gate he superintended. Although not in charge of their interment, he was responsible for paying the cost from the public fund and had to keep a reckoning. Many more had been taken out by relations. In all cases, interment merely consisted of removing them from the city. Other upper-class deserters who got out after Mannaeus said that the bodies of 600,000 poor men and women had been thrown out, but clearly it was impossible for anyone to arrive at an accurate estimate of the true figure. When it became too difficult to remove the paupers' corpses, they were piled inside some of the larger houses, whose doors were kept locked.

Josephus claims that when the Romans learned how dreadful life was in Jerusalem, despite the hatred that they had by now developed for Jews, even the tough legionaries could not help feeling a certain pity. He says that in contrast, the rebels remained totally unshaken by their fellow countrymen's sufferings, although after their private supplies of food had been eaten, they knew that they too would have to starve. They were blind to the horror that was about to come upon the city and upon themselves.

Bad as it already was, the misery within the great city deepened every day. For a long time, tiny amounts of wheat had fetched astronomical sums, and after the building of the wooden wall it became impossible to creep out at night and gather herbs. People were reduced to such misery that to find something to eat they scoured the sewers or sifted through cow dung, eating whatever they could find. What had once revolted them now became their normal diet.

When the rebels themselves ran short of food, they became still more savage. The piles of rotting dead bodies all over the city, daily growing higher and giving off a sickening stench, lay in their way whenever they went out to do battle. Yet although they had to walk over corpses as if on a battlefield, they showed no emotion. Nor did they seem to realize just how ill-omened it was to insult the dead so grossly when charging out to fight foreigners with their hands stained by the blood of fellow country-men. It was "as if they themselves were rebuking God for having taken so long to punish them," comments Josephus.[10] In his view, they went on fighting not because they still hoped to win regardless of the odds, but be-cause they were frightened of what was going to happen to them after their inevitable defeat. He refuses to admit that the Zealots fought on because they were convinced that the God of Israel was on their side.

Meanwhile, the Romans finished the new siege ramps in only three weeks, after turning the country outside the walls into a blasted heath of craters and tree stumps. What had been a landscape of woodland alternating with pleasure gardens was turned into a desert by tree felling. Even a for-eigner who had seen Jerusalem's enchanting suburbs would have been re-duced to tears at the spectacle, says *The Jewish War*.[11] Above all, the doomed city was shut off from the outside world by that terrible wooden wall.

For Romans as well as Jews, the completion of the new siege works was a moment of terror. The defenders knew very well that if they failed to destroy them, Jerusalem was going to fall, while the besiegers realized that should the ramps go up in flames like the previous ramps, they would lose all chance of capturing the place. Their timber was exhausted; it would be impossible to obtain further supplies before winter. Not only were the Roman troops worn out, but they were demoralized by the Jews' ferocious resistance. Rumors of awful suffering inside the city were largely discounted, since the defenders seemed in no way cast down. The legionaries remembered only too well how the Jews had demolished their previous ramps, had stood up to their siege engines, and had launched such lethally effective sorties.

Above all, the Romans were daunted by the extraordinary courage of the Zealots, who were seemingly unaffected by desertion, famine, or the most formidable onslaughts. They were equally shaken by their resource-fulness and resilience in the face of disaster; after any reverse they fought more fiercely than ever. Yet in the long run this despondency was going to work in the legionaries' favor, since it made them keep a sharper lookout for sorties and drove them to strengthen as much as possible the fortifications around the ramps.

Josephus hints eloquently at the feverish atmosphere in the Roman camps during these anxious days when the future of the siege hung in the balance. Although he does not mention it, this must have been a time when he felt more than ever threatened by the legionaries, who were still convinced that this ubiquitous, smooth-talking renegade Jew could only be a Zealot spy.

John of Gischala and his followers, who were based in the Antonia and manned its fortifications, made preparations for a new line of defense in case the Old Wall should fall. In the meantime, however, they intended to do their utmost to stop it from happening. During the night of 1 July— "on the new moon of the month Panemus"—a band of Zealots charged out by torchlight and attacked the Roman siege works, which they hoped to destroy before those terrible rams could start battering the wall.

The sortie was badly coordinated, however, and the Zealots rushed forward at intervals in disorganized groups without proper orders. They showed "a good deal of hesitation and fear, not a bit like Jews," comments Josephus, who adds that this time they seemed to lack their nation's natural fighting qualities of daring and impetuosity, of charging as though they were one man and, if beaten back, of retreating only step by step.[12]

Already on the alert and ready for the attack, the Romans were undeterred by the Zealots' frenzied gallantry. Commanded on the spot by some exceptionally good junior officers, they fought with cool determination to protect the siege engines. Their armor and swords gave them a big advantage at close quarters, while their artillery—instead of firing into the Jews en masse as it had on previous occasions—concentrated on the front ranks so that the bodies of dead and wounded slowed up those behind. The attack lost momentum, as some Zealots recoiled when they came up against the disciplined ranks of armored legionaries in row upon row, while others bolted on receiving a mere scratch from a javelin. Demoralization turned into panic, as the men hurled accusations of cowardice at each other. The sortie disintegrated and the attackers ran back behind the Old Wall.

As soon as it was clear that the Zealots had been beaten back— presumably about dawn—the Romans brought up their storming towers, which became a target for stones, javelins, firebrands, and anything else the Jews could find to throw at them. Although the defenders still had complete confidence in their ramparts, which were built of huge, finely cut, carefully mortised blocks of marble, they were nonetheless afraid of the great rams inside the towers. This encouraged the legionaries, who began to suspect that the defenders knew that their ramparts were not so indestructible after all. Throughout the day the Antonia resisted the fiercest battering, as many besiegers were killed by the unceasing hail of missiles, especially by the rocks thrown down on them.

One group of legionaries formed a tortoise, their shields interlocked above them, while they tried to dislodge the masonry with picks and crowbars and even their bare hands. After superhuman efforts, they managed to prize out just four stone blocks, but the wall stayed firmly intact. At nightfall, the discouraged Romans called off the attack until the next day.

However, in countermining one of the besiegers' ramps with a tunnel, John's men had unknowingly weakened a stretch of the wall's foundations, which were further sapped by heavy rain. During the night, a segment collapsed without warning. With his usual interest in the combatants' psychology, Josephus was struck by the unexpected reaction on both sides. The Zealots were undaunted because the Antonia was still standing, whereas the legionaries' delight at such a piece of luck vanished when they saw that a new wall had been built behind the old one, blocking the breach. Even if it was a ramshackle structure, made easier to climb by the debris of the old wall, the first men in would almost certainly lose their lives.

Both sides knew that this was the critical moment of the siege. If the Antonia fell, then Jerusalem would fall. If the Romans should fail, however, then they would have to pack up and go home. Before launching any important assault, Titus must have consulted Josephus about the Zealots' morale. Like all intelligence officers it was the former Jewish general's job to find out what the enemy was thinking, and his report would have been thoroughly discouraging: they were as ready as ever to fight to the death.

Predictably, *The Jewish War* contains an oration by Titus that reads just like a set piece from Livy. No doubt, Josephus would have supplied one even if the Roman had remained silent. Nevertheless, the speech is plausible enough when stripped down into plain language—the sort of thing a commander might well have said to his men before going into action against a very strong position.

Soldiers, using fine words to ask men to do a job that does not involve
danger is talking down to them and makes the speaker look an idiot. In
my book, encouragement is needed only when the job is really dangerous, because otherwise men just get on with it. So I am admitting to you
frankly that climbing that wall will certainly be a very nasty business indeed. On the other hand, I should like to remind you that anyone who
wants to make a name for himself always has to beat a challenge, that it
is a glorious thing to die a hero and that people who show guts by going
in first earn big rewards.

First of all, what ought to make you keener, even if it puts a few of you
off, is the Jews' sheer toughness, the grit they show when things go
wrong. Wouldn't you be ashamed of yourselves, as Romans and as my
soldiers, men who spend peace time in training and war time in winning,
to find yourselves inferior to Jews in courage and staying power at a moment when you're on the brink of victory and getting help from above?
We're held back only by the Jews fighting desperately—they find everything much harder than we do, because of our combat skills and the gods
being on our side. Feuding, famine, siege, walls falling down without
being battered, things like that only happen if the gods are angry with
them and are helping us.

Allowing ourselves to be beaten by inferiors, and letting down all those
gods who are our allies, is out of the question. It would be an unforgiv-
able disgrace. Defeat means nothing to Jews, since they know what it is
to be slaves and make sorties not because they hope to win but to show
their courage. But you are men who have conquered every land and every
sea, men who feel humiliated if they don't win. Yet now it looks as if you
would prefer not to risk your lives in hand-to-hand combat, but simply
sit here with your first rate weaponry, waiting for famine and fate to do
your work, when at comparatively small risk it is within our power to
finish the job. Because if we get into the Antonia, we capture the city.
Even if there is any further resistance from the people inside, which personally I don't expect, we shall be looking down on them, controlling the
air they breathe, which will guarantee us a quick and complete victory.

I'm not going to talk about how wonderful war is, how people who die
drunk with battle fever live on forever. But I hope that anyone who feels
differently and wants to die in bed from illness does it in a living grave.

Every brave man knows that souls set free from the flesh by the sword on the battlefield are welcomed on the other side by souls of the same sort and by ether, purest of elements, and placed among the stars where they shine down on their children as good spirits and benign heroes. In contrast, souls that fade away in bodies wasted by disease, however blameless and undefiled they may be, disappear into an underground night and oblivion, while their lives, their bodies and all memory of them pass away together. But if death is man's inevitable fate, and as the sword brings it more gently than sickness, then it is obscene to refuse to accept it for the common good since all of us are going to die in the end.

So far I've been talking as though anybody who makes the attempt is bound to be killed. Yet survival is far from impossible for a brave man, even when he's at such close quarters with danger. It won't be too hard getting up on to the wall where it has collapsed while the new one has been thrown together so quickly that it should not be too difficult to pull down. The more of you who can find the courage needed, the easier it is going to be for you to cheer each other on, so that your impetus will soon knock the stuffing out of the enemy. You may even win a bloodless victory, if only you'll make the effort. No doubt, they will try to stop you climbing up, but if you can do it without being seen, then it is quite possible that they won't be able to put up much of a fight so long as a handful of you take them by surprise. As for the man who leads the attack, I should blush for shame if my rewards didn't make him envied while any man who survives will receive instant promotion. Those who die in the attempt are going to be buried with every conceivable honor.[13]

Josephus comments that this rousing offer of immortality failed to reassure the army, who were appalled by what lay ahead. Even their commander had said openly that the Zealots were superb fighting men, more or less admitting that in some respects they were better than legionaries. His troops knew it already, from painful experience.

The first to respond was a wizened, black-skinned little legionary called Sabinus, a Syrian, so emaciated that he looked unfit to be a soldier, yet "there was a certain heroic soul in this small body," Josephus tells us.[14] "I will cheerfully do what you want, Caesar," he announced. "I shall be the first to scale the wall and I hope your accustomed good luck will help my physical strength and determination, but if fortune goes against me, then please remember that it was scarcely unexpected and that I chose death for your sake."[15] Having said this, he held his shield over his head with his left hand and drawing his sword with his right marched up to the new wall, followed by only eleven others. It was about midday. The Jews immediately began to hurl rocks and javelins at him, but Sabinus pushed on until he reached the top.

Under the delusion that he was being followed by a large detachment of legionaries, the enemy lost their nerve and ran. However, when he fell over a rock onto his face with a loud crash, they turned round and attacked him. He got up on one knee, protecting himself with his shield, and fought back, wounding several of them, but was eventually overwhelmed by javelins—"covered in darts." Three of his comrades were killed by the stones, and the remaining eight were badly wounded and pulled down to safety. Josephus comments that he was "a man whose gallantry deserved a better fate but whose death was only to be expected from such audacity."[16]

It was two days before the Romans tried again. Twenty of the legionaries who were guarding the siege engines invited the standard-bearer of the Fifth Legion to accompany them in a further attempt on the new wall. On 5 July at about two o'clock in the morning, joined by two cavalrymen and a trumpeter, they climbed over the ruined wall and then up the new one into the Antonia. Finding the sentries asleep, they knifed them and took control of the new wall, after which they ordered the trumpeter to sound the alarm. Other guards nearby bolted, convinced it was a full-scale attack. Hearing the trumpet call, Titus reacted quickly, charging into the Antonia with his senior officers and bodyguard and bringing up the rest of his troops as fast as possible, some entering the fortress through John's ill-fated tunnel. The defenders of the Antonia fled to the Temple.

As so often, the Zealots, despite all their bravery, were fatally handicapped by lack of discipline. They possessed no proper command structure that might have enabled them to respond faster and drive the legionaries from the Antonia. Now it was too late. Nonetheless, when the Romans tried to push on into the Temple, they rushed to meet them and fought it out hand to hand. At such close quarters, both sides could use only their swords. Even Josephus has to admit that the Zealots behaved magnificently, forcing the legionaries back to the Antonia. The crush was so great at the Temple entrance that there was no possibility of retreat. The men in front on both sides fought to kill or be killed, forced on by those behind them, trampling on dead bodies, deafened by the clash of weapons and the yelling. The struggle went on for twelve hours, from two in the morning until one o'clock in the afternoon. The legionaries were unable to exploit their superior weaponry in such a confined space, and in the end the Zealots' fury got the better of their opponents' discipline. The entire Roman line gave way, and the legionaries retreated. But they kept possession of the Antonia.

For a moment, however, the Zealots were almost driven back once again during a Homeric episode. When the Roman line collapsed, a Greek centurion from Bithynia called Julianus, who had been standing at Titus's side inside the Antonia, tried to retrieve the situation by charging forward alone. Rushing into the enemy, he cut down Jew after Jew, until their comrades began to run from this terrifying swordsman, much to Titus's delight. Then his hob-nailed army boots slipped on the marble pavement, and he fell on his back with a loud crash. Recovering their nerve, the Zealots rallied. Crowding around Julianus as he lay on his back, they aimed blows at him from all sides with their spears and swords. Trying unsuccessfully to get back on his feet, he warded off many of their thrusts with his shield and, protected by his helmet and breastplate, even managed to wound several of them with his sword. However, hacking at his arms and legs, the enemy soon finished him off. Titus was deeply upset at losing such a gallant officer, who seems to have been attached to his staff.

"A man of good birth and one of the genuinely outstanding soldiers whom I got to know during the campaign, distinguished by his knowledge of warfare, his physical strength and his unfailing courage," is Josephus's encomium. Clearly, he was not only a friend of Julianus but must have watched his heroic death, just as he had seen Sabinus die, either while he was standing beside Titus or from a vantage point on one of the towers of the wooden wall.[17]

20

The Destruction of
the Temple

*"And they shall pollute the sanctuary of strength, and shall take
away the daily sacrifice, and they shall place the abomination that
maketh desolate."*

DANIEL, XI, 31

THE ZEALOTS REMAINED undismayed when on 17 July, ten days after
the loss of the Antonia, the daily sacrifice at the Temple was discontinued. Despite the famine, and at the cost of heroic self-denial, sufficient
sheep and oxen remained for the offerings, but there were not enough
priests loyal to John who could perform them properly. The sacrifice had
been taking place here each morning and evening for hundreds of years,
ever since the Jews had returned from their Babylonian captivity. Many
who were not committed Zealots must have seen its cessation as proof that
God had abandoned Israel.

Titus tried to exploit the mood of depression, with a message he gave
Josephus to shout at John of Gischala. If John was so bloodthirsty that he
wanted to go on fighting for its own sake, then why didn't he march out
with his men and settle his quarrel with the Romans in the open, without
putting the city and the Sanctuary in danger? Whatever happened, he

must stop polluting the Holy Places and insulting God. Surely he had sufficient priests to resume the sacrifice? But the Zealot hold was too strong for the appeal to have any effect.[1]

After delivering Titus's message, Josephus made another of his speeches. He says he spoke in Hebrew and not Aramaic, which presumably he considered more impressive. The speech was designed to highlight the difference between John and the remaining moderates. He begged the people of Jerusalem to save their city and stop the flames from reaching the Temple, to resume the sacrifice. "At his words a great sadness and silence spread among the people." Just as he intended, John of Gischala—whom here Josephus calls "the tyrant"—lost his temper, cursing him and shouting that the city could never be captured because it belonged to God.

"How wonderfully pure you have kept this city on God's behalf, with the Temple quite unpolluted," Josephus yelled back at the Zealot leader.

No one can say you've been guilty of any impiety towards Him from whom you hope for help, can they? Of course, he still gets his usual Sacrifice! But if someone stopped your daily meals, you filthy brute, wouldn't you start seeing him as an enemy? Are you really expecting God to be your ally in this war when you take away his everlasting worship? And why blame your own crimes on the Romans, who respect our laws and want to restore the Sacrifice to God that you have stopped? Who would not feel sorry for a city plunged into such an upheaval, when foreigners and foes have to try and undo your blasphemies, when you, despite being a Jew bred up in our laws, are its worst enemy?

All the same, John, there is nothing wrong with repenting and putting things right at the last moment. If you really want to save the city, then you have been set an excellent precedent by King Jechoniah of the Jews who, when the King of Babylon arrived outside with an army, surrendered with his whole family rather than see it destroyed and see the House of God go up in flames—as a result, he is still remembered by the Jews, famous in history, while his story is more admired each time it is told and will be handed on forever. He is the right model for you, John, if somewhat difficult to follow, although I guarantee it will earn you a pardon from the Romans. Remember, I'm asking you to do this as one of your own nation, that I'm making these promises as a Jew myself, and that it might be wise for you to reflect on just who is advising you and to what nation he belongs. Because for as long as I live, I should never be such a poor creature as to disown my own people or forget the laws of my forefathers.

Then Josephus reverted to his role as prophet:

Are you growing wrathful at me again, John, is that why you curse me so horribly? Well, I dare say I deserve much worse for flying in the face of fate by giving you good advice and trying to save men who have been damned by God. Everybody here knows what is in the writings of the old prophets and that their forecast about this miserable city is about to come true. Because they foretold it would be captured when somebody began slaughtering his fellow countrymen. And are not the city and the entire Temple heaped with the bodies of your fellow countrymen? So, it is God then, God himself, who is using the Romans to bring his purifying fire down on the place, and about to sweep away a city that has been almost drowned by your pollution.[2]

Despite his jibes at John, Josephus says he groaned and wept throughout his entire speech and that the Romans were full of pity, even if they had to guess what he was saying. In contrast, John and his friends were beside themselves with rage.

His words had a profound effect on many of the remaining magnates and their families—far more of whom still survived than one might expect from the massacres he describes so luridly. Most were too frightened of the guards to try and escape, although they were convinced that they and the city were doomed. However, some risked it. Among those who managed to flee to the Romans were the high priests Joseph and Jesus with several men whose fathers had been high priests. Three of these were the sons of Ishmael who was beheaded in Cyrene, four were the sons of Matthias, and one was the son of the Matthias murdered by Simon bar Giora—somehow he had evaded his brethren's fate. They were accompanied by other members of the Jewish nobility.

Titus gave them an especially kind welcome, we are told in *The Jewish War*. Aware that they would feel polluted if they had to live with Romans in the Roman way, he sent them en masse to Gophna where they could live according to Jewish custom, telling them to stay there until the war was over and promising to restore their property. With the indispensable Josephus beside him, he was able to identify them as members of the old upper class who had once collaborated with Rome and whose cooperation might be of considerable value in reconstructing Judea when the war was over—and also in ensuring its prosperity as a source of taxes.

When these well-known figures disappeared from Jerusalem, the defenders, concerned that others might run away as well, spread a rumor that they had been butchered by the Romans. In response, Titus brought back the fugitives from Gophna and made them walk all around the city walls, led by Josephus who must have told them how to behave. Standing in mournful little groups below the ramparts, weeping, they begged the Zealots to let the Romans into the city and save their birthplace or, at the very least, evacuate the Temple and save the Sanctuary. At the same time they assured everybody that the besiegers were most reluctant to set fire to it. The demonstration infuriated the defenders on the walls, who yelled curses and insults at the deserters and trained scorpions and stone-projectors on them.

The Zealots had mounted their artillery on top of the gates of the Temple, which by now had the appearance of an overcrowded morgue because of all the corpses that littered it, while the Sanctuary was full of heavily armed men and looked like a gilded bunker. Traditionalist Jews were appalled at such an intrusion by ritually unclean soldiers, many of them bloodstained and with more than a few murders on their conscience. It was a profanation that shocked even the Romans.

According to Josephus, Titus himself was horrified. "You miserable men, didn't your own people build that portico in front of your Sanctuary?" he shouted up at John and his followers, using Josephus as his interpreter.

Wasn't it your people who set up all those tablets in Greek and Latin, forbidding anybody to go in. Didn't we give you leave to execute anyone who did? So why, you unclean creatures, are you trampling over dead bodies inside it? Why are you polluting your Holy House with the blood of foreigners and even of Jews? I call upon the gods of my fathers, and on any other gods who once watched over this place—although I doubt if any of them is still doing so now—to bear witness, as I do on my army and on the Jews standing beside me, that it was not I who forced you to defile your Sanctuary. If only you would change the battle-ground, no Roman would go near the Holy Places, let alone profane them. Whether you like it or not, I'm going to save the Sanctuary.[3]

The Jewish War tells us that the Zealots reacted with contempt. Under the delusion that they could never be defeated, they were genuinely convinced that the Roman general was speaking from cowardice, because he realized that he would never succeed in taking Jerusalem.

Titus had always known they were unlikely to listen to reason, so in the meantime, in order to attack the Temple on as broad a front as possible, he had ordered the Antonia to be razed to the ground. Although the fortress was very strongly built, it took his troops only a week. Once the area had been leveled, he ordered each of the four legions to construct yet another siege ramp. Unfortunately for the Romans, the Temple was guarded by the thickest walls in Jerusalem, and its inner forecourt was protected by its own massive ramparts, making a fortress inside a fortress, so there was not enough room to use all their troops, as "the place was so narrow."[4] Titus's solution was to pick thirty of the best men in every century, which he grouped in storm troops of a thousand under a tribune. The commander of this crack force was Sextus Cerealis, legate of the Fifth Legion, who had already distinguished himself by his ruthless efficiency.

Although the ramps were far from ready, Titus had given orders to launch an attack on the Temple outposts, at an hour before sunrise. He had to be restrained from leading it himself.

As he was putting on his armor and getting ready to accompany his soldiers, his friends stopped him, saying it was too dangerous. The generals insisted, "he would be of far more use if he remained in a command-post in the Antonia directing troop movements than if he came down and risked his life leading the attack—when they knew he was able to watch them, the men would fight better." Reluctantly, Titus agreed, commenting that "the only reason for his staying behind was to see how gallantly they fought, so that no act of bravery should go undecorated and no cowardly behavior escape punishment—as a spectator he would know how to reward or punish the troops."[5]

It sounds very much as if Tiberius Alexander was among the generals who insisted that this time Titus had to be cautious. It also sounds as though Josephus was among the friends at his side—presumably his staff—when, by the dim light of minute oil lamps, he was putting on his armor in his big leather tent.

In the event, it was lucky for Titus that he had decided to remain in the Antonia. He would have been risking his life to no purpose. When the legionaries reached the enemy guard posts, the Zealot sentries were far from being asleep as they had hoped and immediately sounded the alarm, whereupon more Jews ran to their help at the double. In the darkness, the confusion and din were so overwhelming that some Romans began to fight each other. However, they were crack troops, highly trained and experienced, who soon recovered their wits, locking shields together and charging in compact groups. Although not so disciplined as their opponents, the Zealots did not budge an inch, urged on by their "tyrant" John with threats or encouragement. The Romans were cheered on from the Antonia by their commander. The battle raged on from the small hours until midday when Titus finally called off the assault, neither side having gained any ground.

Many of the Romans had fought superbly, Josephus tells us, but so had the defenders. "Among the Jews, heroes [in this engagement] were Judes ben Mareotes and Simon ben Hosias from Simon bar Giora's party; James and Simon—the latter being Acatelas's son—from the Idumeans; and Gyphthaeus and Alexas, and also another Zealot Simon ben Ari." He means that Simon ben Ari had been one of Eleazar's men since he cannot bring himself to extend the name of Zealot, much as he dislikes it, to the others, whom he simply calls "robbers" when he is not calling them heroes, as he does here.[6]

In the meantime, the legionaries who were not in the storming parties had almost completed the new ramps. One of these was opposite the northwestern corner of the inner Temple, the second was opposite a spot between its two outer gates, the third was opposite the western colonnade of the outer court, and the fourth was opposite the northern colonnade. Building these latest assault platforms beneath the summer sun of Judea meant grinding fatigue for all troops involved, since the enormous amounts of timber needed for their construction had to be brought from at least twelve miles away. They were harried by Jews who stole their horses when the animals were left to graze, until Titus made them more careful by executing a man who lost his mount in this way.

On the day after the abortive assault, the Zealots, starving but undaunted, launched yet another of the formidable sorties that the legionaries had learned to dread. They attacked the Roman outposts on the Mount of Olives at a time of day when they expected to find the legionaries eating and off their guard, so that they could smash their way through the wooden wall. However, the lookouts saw them coming, and reinforcements were rushed over from the other camps. Another savage hand-to-hand combat took place, until the Jews were pushed back down the ravine at the bottom of the hill.

A cavalryman from one of the legions called Pedanius, a member of a squadron of horse whom the Jews had driven off, performed a remarkable feat of strength. Galloping back and into the Jews from the flank, he bent down from the saddle and seized a retreating Zealot by the ankle, a sizeable young man in armor, whom he carried back like a parcel and dropped at Titus's feet. After warmly congratulating Pedanius on his strength, the commander gave orders for the prisoner's immediate execution, presumably by crucifixion. Then he told his troops to get on with finishing the mounds.

Aware that another—and this time full-scale—assault might come at any moment, the Zealots made drastic preparations for it, burning down the northwestern colonnade that joined the Temple to the Antonia and demolishing a stretch about thirty feet long. Thus began the destruction of the Holy Place of Israel—by Jews. Two days later, the adjoining colonnade was set on fire by the Romans, and when the flames destroyed another twenty feet, the defenders pulled down the roof so as to destroy any remaining communication with the Antonia. Josephus observes sadly that they might have tried to stop the enemy, but "when the fire caught hold they calmly looked on, since they thought it was to their advantage."[7] All they could think of now was a last-ditch defense.

While all this was going on, minor engagements were taking place in front of the Temple, where small parties of Zealots and Romans fought each other with unremitting savagery. Josephus records yet another incident, typical of the siege, one that he must have seen with his own eyes.

"A Jew called Jonathan, a man of small size and despicable appearance, low born and low in every other way, too," came out in front of the monument of John the High Priest where, after shouting a stream of abuse, he challenged the Romans to single combat. Despite his puny appearance, there was no response for some time as his readiness to die looked uncanny, so he went on taunting the legionaries. Eventually a cavalryman named Pudens ran forward, but to everybody's surprise he was cut down by the little Jew. After finishing him off, Jonathan trampled on Pudens's corpse, brandishing his bloodstained sword and yelling insults at the Romans, "insanely dancing up and down and waving his arms." In the end a centurion called Priscus sent a well-aimed javelin through him.[8]

The Zealots never stopped trying to trap their opponents, exploiting their ignorance of the terrain. A few days later, on 27 July, they packed the crevices between the joists supporting the western colonnade and the ceiling below with tinder wood, bitumen, and pitch and then beat an ostentatious retreat as if they had lost hope of defending it. Some of the legionaries rushed after them, bringing ladders to climb the colonnade, although wiser men were suspicious and held back. As soon as the Romans crowded on top, the Jews set it alight, and the whole structure burst into flames. Many died in the fire or were hacked to pieces by the enemy after jumping off or were killed when they hit the ground, while some stabbed themselves. One can believe *The Jewish War* when it says the legionaries were deeply upset by the incident.

Cynical as always, Josephus was amused by the trick with which a certain Artorius managed to save himself after being cut off by the flames. He did so by shouting to a fellow soldier with whom he shared a tent, "Lucius, I'll leave you all I have if you'll catch me when I drop down." Running forward eagerly to catch Artorius, who survived, Lucius was himself killed through being dashed to pieces onto the stone pavement by the sheer weight of his friend's body.[9]

The western colonnade now burned down as far as the tower that had been built by John of Gischala as a defense against Simon bar Giora, on top of the gates opposite the Gymnasium, while the remainder was demolished by the Jews. The next day, the Romans fired the whole of the northern colonnade, right up to where it joined the eastern at the angle overlooking the Kedron valley where there was a fearsome drop down into the ravine. The scene had been set for the destruction of the entire Temple.

Meanwhile, there was even more dreadful suffering inside Jerusalem. *The Jewish War* tells us that an incalculable number were dying from famine, not even the brigands being exempt by now. "Gaping with hunger, stumbling and staggering along like maddened dogs, reeling against the house doors as if they were drunk, the robbers were in such a dazed state that they would burst into the same house several times a day," says Josephus. "Their hunger was so terrible that they chewed anything, picking up and swallowing things rejected by the filthiest of animals. In the end they were gnawing at belts and shoes, even at leather torn off their shields."[10]

Josephus then tells us the most appalling of all his grim stories. A woman of rich and distinguished family called Mary, the daughter of Eleazar, had fled from Perea on the other side of the Jordan to take refuge in Jerusalem. It looks as though she belonged to Josephus's own class, which was an added reason for his finding her history so shocking. Just the sort to arouse their hostility, not only was she robbed of all the property she had brought with her by the "tyrants"—Simon and John—but their bodyguards made a point of stealing any food she was able to find, and although she shrieked curses at them at the top of her voice, they did not bother to kill her.

In the end, "the famine pierced through her very bowels and marrow," sending Mary out of her mind. She killed the baby that was sucking at her breast, roasted the body, and devoured half of it. Attracted by the smell of cooking, some troops rushed into her house, so she showed them the remains. "This is my child and that's what I have done," she told them. "Eat as much as you like since I have had enough already. You men can't possibly be more fastidious than a woman or more tender-hearted than a mother. But if you don't want to eat from religious scruples and won't accept my sacrifice, then you can leave what's left to me." The troops ran from the house in horror, leaving Mary to her meal. The story spread throughout the city, everyone shuddering as though he or she had committed the crime. All longed for death, envying anyone who had died before hearing so horrible a tale.[11]

The news of this ghastly incident reached the Romans, brought either by deserters or by Josephus's spies, the result being that most of them hated the Jews more than ever. Titus swore before the Gods that he was not responsible. He also declared that he was going to bury the abomination of a mother eating her own child beneath the ruins of Judea, and that he would not leave standing on the face of the earth a city in which mothers fed in such a way.

And that is precisely what Titus Caesar and his men were about to do.

∽

Well aware that by taking the Antonia Fortress the Romans had seized the key to Jerusalem, the Zealots never had any thought of surrender. Nothing could shake their courage, although the sacrifice was no longer offered. They still held the Temple, which was a citadel in itself. Should the city fall, then it would be God's will, and they were ready to fall with it. Whatever happened, they would never yield to the pagan *Khittim*.

On 8 August two of the assault platforms were completed, so on the same day Titus gave orders for new battering rams to set to work on the western side of the outer Temple. For the last week, the great ram inside the largest of the siege towers had been doing its best to smash down the wall here but without any effect, and when the rams that replaced it went into action they also found they could make no impression—the stones were too big, too neatly put together. Some of the troops tried undermining the foundations of the northern gate, and although after enormous labor they succeeded in prizing out one or two of the stones at the front, the inner ones on which the gate rested stood firm. The Romans then decided that battering rams and crowbars were of no further use and put their trust in scaling ladders.

The Zealots made no attempt to stop the ladders being put in place, but as soon as the legionaries tried to climb up, they attacked them ferociously. Some were shaken off and hurled to the ground, and many were cut down as they stepped off, before they could cover themselves with their shields. Several ladders laden with armed men were pushed over with poles, throwing the climbers headlong down, while the Jews remained undaunted despite suffering heavy casualties themselves. The Romans tried bringing their eagles up the ladders, in the belief that any legionary would die rather than suffer the indelible disgrace of their loss, but to general astonishment the eagles were captured by the defenders, who succeeded in killing everybody who tried to scale the wall. Disheartened, the besiegers abandoned the assault. Although almost every Roman soldier who died had taken an enemy with him, the Zealots had fought even more effectively, one of their champions being Eleazar, a nephew of Simon bar Giora. Furious at having made no progress whatever, Titus ordered his men to pile wood against the Temple gates and set fire to them.

A few important deserters continued to drift over to the Romans. Among them was Ananus of Ammaus, a notoriously bloodstained member of Simon's bodyguard, and Archelaus ben Maggadatus. They chose a moment when the Jews were doing well, hoping that it might earn them a pardon, but Titus was strongly inclined to put these men to death, as he had heard how cruelly they had behaved in Jerusalem. He told the pair they were deserting to save their skins, not from conviction. "People who are in such a hurry to leave their native city when it's in flames through their own fault do not deserve mercy," he commented. Since he had given his word, he allowed the two to go free, but he would not let them be as well treated as other refugees.[12]

Meanwhile, the fire had quickly taken hold of the Temple gates, melting the silver ornaments, which set the doors alight, and soon the blaze reached the wooden galleries. After their recent victory this was a terrible shock to the Jews, who watched in horror as flames and smoke spread around them along the passages. The fire burned through the day and the following night, but it destroyed only parts of the galleries. What was left was quickly reoccupied by the defenders.

The next morning, that of 9 August, after detailing troops to put out the flames and clear the ground in front of the Temple gates in readiness for a general assault, Titus held a council of war with his generals. Among those whom Josephus lists as being present at the meeting were Tiberius Alexander, second in command; Sextus Cerealis, Larcius Lepidus, and

Titus Frigius, the commanders of the Fifth, Tenth, and Fifteenth Legions; Aeternius Fronto, commander of the two legions from Alexandria; and Marcus Antonius Julianus, who was the new procurator of Judea. The council was also attended by all the tribunes—next in rank below the legates or legion commanders.

The main problem raised by Titus was how they ought to deal with the Sanctuary. Some officers wanted to destroy the shrine under the rules of war, arguing that the Jews would never stop rebelling while it remained as a rallying point. Others advised that it should be spared, so long as the Jews did not try to use it for military purposes; if they did, then it would turn into a fortress instead of a shrine and should be torched. Titus took a different view. Even if the Jews used it as a strong point, the troops should not try to revenge themselves on objects instead of men or burn down such a magnificent structure. Its destruction would be a loss to the whole empire. Tiberius Alexander, Cerealis, and Fronto, the three most senior officers, agreed with him.

Before dismissing the meeting, Titus told the generals to tell the men to get some rest and recover their strength so that they would be ready for what was going to be an unusually grueling action. At the same time he gave orders for the thousand-strong storm troop—organized earlier—to make preparations for a final assault on the Temple.

On the following day, having recovered from the shock of the fire set by the Romans, the Jews made a fierce sortie through the eastern gate of the Temple at about eight o'clock in the morning, attacking a large Roman guard post in the outer court. Although the legionaries closed ranks to form a wall with their shields and fought back gallantly, the Zealots charged them with such fury that it was obvious they would soon be overwhelmed. Titus galloped to their rescue with his bodyguard, driving away the Jews. They retreated very slowly and reluctantly, turning around to beat off their pursuers again and again, until finally they were forced back into the Temple's inner court.

This was the day, 10 August, when Titus started to assemble his entire army on the area where the Antonia Fortress had stood, with the intention of attacking the Temple from all sides with every single man available. The grand assault was planned to take place the next day. Portentously, Josephus observes that 10 August was the anniversary of the date when, centuries

earlier, the Temple had been burned down by the King of Babylon. Uncowed by these menacing preparations and the vast force that was massing
outside, the Zealots made another sortie. At the same time, quite indepen-
dently of the sortie, fighting broke out between the Jewish guards around
the Sanctuary and a small detachment of Roman troops, who, in trying to
put out the fires, had somehow penetrated unobserved into the inner court.
Routing the guards, they ran after them toward the Sanctuary. Then the ultimate disaster took place.

Without any orders, but "moved by a supernatural impulse," an unknown legionary picked up a piece of burning wood that had fallen down
from a gallery.[13] Approaching the Sanctuary and climbing on the back of
a comrade, he threw it through a "golden window" that opened into the
cedar-lined chambers around the Holy of Holies, setting the curtains
alight. As the blaze took hold, the Jews raised an anguished cry, hurling
themselves in desperation at the fire.

Titus was resting in his tent when someone burst in with the news.
Rushing to the Temple with his staff, he shouted orders to save the shrine,
as the legionaries ran up in large numbers. Unfortunately, the crowd was by
now so big that they could not hear him. Not only did they begin fighting
the Jews instead of helping them, but they threw flaming torches to stoke
the fire, which spread swiftly. Before it reached the Holy of Holies, Titus
went in to marvel at the beauty of its furnishings and to order the removal
of its treasures, such as the great gold table of the shewbread, which
weighed several hundred-weight, and the seven-branched gold lamp—the
menorah. Going back outside, if Josephus is to be believed, he did his utmost to save the building, telling a centurion to have the legionaries beaten
off with clubs. They were out of control, however, in a frenzy of excitement,
and took no notice. One lunatic put a light to the hinges of the door to the
shrine, which was burned to the ground in a very short space of time.

This is how Tacitus, who can have heard only a very garbled version of
the tragedy, describes the impression that the shrine's destruction made on
the Romans: "Suddenly the doors of the Sanctuary were flung open and a
more than human voice was heard announcing that the gods were going
forth, while at the same time there was a tremendous noise of people leaving." Even men who did not understand the Jewish religion were aware
that the Jews had suffered some appalling disaster.[14]

Yet Josephus accepted the loss with all the fatalism of the convinced Pharisee. "As for that holy house, long ago God had undoubtedly doomed it to the fire," he writes.[15] "We can comfort ourselves with the thought that there is no escape from fate."[16] Even so, he admits that he mourned deeply for the loss of not just the Holy of Holies but for that of the entire Temple, "the most marvelous building that was ever seen or heard of, with its amazing architecture and its vast size, and wonderfully rich ornamentation, not to mention the glory of its holy places." He adds sadly, "from the second building of it, which was done by Haggai in the second year of Cyrus the King, till its destruction under Vespasian, there were six hundred and thirty-nine years and forty-five days."[17]

His portrayal of Titus verges on idolatry. But for his protection, Josephus would almost certainly have been put to death as a Zealot spy. Moreover, Titus later enabled him to embark on a prosperous career as a writer in Rome. As a Jew who never forgot a kindness, Josephus wanted to repay him by showing his generalship in the best light possible. Unfortunately, he is often suspected of sycophancy, and over the centuries, a number of critics have dismissed *The Jewish War*'s account of the Roman general's attempt to save the Holy of Holies as the purest flattery. Did he really try to save it, as Josephus claims so eloquently?

The first known critic is the Christian historian Sulpicius Severus, who wrote in the late fourth century and who insists that Titus gave orders for the shrine to be torched, as a blow against both Judaism and Christianity—an anachronistic suggestion that weakens Sulpicius's credibility, even if Orosius in the fifth century seems to agree with him. Since the nineteenth century, numerous scholars have nonetheless accepted Sulpicius's version, on the grounds that he may have had access to the account of the siege of Jerusalem in Tacitus's lost *Histories*. A recent biographer of Vespasian has expressed doubts about Josephus's account as well.[18]

There is also a passage in the Talmud that insists that Titus was determined to profane the Sanctuary. It claims that the Roman commander went into the Holy of Holies and copulated with a prostitute on an unrolled scroll of the Torah. Yet this is too crude and lurid a tale to carry conviction.[19]

However, one of the most authoritative modern historians of Josephus, Tessa Rajak, disagrees with the critics, arguing that the Temple was of such importance in Josephus's life that he would never have forgiven even Titus had he been guilty of such a crime. She observes, rightly, that the story of the burning of the Sanctuary is a test of the author's veracity as a whole; if we cannot accept his account of how the Holy of Holies perished, then we must question a lot more of what he tells us in *The Jewish War* and in his other books. In Rajak's view, Josephus's story is the best we have and, as it cannot be convincingly demolished, should be accepted.[20] Certainly, a wish to save the beautiful, mysterious shrine was not out of keeping with what we know of Titus's imaginative and often—if not invariably—generous character.

In addition, there is a theory that Queen Berenice was living in the camp, and she begged Titus to save the Sanctuary. He had already begun his long affair with this fascinating Jewess, whom he may have first met at Ptolemais in early 67 when preparing for the Judean campaign.[21] Tacitus thought that one reason why Titus failed to complete his journey to Rome during the dangerous year of 68 was because he wanted to go back to the seductive Berenice.[22] If she really had been in the camp, he might conceivably have done his best to spare the Holy of Holies in order to please her. Yet Josephus makes no mention of Berenice's presence, although this could be explained by a wish to say nothing that might damage his patron's reputation. But it was unheard of for a Roman general to live with his mistress on campaign. However intriguing, the suggestion is rejected by every modern historian.

Josephus's account of the burning of the Sanctuary is a testimony to his belief that everything that happens does so because it is the will of God. This explains the strange detachment with which he describes the burning of the Holy of Holies. He was convinced it was a divine punishment, because in his view, those who fought the Romans had betrayed the Law.[23] Even so, the sight of the Temple going up in flames must have horrified him, and he suffered with every other Jew. (Even today, the grief they felt is commemorated by an annual day of mourning, Tish B'av.) Yet he was sure that another Temple would arise, where his people would again worship God in the ancient way.

21

A Holocaust

"And many nations shall pass by this city, and they shall say every man to his neighbor, 'Wherefore hath the Lord done thus unto this great city?'"

JEREMIAH, XXII, 8

I N FORMER TIMES the prophets had exulted over the fall of Niniveh and Babylon, but now it was Jerusalem's turn. There was no need for the Romans to mount a full-scale assault on the Temple. They simply overran the entire compound, the defenders being by now too demoralized by the fate of the Sanctuary to put up a proper fight. No pity was shown to children or the old, no distinction made between rich and poor, between those begging for mercy and those with swords. The Jews' throats were cut wherever they were caught. The din was ear-splitting— clashing weapons, war cries, women screaming, the groans of the dying. Even those expiring from hunger found strength to bewail the Holy of Holies. Whipped up by heat from the flames, the clamor echoed from the surrounding hills.

"The suffering was still more terrible than the noise," recalls Josephus who had watched it. "You would have thought the hill on which the Temple stood was boiling from the bottom upwards, that everywhere was a mass of flames, that there lay a sea of blood deeper than the fire, that there were more killed than killers. You could not see a single piece of ground anywhere because it was so thickly covered with bodies, forcing the soldiers to climb over them in order to reach further victims."[1]

In the end, a large number of the Zealots in the Temple broke through the Romans, forcing a way out of the inner court into the outer and from there into the city. Most of the noncombatants in the precincts stayed behind, however, climbing up onto the outer colonnade, which was twelve feet wide, some priests among them tearing railings from the Sanctuary to hurl down at their enemies.

As the Sanctuary had been destroyed, the legionaries could see little point in preserving the Temple's other buildings so they torched the lot, including what was left of the colonnades and the gates. They lit fires beneath the terrified people cowering on top of the outer colonnade, mainly women and children, many of whom jumped to their deaths to escape the flames; Josephus says that about 6,000 perished in this way. They had taken refuge here because earlier in the day yet another so-called prophet had told them, "Go up onto the Temple where you will receive a sign of your deliverance."[2]

The troops also burned down the Temple's treasure chambers after plundering them. These had been used as strong rooms by Jerusalem's richer citizens, and they contained immense amounts of coin, gold and silver plate, jewelry, robes, and other valuables, together with goods stolen from the houses of murdered magnates. According to *The Jewish War*, the plunder taken in the city by the Romans was so great that its sale halved the price of gold throughout Syria.[3] Later, they would systematically raze the entire precincts of the Temple above foundation level.

"A large number of false prophets had been hired by the tyrants to delude the people, by telling them to wait for help from God, so that there would be less desertions, and that those who could not be frightened or controlled would respond to hope instead," says Josephus.[4] Yet it is more than likely that Simon and John had themselves believed fervently in "these impostors and pretended messengers of heaven."[5]

The Jewish War castigates such prophets for not heeding the "obvious portents that had foreshadowed the coming desolation."[6] It lists a sword-shaped star hanging over Jerusalem, a comet staying in the sky above for a whole year, a light hovering around the Holy of Holies, a sacrificial cow giving birth to a lamb in the Temple, and a bronze door into the Sanctuary that took normally twenty men to open doing so of its own accord, besides chariots and an armed host in the sky that encircled the city on a day in May 66—"a phenomenon so amazing as to stagger belief." One night before an important feast the priests had gone into the inner court of the Temple to make their customary preparations, when they felt the ground moving and heard a ringing noise, and then the sound of many voices that seemed to cry, "Let us go hence." (Tacitus repeats this story, perhaps told to him by someone who had read *The Jewish War*, a book that was not among his sources.)

Josephus also tells of an illiterate peasant farmer and holy man, Jesus ben Ananus, who had stood outside the Temple crying, "A voice from the east, a voice from the west, a voice from the four winds, a voice against Jerusalem and the Sanctuary, a voice against bride and bride-groom, a voice against the people!" Everyday he went through the streets of Jerusalem shouting this message. People grew so angry that they had him arrested and whipped, but he went on. Believing he was under some demonic influence, they dragged him before the procurator Albinus. Scourged until the bones showed, the man neither wept nor begged for mercy, but whispered at every stroke, "Woe! Woe unto Jerusalem!" The procurator demanded that he explain who he was and what he meant, but he did not answer, only continuing his lament. Albinus decided he was a lunatic and let him go. When the war broke out, Jesus went on crying his lament every day, speaking to no one. He never cursed anybody who hit him, never thanked anybody who fed him, his only reply being, "Woe! Woe unto Jerusalem." When the siege intensified, he changed his cry to, "Woe! Woe once more to the city, to the people and to the Sanctuary!" When he added to his litany the words, "Woe! Woe to myself as well," he was killed by a stone from a ballista.[7]

Another of the portents that Josephus describes must have been highly satisfactory to his Roman patrons. He explains that one reason why the Jews went to war so eagerly in 66 CE was an ambiguous prophecy in their sacred writings, which predicted that at about this time someone from their country was going to become ruler of the entire world. Many Jewish scholars thought it applied to their own race, but obviously the prophecy had referred to Vespasian.

Now, the triumphant Romans carried their eagles into the Temple, placing them opposite the east gate. Then they sacrificed to them, cheering Titus, whom they hailed as "Imperator!" "Victorious General!"

A few priests still held out on top of what was left of the walls of the Sanctuary, without food or water. After four days they were forced to come down by hunger and were taken into Titus's presence. When they begged him to spare their lives, he told them that the time for pardon was over and that since the one thing that might have given him a reason for sparing them had been destroyed, it was fitting they should die with their Temple. Then he gave orders for their execution. This seems out of keeping with his usual clemency toward upper-class Jews, but Josephus may have explained to him that, far from being members of the nobility, these were men from the ranks of the lower clergy. As such, they are likely to have been committed Zealots.

Now that they had been defeated and were completely surrounded, Simon bar Giora and John of Gischala tried to make terms. Accordingly, Titus went to a place at the west of the outer Temple, where a bridge joined the Temple to the Upper City. The Zealot leaders stood at the far end of the bridge, on the other side of the Tyropoeon Valley, surrounded by their followers, hoping against hope for a pardon. Titus had some difficulty in making his troops restrain their anger and keep their swords in their scabbards, and only did so by issuing the strictest orders. His interpreter was almost certainly Josephus, who must have relished the abasement of the two men he hated most in the world.

Titus spoke first.

So, are you at last satisfied with your country's misery? You never bothered to think about how strong we were or your own weakness, but through your reckless impetuosity and madness you've destroyed your people, your city and your Holy House. Because of it, you're going to die as you deserve! Your nation had never stopped rebelling against the Romans since the time Pompey's troops crushed you, until you finally declared open war. Was it because you were so confident about your numbers? Well, only a tiny part of the Roman army has been more than able to cope with you. Or was it because you thought you might have allies, although what nation outside our empire prefers Jews to Romans? Did you rely on your physical strength, despite our having made slaves of the Germans, or on the thickness of your walls? No walls can be more of an obstacle than an ocean, yet the Britons have had to surrender to the Roman army! Or were you intoxicated by your leaders' determination and cleverness? Yet you must have heard how we defeated even the Carthaginians.[8]

Titus's speech contains some very interesting information. The reference to "allies" is highly significant, since it reveals that the Romans had been more worried than they liked to admit about the possibility that Parthia might join the Zealots' side, especially during Rome's recent civil wars. The comparison of the Jews' physique with that of the Germans shows that they must have been a big and well-built race, because we know that contemporaries always thought of the Teutons as giants.

He went on to rebuke the Jews for turning against the Romans after they had treated them with so much kindness, allowing them to observe the laws of their fathers and levy taxes for their God. However, they were untamable reptiles, biting the hand that fed them. His father had come to Judea not to punish but to caution them, but they had despised his benevolence as weakness. He accused them of taking advantage of the Roman civil war and sending embassies to fellow Jews on the other side of the Euphrates, implying that the envoys had not merely asked them to come and fight but tried to persuade the Parthians to send an army.

He claimed he had been exceptionally merciful and had tried to make peace every time he won a victory, that he had begged them to save the Sanctuary, their Holy House, that he had invited them to leave Jerusalem with permission to resume the war elsewhere. They had spurned every one of his offers. They themselves had set fire to the Sanctuary "with their own hands," insisted Titus, a charge he must have known was untrue. The fact that he made it reveals his sensitivity on the subject, besides showing that he genuinely regretted the destruction of the Holy of Holies; he may even have felt a certain guilt.

After all this, you miserable men, you actually invite me to a conference! What is the point when you've destroyed your Sanctuary? Why do you hope to survive your Temple when it lies in ruins? Yet here you are, in your armor, unable to bring yourselves to beg for mercy when you're at your last gasp. You abominable animals, what makes you so deluded? Aren't your people dead? Haven't you lost your Holy House? Isn't your city in my power? Aren't your lives in my hands? And yet you still believe it's glorious to fight to the death? But there is no reason for me to share your madness. Throw down your weapons and surrender unconditionally, and I will let you keep your lives. I shall act like the master of a household with a name for kindness, punishing the real sinners among you and sparing the rest of you for my own uses.[9]

Intoxicated by his victory, Titus was scarcely magnanimous. Yet Josephus could see nothing wrong with his harangue, since he includes it in *The Jewish War*. Never a forgiving man, he himself plainly felt the same way, and no doubt he inserted a few extra insults while interpreting Titus's words.

The Zealots replied that they could not accept Titus's demand for surrender because they had all taken an oath that they would never surrender under any circumstances, however desperate. Instead, they asked to be allowed to go out through the wooden wall into the desert, taking their women and children with them, and leaving the city to him. They must have known that their request was bound to be refused by a people so merciless as the Romans, but despite their hopeless situation, they had not lost their dignity.

Enraged that men whom by now he regarded as no better than prisoners of war should dare to try and make terms with him, Titus had a proclamation read out. The gist of it was that deserters would no longer find a welcome among the Romans, since he had no intention of sparing anybody but was preparing to attack them all with his entire army. Would-be refugees must fend for themselves as best they could, since from now on he was going to treat everyone according to the rules of war, without any exceptions. His troops would receive orders to burn down and plunder what was left of Jerusalem.

The next morning the legionaries overran the whole of the Lower City. They set fire to the building that housed the magistrates and the archives, to the council chamber in the part known as Acra where the Sanhedrin had met, and to the area called Ophel. Soon the blaze spread to the palace of the late Queen Helena of Adiabene, which was in the center of Acra. The streets went up in flames as well, destroying many houses that were full of dead bodies, filling the air with the smell of burning human flesh.

On the day their grandmother's palace was burned down, the sons of King Azates of Adiabene and their uncles, who had been fighting with the fury of converts at the side of the Zealots, came with a group of leading citizens to beseech Titus to give them his protection. Despite his proclamation and although very angry, he spared their lives. All were kept under guard, however, and the king's sons and kinsmen were put in chains and later taken as hostages to Rome, to ensure their countrymen's loyalty.

In the Upper City the Zealots used the Royal Palace as a last-ditch bastion because it was so strongly built and because a considerable number of rich citizens had stored their valuables in it. They drove out the Roman troops who had occupied it and then murdered "8,400" people who had taken refuge inside, besides looting the place. (The figure that Josephus gives for those killed looks like yet another of his exaggerations.)

The Jews captured a legionary and a Roman cavalryman, cutting the legionary's throat and then dragging his body through the streets, kicking and cursing it. However, the cavalryman said he had a wonderful idea that might save the defenders' lives, so they took him to Simon, who quickly discovered he was lying and handed him over for execution to Ardalas, one of his officers. Intending to cut off his head, Ardalas blindfolded the man and took him in front of the Romans, but while he was drawing his sword, the trooper broke free and ran, reaching his comrades in safety. Titus had him stripped of his weapons and dismissed from his legion, however, saying that it was a disgrace for a Roman soldier to let himself be taken prisoner. Josephus, who after months on the staff had absorbed the army's harsh ethos, comments that being expelled from a legion was worse than death for a man with self-respect.

Meanwhile, the Romans methodically drove the Zealots out of the Lower City, which they torched all the way down to the Pool of Siloam. They were delighted to see it go up in flames, but very disappointed at finding such a small amount of loot, since everything of value had been moved into the Upper City. Here, the defenders put on a brave face, declaring bravely if unconvincingly that they were overjoyed by the sight of so many buildings burning, since it showed how little would be left standing for their enemies.

Josephus tells us that even now he did not stop begging the Zealots to surrender and save what was left of Jerusalem. While he could not stop himself from reminding them of how savage and impious he thought they had been, he suggested that they might save their lives, but his advice was greeted with contempt. Although they could no longer fight the Romans on equal terms, they kept their oath never to surrender. Some of them were no less active than the enemy in setting buildings alight. Others hid among the ruins on the edge of the city, killing any deserters they could catch, for people were still trying to go over to the Romans, regardless of Titus's announcement that they would no longer be welcome. Fugitives too weak from hunger to run were butchered on the spot, their bodies thrown to the dogs.

One reason why Zealots in the Upper City went on fighting for so long was a belief that they would be able to escape through the labyrinth of caves beneath them. Anybody not a Zealot who fled into the sewers was killed and robbed; if he had food, they snatched it from him and devoured it, although covered with blood. They were on the point of eating dead bodies, says Josephus who takes a horrid pleasure in recording these last minute agonies. As he saw it, such uncleanliness meant that they could not possibly be true Jews.

On its hilltop, behind massive walls that were reinforced by a very steep ascent, the Upper City was a formidable fortress in itself. The place could only be captured by a full-scale siege operation, for which Titus gave orders on 20 August. Once again, the troops had to build ramps equipped with assault platforms. The legionaries built mounds on the western side opposite the Royal Palace, while auxiliaries and allied troops erected other ramps on the eastern side near the gymnasium and where Simon had built his tower.

The Idumeans realized that the situation was beyond hope and sent five men through the lines to Titus to see if he would give them terms. After some hesitation, knowing that they were among the toughest elements in the Zealot army and hoping that their defection might force Simon and John to surrender, he sent the five back to say he was ready to guarantee their lives and their freedom. As they were preparing to go over, Simon learned what was happening and executed the messengers, placing the Idumean leaders under arrest. Deprived of their officers, their men did not know what to do and stayed put. Simon watched them closely, placing guards on the ramparts; at this desperate moment he could not afford to lose such good troops.

But Zealot efforts to prevent further desertion proved unavailing. Although many people were killed when trying to escape, an even larger number got away. Ignoring his own proclamation, Titus spared their lives. Male citizens were kept as captives, while their women and children were sold as slaves, although they fetched a very low price since there was a glut of slaves from the city. *The Jewish War* says that during the siege an "incalculable" number of deserters had been packed off to the slave markets, yet it also tells us that even at this late stage 40,000 citizens were given their lives and allowed to go wherever they liked in Judea.[10] This was after they had been examined by specially appointed officers to make sure they were not Zealots, an operation perhaps organized by Josephus.

During the last phase of the siege a priest named Jesus ben Thebuthi obtained a pardon from Titus on the condition that he hand over the Temple's treasures. From a hiding place in a wall of the Sanctuary, he produced two seven-branch gold candlesticks similar to those that had lit the shrine, as well as golden tables, basins, and cups, and the high priest's jewel-studded vestments. The keeper of the Temple treasury, whose name was Phineas, also cooperated, leading his captors to where the priests' tunics and girdles were concealed, together with a stock of priceless purple and scarlet cloth for repairing the Veil of the Temple, a huge quantity of cinnamon and cassia and other spices intended for use as incense, and various sacred ornaments. In reward, he was granted the pardon given to genuine fugitives, although he had been taken prisoner.

After eighteen days the ramps against the Upper City were at last ready for use, and by 8 September the Romans had all their siege engines in place. As soon as they went into action, some of the defenders fled from the walls to hide in the citadel, while others dived into the sewers. There was a general mood of despair inside the Upper City yet there were still enough Zealots to man the ramparts, and they did their best to shoot down the troops bringing up the siege towers. This time the defenders proved no match for the Romans, who knew that they were dealing with beaten men. When the rams brought down part of the wall with several of its towers, panic set in, and there was no attempt to defend the breach.

During this final attack, Titus shot at the Jews himself with a bow, killing twelve. The entire Roman army knew that it was the day of his daughter's birthday, which delighted the troops.[11]

Even Simon and John lost their nerve as the legionaries climbed toward them over the rubble. "Watching these two men, who had once been so arrogant and boastful about their crimes, suddenly become so abject, trembling with fear, would have made you pity them, vile as they were," we are told by a gloating Josephus. "For a moment they thought of charging the enemy, with some idea of breaking through the guards, smashing down the wooden wall and escaping. But there was no sign of their supposedly faithful followers, who had all fled, while messengers came rushing up to say that the entire western wall had collapsed and the Romans were everywhere, and with their own eyes they must have realized that the enemy were looking for them. When somebody, bewildered by terror, said he could see legionaries on top of one of the three great towers, they fell on their faces and cursed their folly. Paralyzed with fear, they could not even run away."[12]

When they recovered their wits, they made the disastrous mistake of abandoning the impregnable towers that were their headquarters, against which the most powerful siege engines would have been useless. Rushing into the ravine below the Pool of Siloam, they tried to break out of the city but were driven back by the Romans. Having failed to escape, they hid in the sewers.

When they discovered they were masters of the Upper City—and therefore of all Jerusalem—the Romans could scarcely believe their final success. After planting the eagles of all the legions on the towers, they began cheering, clapping, and singing. As *The Jewish War* says, they were finding the end of the war much easier than the way in which it started. Their last assault through the breach had not cost them a single casualty, and after so much savage hand-to-hand combat with the Zealots, they were astonished at finding no further resistance inside the walls.

After a few minutes of rejoicing, the Romans began to celebrate victory in their own special way. Pouring into the streets, sword in hand, they butchered anyone they saw so that the thoroughfares became blocked by bodies, and they burned down buildings in which fugitives had taken refuge with everybody inside. When they broke into houses in search of plunder, they often found whole families dead from hunger and recoiled in horror empty-handed. Despite their pity for the dead, they had no mercy on the living, Josephus tells us, but killed every living soul they met, so that the whole city ran with blood that in some places even put out the fire. For on all sides there were flames, which during the night engulfed the entire city.

When Titus made his entry into the Upper City, he was astonished to find that it was so strong. In particular he was impressed by the three great towers that Simon and John had so insanely abandoned. Noticing their height, the massive solidity of their construction throughout, the size of the stone blocks with which they were built and how neatly these fitted, he exclaimed, "We must have had the gods on our side when we were fighting for it can only have been the gods who overcame the Jews, since how could human hands or human machines be of any possible use against such [mighty] towers?"[13] He set free all the people who had been imprisoned in them by the two leaders, and when he later destroyed the remainder of the city, he left the towers standing as a monument to the good fortune that had enabled him to triumph over what had at first seemed to be impregnable defenses.

As his troops were finally beginning to growing tired of such unending slaughter, and as there was a surprisingly large number of survivors, Titus ordered that only men with weapons in their hands were to be killed; the rest were to be made prisoners. The troops interpreted the order as they pleased, massacring all who were old or feeble. Those in the prime of life and fit for work were herded into the Temple and penned in the Court of Women, where officers interrogated them, a task that was made easier by the prisoners' readiness to inform against each other. Anybody identified as a committed Zealot was executed on the spot.

The Romans searched the sewers and caves beneath the city, digging up the ground and killing everyone they found. Over 2,000 dead Zealots were discovered; some had killed themselves or been killed by a comrade, but most had died from hunger. The revolting stench from dead bodies that met those who entered the tunnels caused many of the pursuers to turn back in disgust, although a few of the greedier soldiers climbed over the corpses to look for loot.

The tunnels underground proved to be not such a refuge after all. Rather than die of starvation John of Gischala, who had been hiding in a sewer with his brothers, crawled out and gave himself up. It took a little longer for Simon bar Giora to surrender. Taking a few friends and some miners, bringing picks, stonecutters, and food for several weeks, they had gone down into a secret cave, hoping to dig their way out of the city. Although the miners did their best, the food ran out. Simon went up to look for further supplies, dressing himself in white to look like a ghost and emerging where the Temple had stood. Arrested, he demanded to be taken to a general, who put him in chains.

"Thus was Jerusalem captured in the second year of the reign of Vespasian, on the eighth day of the month Gorpiaeus [8 September]," says Josephus with a fine rhetorical flourish.[14] Although their defense of Jerusalem had ended in horror, the Zealots nonetheless deserve credit for a heroic feat of arms, however passionately *The Jewish War* may insist that the city fell because it was a "victim of revolutionary frenzy."[15] The siege was one of the great sieges of history. What had begun as a rabble transformed itself into a formidable army that for nearly five months kept at bay the best troops in the world. Despite their leaders' rivalry having deprived them of proper leadership and a unified central command, they had to a large extent made up for it by sheer bravery. Josephus tactfully omits to give a figure, but they must have inflicted tens of thousands of casualties on the Romans. Under another Judas Maccabeus, the Zealots might well have beaten off the besiegers, humbled the Flavians, and brought the Roman Empire crashing down. Their modern fellow countrymen should take pride in their fighting qualities.

Now that the capital had fallen, the Romans had almost wrested back control of Judea. They had already recovered every other Jewish city. Only the isolated fortresses of Herodium, Machaerus, and Masada remained in Zealot hands.

⸛

Citizens of Jerusalem who perished during the siege were lucky. While the Romans were deciding what to do with their captives, 11,000 of those penned inside the Temple ruins died from hunger—some because the guards deliberately starved them, others because they refused to eat. In any case, as Josephus tells us, there was not enough food to feed so many prisoners.[16]

The conquerors kept 700 of the tallest and best-looking young men for Titus's triumph at Rome. Of the remaining men, those over seventeen were sent in chains to a living death as forced labor in Egypt or to arenas all over the Roman Empire where they would die in gladiatorial combats or be fed to wild animals. Women and children were packed off to the slave markets.

Josephus says that only 97,000 prisoners of war had been taken in the entire Judean campaign, while 1,100,000 people had died during the siege.[17] As he is so prone to exaggeration, the estimate of 600,000 dead given by Tacitus seems more plausible, even if still enormous. On the other hand, Josephus justifies his figure by explaining that a large number of the casualties were pilgrims who had been trapped in the city while visiting it for the feast of Passover. In addition, there were all those who had come in from the countryside for miles around in order to take refuge.

He tells us that on Titus's instructions, all Jerusalem, including the Temple and the Sanctuary, was razed to the foundations. Only the three great towers—Phasaelus, Hippicus, and Mariamne—were left standing, with a small stretch of the fortifications at the western side, which was turned into a barracks. The rest of the walls were leveled to the ground so that according to Josephus there was nothing to suggest the place had once been a city. This is an exaggeration; although the city walls and the Temple were demolished, much of Jerusalem survived until the Bar Kokhba revolt. Moreover, the "wailing wall" of the Temple Mount still exists. The statement may be due to faulty information, suggesting that he never again saw his birthplace with his own eyes.

A victory parade was held at the headquarters' camp, Titus and his staff standing on a dais. After a speech in which he congratulated his legionaries on their skill and courage during "a war that had lasted so long," he announced that he was more interested in rewarding gallantry than in punishing cowardice. He then decorated all those men who had performed an outstanding act of bravery. When their names had been read out, they marched up to the dais where golden crowns where placed on their heads and gold chains around their necks, while long gold lances and silver standards were put in their hands, and they were promoted. In addition, they were each given large amounts of the booty—gold and silver, valuable clothing. Finally, Titus sacrificed a large number of oxen to the gods in thanksgiving, the meat being distributed to the troops to be eaten at a banquet. He himself joined in the party, which went on for three days.

Just before the final assault, Titus had told Josephus to take anything that he liked "from the wreck of my country."[18] He also presented him with some "sacred books," which seem to have included an especially fine copy of the Torah, presumably found in the Temple. Josephus was more interested in saving Jewish lives than in loot, however, and begged Titus to free some of his fellow countrymen who had been taken prisoner, in particular his brother and fifty friends. (His father seems to have died.) The request was granted. Still hoping to rebuild a pliant ruling class, who would cooperate in rebuilding Judea, his amiability was due to more than a wish to please his protégé. In addition, Josephus tells us in the *Vita* that he went into the prison camp in the Temple and got possession of every acquaintance he saw there, about a hundred and ninety people. They were handed over to him as slaves, but he refused to let them buy their freedom and set them at liberty.

Shortly after, he was sent by Titus with Sextus Cerealis, the legate of Syria, and a thousand cavalry to a village called Tekoa, twelve miles south of Jerusalem. The purpose of their journey was to see whether the place would be suitable for a legionary camp, yet another of the jobs he was called on to do as an unofficial staff officer. At Tekoa he found a large number of prisoners who had been crucified, including three old friends. Galloping back to headquarters in tears, he told Titus, who immediately gave orders for them to be taken down and given the best medical treatment. One survived, but the others died in the surgeons' hands.[19]

The autumn storms had set in by now, making the Mediterranean too dangerous for Titus to risk shipping his prisoners and wagon loads of plunder back to Italy. He spent the winter in Judea. When he was at Caesarea, Simon bar Giora was brought to him, and he gave orders for the Jewish leader to be taken to Rome to feature in his triumph—just as the Gallic leader Vercingetorix had featured in Julius Caesar's. The Fifth Legion and the Fifteenth Legion guarded the loot and the prisoners, who were confined outside the city. The Tenth Legion was left to garrison ruined Jerusalem and was entrusted with keeping the peace in Judea. The emblem on its eagle was a wild boar—a pig.

Many of the captives died in a succession of "games" at the city's amphitheater, where they were thrown to starving animals to be eaten alive or made to fight each other to the death in large numbers. On 24 October there was a particularly splendid entertainment to celebrate Titus's brother Domitian's birthday. On that day, "the number of those [Jews] who were killed in fights with wild beasts, burned alive or slain in combats with each other was more than 2,500," Josephus informs us. He adds, in what is probably an attempt to excuse Titus's abominable cruelty, "Although the prisoners were dying in countless [cruel] ways, all the Romans thought it was far too mild a punishment [for Jews]."[20] On 17 November Titus celebrated his father the Emperor Vespasian's birthday at Beirut in the same way, a further 2,500 dying a terrible death in the arena.

More Jews died in the entertainments that he gave at various Syrian cities, including Antioch. Only recently that city had witnessed a pogrom, in which its Jewish inhabitants became scapegoats for a fire that devastated the city center and were persecuted for refusing to sacrifice to the pagan gods. However, when the Antiochenes asked Titus to expel all Jews from the city, he refused, saying they could only be sent back to their own country, which had been destroyed, and no other place was prepared to take them. Nor would he agree to withdraw their privileges. When he left Antioch, the city's Jews were in a better position than ever before, since the Antiochenes dared not disobey him. Titus became famous throughout the East. King Vologaeses, the one man who might have saved the Zealots, sent him a golden crown as a sign of respect.

During the winter, Titus paid a last visit to Jerusalem. Instead of boasting of his victory, he deplored the destruction of such a wonderful city, cursing the men who had brought ruin upon it by rebelling against Rome. Josephus, who was with him, tells us that the Romans were still digging up large quantities of gold and silver hidden during the siege. But he reveals nothing about his own feelings.

Titus's melancholy mood may have had to do with more than the sight of a ruined Jerusalem. There was worrying news from Europe. The Germans and the northern Gauls had revolted, encouraged by the recent civil war and the hope that Vespasian would not last long. At the same time, the Scythians had launched a serious raid across the Danube into Moesia.

However, the Germans and Gauls were quickly defeated, the Scythians were checked, and peace was restored to the entire empire.

Accompanied by Josephus, Titus marched into Egypt across the desert, attending the consecration of the sacred bull Apis in the temple at Memphis. During the service he wore a diadem, which seemed to confirm rumors of his planning to invade Italy and replace his father. During the siege the legionaries had hailed him as "Imperator," and although they were only acclaiming him as a victorious general, it had aroused suspicion. His troops were so devoted to him that when he was leaving Judea they begged him to stay, which made some think that he intended to revolt against Vespasian and make himself ruler of the East. Josephus must have listened to these rumors with horror. He had no wish to find himself in the middle of another dangerous civil war in which once again he would have to choose sides.

But Titus was much too sensible to rebel and risk losing his chance of inheriting the empire. Sending ahead of him the 700 prisoners who had been chosen for their fine appearance, together with Simon and John, he sailed from Alexandria to Italy in the spring of 71. It was a pleasant voyage, according to *The Jewish War*.[21] Josephus writes from personal experience, since he says in the *Vita*, Titus "took me on board with him, treating me with every mark of esteem."[22] Their ship put in at Regium, then at Puteoli. From there, Titus rushed up to Rome where, to show that the rumors about him were groundless, he burst into Vespasian's presence with the words, "Here I am, father, here I am!"[23] "From that time on he never ceased to act as the emperor's partner, even as his protector," Suetonius tells us.[24]

"On our arrival in Rome, I was treated with the greatest consideration by Vespasian," Josephus informs us in his autobiography. "He gave me a lodging in the house in which he had lived before becoming Emperor, honored me by making me a Roman citizen, and bestowed a pension on me. He continued his benevolence towards me until the day he left this life, without any lessening in his kindness."[25] That inspired prophecy at Jotapata was certainly paying dividends. Becoming a Roman citizen meant a considerable rise in his legal and social status and was particularly useful in any dealings with the authorities. He was no longer just a Jewish refugee.

In June, Titus and Vespasian shared a joint triumph, which was almost a coronation. Josephus records every detail in *The Jewish War* with such en-

thusiasm that one has to remind oneself that he was a Jew, since it celebrated the humiliation of his nation and his faith. However, by then he
was writing for a non-Jewish readership and had been a Roman citizen for
several years.

The entire Roman army paraded before dawn in front of the Temple of
Isis, where father and son had spent the night. The pair came out at daybreak, in purple robes and crowned with laurel wreaths, and then proceeded to the Octavian Walks where the Senate and chief magistrates were
waiting. Here they seated themselves on two ivory chairs on a tribune.
After offering sacrifice and prayers, they put on triumphal robes before
taking their places in the pageant.

The plunder was carried in procession, "like some flowing river,"
masses of gold and silver, rare jewels set in crowns or simply in heaps. Even
the robes worn by the 700 prisoners were beyond price. There were floats,
some of them four stories high, depicting battles by sea and land, the
storming of fortresses and towns, all deluged in blood, temples burning
down, houses being demolished and burying their owners in their ruins,
warships sinking. A captured city governor was made to sit on each float.
Then came the crimson veils, the great gold table of the shewbread, and
the seven-branched candlestick that had once adorned the Sanctuary, with
a copy of the Torah, after which followed ivory and gold statues of the
Roman gods who had supposedly conquered the God of the Jews. As a climax, Vespasian and Titus brought up the rear of the procession, riding superb chargers.[26]

The procession ended at the Temple of Jupiter Capitolinus, where it
was a hallowed Roman tradition to await the news that an enemy leader
was dead. This time the leader was Simon bar Giora, who had been forced
to walk in the pageant with a halter tied round his neck. Beaten as he
went, he was dragged along by the halter into the Forum and then into the
Mammertine prison at its northeastern end where he was ceremonially
scourged and tortured before finally being put to death. When the news
that he had been killed reached the Temple of Jupiter, the crowd broke
into a great shout of joy.

There is a mystery about what happened to John of Gischala, who also
marched in the triumph. All we know from *The Jewish War* is that he was
sentenced to lifelong captivity. The novelist Lion Feuchtwanger makes an

oddly convincing case for it having been far from unpleasant, although he would never again see Gush Halav. One wonders how he escaped the ghastly fate of his fellow commander, Simon. For all his savagery, the Romans may have recognized a certain greatness of spirit in the man.

Josephus tells us that afterward, Vespasian built a Temple of Peace, which he lavishly embellished with marvelous paintings and statues. Here he placed the golden ornaments from the Sanctuary, although he kept the Torah from the Holy of Holies and the crimson veil in the Palace. The seven-branched candlestick appears in one of the reliefs of the Arch of Titus. Nearly five hundred years later, King Genseric of the Vandals took the menorah and the golden table to Carthage, from where they were recovered by Belisarius in 533. Then the Emperor Justinian sent them back to Jerusalem. They vanished for good during the seventh century.

Despite Josephus's glowing account, the triumph must have been a dreadful experience for him. The crowd's mood was not just one of rejoicing; it was also one of bitter hatred for the race that had more than once humiliated their supposedly invincible army. No doubt, the new Roman citizen was reassured by his patron's popularity, and presumably he felt satisfaction at the death of the "tyrant" Simon bar Giora. But throughout his entire life he can have seen no more harrowing spectacle than this reenactment of his country's defeat and destruction, together with the parade of the sacred ornaments from the Holy of Holies.

What happened at the fall of Jerusalem was genocide. No other word can describe what took place. The Romans never showed mercy to defeated enemies, and the realization that the siege had almost failed—which could have meant the fall of the Flavian dynasty and renewed civil war—made them still more merciless. In any case, after suffering so many casualties the legionaries were determined to exact a memorably vicious reckoning, while as usual the Syrian and Arab auxiliaries were bent on doing as much harm to Jews as they could. Titus's prolonged cruelty to prisoners was excessive, even by Roman standards. Far more dreadful than the Babylonian sack of the city six centuries earlier, the siege and fall of Jerusalem was the worst disaster suffered by the Jewish people until the twentieth century. It is no exaggeration to call it a holocaust.

22

The Propagandist

"I shall describe the cruelty of the [Jewish] tyrants to their fellow countrymen, in contrast to the clemency of the Romans towards a race of foreigners, and how often Titus showed his eagerness to save the City and the Temple by inviting the rebels to make terms."

JOSEPHUS, *THE JEWISH WAR*, 1, 27

FOR AN AMBITIOUS young man who still had a career to make there could be no point in staying in a wrecked Judea. Josephus does not tell us whether Vespasian had invited him to settle in Rome, but it seems more than probable in view of his "lodging" in the former Flavian mansion on the Quirinal, his Roman citizenship, and his pension. Since his family's estate outside Jerusalem had been appropriated (presumably to supply the garrison with food), Titus gave him as compensation another estate, "in the plain," which meant the fertile *shefelah* near the sea.[1] Vespasian also presented him with another large tract of good Judean land.

Yet we should not read too much into such gifts. Although he took the emperor's name, so did many other new citizens, and it is likely that Flavius Josephus was never quite as high in favor as he would have us believe. It is also possible that his lodging in the Flavian mansion was just a room for a short period. He did not receive the title of "Friend of Caesar" (*amicus Caesaris*), nor was he among the *comites*, the emperor's formally

acknowledged companions. It has even been suggested by a modern historian that he had a comparatively low place at court, in the same category
as magicians and buffoons.[2]

Nobody could claim that Vespasian's Rome was a tranquil haven of security during its early years. When Josephus arrived with Titus in 71, he
must have noticed the uneasy atmosphere all over the city. Everybody remembered how the Roman Empire had nearly disintegrated only a few
months earlier. The public buildings that burned down during Vitellius's
overthrow had not yet been rebuilt, while the civil war, the uprisings in
Gaul and Germany, and the need to reward the troops had left the administration desperately short of money. Despite the victories of Vespasian and
Titus, and their triumph in Rome, the new dynasty was still very insecure.
The Senate dreamed of regaining the right to choose emperors, so much so
that Vespasian ordered the execution of one of its members, Helvidius
Priscus, and sent other senators into exile.[3]

The problem of who would succeed Vespasian was far more dangerous
than any senatorial nostalgia for a republic, however. Even after he gave his
elder son titles to show that he was his heir, the succession remained in
doubt. The events of 69 had shown that an emperor might be elected by
the army. Licinius Mucianus, the extremely able general who, after establishing an alliance with Titus had captured Rome for Vespasian in 70,
thought he had not been properly rewarded, and there is some evidence
that he was trying to turn the new emperor against Titus, even hoping to
become his heir, which may be why Titus had suddenly come rushing back
to Rome. Fortunately for Titus, Mucianus died in 75. Then Domitian
began to dream of supplanting his elder brother, who in any case had other
secret enemies. Throughout Vespasian's reign there were whispers of con-
spiracy.[4] The politically minded Josephus must have sensed these menacing undercurrents, which scarcely made for peace of mind.

While there is no indication that he spent much time at court, he saw
a lot of King Agrippa II, who came to Rome as a favorite of Vespasian and
was granted the rank of praetor. It looks as if Agrippa was not quite sure
what to make of Josephus; there are hints that sometimes he may have listened to slanders about him. However, we can be sure that Josephus took
great care to flatter the last prince of the House of Herod. Someone else
from Judea was in Rome during these days. Queen Berenice was living

with Titus in his palace, despite her being ten years his senior. The Romans loathed Berenice, seeing her as a new Cleopatra, eager to become empress. They were repelled by rumors of her former incestuous relationship with her brother, Agrippa, and irritated by her glittering panoply of diamonds. Josephus does not refer to receiving any favors from her.

"My privileged position aroused envy and exposed me to dangers," he tells us.[5] He was envied by other Jews, and not only by those in Rome. This became evident in the case of a Jewish weaver called Jonathan, who had stirred up a rising at Cyrene that caused the death of 2,000 Jews whom he persuaded to join him. Promising the usual signs and portents, he had led them into the desert, where they were massacred by the troops of Catullus, governor of the Libyan Pentapolis. When caught, he accused the richest Jewish citizen in Cyrene of having given money to arm the rebels. The governor then forced him to accuse another 3,000 Jews in Libya, who had their property confiscated and were executed. After exhausting this source of plunder, Catullus aimed still higher, and ordered Jonathan to denounce well-known Jews in Alexandria and Rome, among them being Josephus. Hoping to convince Vespasian, the governor went to Rome, bringing Jonathan in chains. Brought before the emperor, the man insisted that Josephus had given him money and weapons. He did not deceive Vespasian, who had him burned alive—"the punishment he deserved," says Josephus. Catullus escaped with a rebuke but was not allowed to return to Cyrene.

Josephus records Catullus's last days with characteristic relish, telling us how the governor was struck down by a disgusting disease. He would dream that those whom he had murdered were standing by his bed, and then he would leap out of it as if he were on fire. In the end his bowels became riddled with ulcers and fell out, "providing unusually striking evidence that God in his providence visits the wicked with punishment."[6]

"Subsequently, many other false accusations were made against me by people who envied my good fortune, but by the providence of God, I survived them all safely," says Josephus.[7] By his own account, his private life suddenly became very happy. "At about this time I divorced my wife, dissatisfied by her behavior," he tells us in the *Vita*. "She had borne me three children, two of whom died although one called Hyrcanus is still alive. Afterwards I married a woman of Jewish extraction, who belonged to a family that had settled in Crete. Her parents were very distinguished, the most prominent people in the country. In character she infinitely surpassed the majority of her sex, as she would show throughout her subsequent life. By her I had two sons—Justus, the elder, and then Simonides, who is surnamed Agrippa."[8]

Shortly after 70 CE, Josephus wrote a history of the recent war in Judea. It was probably little more than a pamphlet written at Vespasian's bidding, but no copy has survived. As Josephus describes it in the preface of *The Jewish War*, it was written in Aramaic and was designed "to give an accurate account of the war and all the miseries that resulted from it, and how it ended, to Parthians, Babylonians and remote Arabians, to our Jewish kindred beyond the Euphrates and to the Assyrians."[9] His goal was to make these potentially troublesome compatriots realize how futile it would be for them to try and encourage any further rebellions in Judea.

Another purpose of the pamphlet was to reinforce the Parthians' fear of Rome. Their king, Vologaeses, remembered all too well the defeats that had been inflicted on his soldiers by the Roman legions during the 60s. Living in terror of a rival for his throne, he had cravenly offered 40,000 troops to Vespasian in 69 when he saw that he was winning, and he had been so impressed by Titus's capture of Jerusalem that he sent him a golden crown during his visit to Zeugma on the Euphrates. The Romans understood perfectly that these friendly gestures were inspired by fear and that the Parthians would not hesitate to attack them if they saw any chance of success.

A third purpose was to explain to the Jews of the Diaspora not only how the Temple itself had been destroyed but why: it was a judgment of God on the people of Jerusalem.[10] This was among Josephus's most fervently held convictions.

Apparently he had a Greek translation made and showed it to Vespasian, who liked what he read. It may have been the emperor and not Josephus who first realized that a book could be useful for his insecure dynasty; lacking the aristocratic background of their blue-blooded Julio-Claudian predecessors, the Flavians needed monuments to give them an air of permanence. This was the reason that the triumph had been so welcome, and why Vespasian had ostentatiously founded his new Temple of Peace. The reconquest of Judea featured prominently on their coins, that vital means of propaganda, and it would later be depicted on the Arch of Titus.

A full-scale chronicle of the war in Judea, written in Greek, with numerous copies made by professional scribes on papyrus rolls (the period's method of publication) could command a wide circulation in the Roman world and would demonstrate that throughout the campaign the Flavians had enjoyed the favor of the gods. The author was expected to make the most of his Jotapata prophecy of Vespasian's future greatness and to praise the heroic exploits of Titus. If no more than conjecture, this is certainly a plausible explanation of the origin of the book that we know as *The Jewish War*.

"There are people who by necessity and force of circumstance are obliged to write history because they took part in what happened and have no excuse for not putting it on paper for posterity's sake," he writes in the preface to his *Antiquities of the Jews*.[11] He adds, "Some people decide to explain little known events on which light needs to be shed, because the general public should be made aware of them on account of their importance, events in which the writers have been involved. These are my reasons [for writing]."[12]

He had his own notebooks, and Vespasian and Titus lent him their war diaries, and these may have been supplemented by the jottings of other soldiers. Yet apart from his booklet, he had no apparent qualifications for such a task, especially for writing in Greek. In the last chapter of the *Antiquities*, written years after *The Jewish War*, he tells us frankly, "I have worked hard to . . . understand the elements of the Greek language, but I am so used to speaking our own tongue that I cannot pronounce Greek properly."[13] Yet if he could not speak Greek with a perfect accent, we know that he wrote it very well indeed.

"In the leisure provided by Rome, with my sources at hand and the aid of assistants to help me with the Greek tongue, I settled down to writing my account of what had taken place," Josephus tells us in *Contra Apionem*, another work written long after *The Jewish War*.[14] This passage has convinced some scholars that he relied on secretaries to write his books for him, and some argue that it is obvious from the different prose styles he uses. However, the "assistant theory" has been demolished by Tessa Rajak, who points out that it was normal for an author to use different styles in a long book, in a period when authors often copied the prose of writers whom they admired.[15]

Clearly, Josephus thoroughly enjoyed writing history, and he may have seen himself as following in the footsteps of giants such as Thucydides and Livy. (It is unlikely that he read Livy in the original since the interminable volumes of the great chronicler of Rome were in Latin, although he may have acquired a superficial, outline knowledge of them from some Greek epitome.) This perhaps explains his desire to be as comprehensive as possible and why *The Jewish War*'s first two books, a third of the entire work, have nothing to do with the war but tell the story of Judea from the Maccabees up to the last rulers of the House of Herod.

His greatest problem, however, was to give an account of the recent conflict with Rome that would absolve the Jews of as much blame as possible. He does so by portraying the Zealot regime as a bloodthirsty jacquerie against the aristocracy, who were the only real Jews. If some of the magnates joined in the revolt, it was only because they were forced into it by Florus; they had always wanted peace. He conceals the fact that many of them had been only too willing to join the Zealots, whom he caricatures as brutish fanatics or godless criminals.

And Josephus has a deeper message: God deserted his Chosen People and used the Romans to destroy the Temple, just as God had used the Babylonians to destroy the first sanctuary. This is why the Jews must never fight the Romans again; they are bound to lose.

Loyal though Josephus may have been to Rome, he can never forget that he is writing about the ruin and humiliation of the country of his birth. Even if he hides it, he must have been deeply distressed at having to tell the story during the years that it took him to write *The Jewish War*. Then, while he was in the middle of his task, in 73 or 74, he heard reports of an incident that would provide an epilogue to restore Jewish pride. It was that of the Zealots' magnificent last stand at Masada.

23

Masada and the Last Zealots

"Our persecutors are swifter than the eagles of the heaven; they pursued us upon the mountains, they laid wait for us in the wilderness."

LAMENTATIONS OF JEREMIAH, IV, 19

F AR MORE PEOPLE HAVE heard of the siege of Masada than have ever heard of Josephus. It has inspired films, novels, and documentaries and attracted one of the most popular archaeological digs of the entire twentieth century. New books on Masada are published nearly every year. Yet we only know its story from *The Jewish War*. No monumental inscription mentions it, let alone any other contemporary historian, and archaeologists have failed to add substantially to our knowledge.

Although Jerusalem had fallen to the Romans, plenty of mopping up remained to be done since there were still three Zealot strongholds: Herodium, Machaerus, and Masada. Their garrisons supported themselves through "banditry," which probably meant rustling livestock and commandeering grain rather than highway robbery. Lucilius Bassus, once commander of the Roman fleet, took over as governor of Judea from Sextus Cerealis in 71 and made their destruction his immediate priority. Despite being heavily fortified and well supplied with water, the fortress of Herodium, which was seven miles south of Bethlehem in the hills facing

Arabia, seems to have surrendered to Bassus's troops fairly promptly, apparently in 71, but we have no details.[1]

Lucilius Bassus then led his army, which included the Tenth Legion with its wild boar eagle, to Machaerus, probably in 72. East of the Dead Sea in Perea, this was regarded as the most formidable stronghold in the whole kingdom of Judea after Jerusalem. (It was where John the Baptist had been beheaded.) It had been in Zealot hands since the start of the war, and its legendary invulnerability made it a rallying point for anyone who had managed to escape from the capital. Built on a huge rock of a hill, it was surrounded by ravines. Stretching as far as the Dead Sea, the ravine on the west side was seven miles long. Although those on the north and south sides were smaller, they presented almost as much of an obstacle. The ravine on the east side was not quite so daunting, although it was at least 150 feet deep.

Machaerus was one of King Herod's favorite refuges, and he had strengthened it with walls and bastions that enclosed an entire town. From the town, a steep path climbed up to a citadel on the summit of the great hill whose ramparts were buttressed at the corners by towers ninety feet high. Inside was a palace "of surpassing beauty." His builders had hacked large cisterns in the rock that stored an inexhaustible supply of rainwater, and Herod had stocked the arsenal with missiles and siege artillery that was still in working order seventy years after his death. But Herod never had to face Roman legionaries.

After examining the fortress, Bassus decided that his best plan would be to fill the smallest ravine on the east side and build an assault ramp on top. Knowing how skillful the legionaries were at siege craft, the Zealot garrison withdrew to the citadel, leaving the town below—crammed with refugees from miles around—to fend off the first attacks. Should the Romans show signs of gaining the upper hand, they intended to use the citadel as a bargaining counter with which to buy their lives. Meanwhile they launched sorties to stop the ravine from being filled, killing large numbers of the enemy as they brought faggots and sacks of earth. Before it could be completed, an accident ended the siege.

Among the bravest of the Zealots was a handsome and much-liked young man named Eleazar, who constantly distinguished himself by his daring during the sorties. He so often emerged unscathed that he grew careless. After one of these engagements he was standing outside the gates, chatting with friends on the ramparts, when a legionary named Rufus, an Egyptian, stole up behind him. Seizing Eleazar around the waist, despite his armor, Rufus succeeded in dragging him all the way back to the Roman lines. Bassus promptly had him stripped, tied to a stake in front of the walls, and scourged. Seeing the defenders' horror, the general ordered a cross to be set up, as if intending to crucify him. Eleazar, who was not as tough as might have been expected, never stopped shrieking. His harrowing screams upset the garrison so much that they sent envoys to the Romans, offering to evacuate the fortress if they were allowed to leave in safety with him. Bassus accepted the conditions.

When they heard of the surrender, the townsmen—guessing they had been left out of the bargain—made up their minds to escape during the night, but as soon as the gates were opened, the garrison told Bassus of the plan to avoid any suspicion of treachery. The general turned his troops loose on the unfortunate townsmen, and only the most determined managed to cut their way out; 1,700 were slaughtered, and the women and children were enslaved. Bassus nonetheless honored his agreement with the garrison, whom he allowed to depart with Eleazar.

However, Bassus immediately followed the garrison at full speed to a wood known as the Forest of Jardes (whose site is unknown but which was somewhere in the Jordan Valley), where its members had taken refuge, joining some survivors from the capital. Together, the Zealots in the wood numbered about 3,000 men, their leader being Judas ben Ari, a former commander of a company of soldiers at Jerusalem during the siege and one of the very few who had succeeded in escaping through the underground passages. Bassus surrounded the forest with his cavalry to prevent anyone from escaping, while his legionaries began to methodically chop down the trees that provided their quarry with cover. When the Jews realized what was happening, they made a desperate effort to break out, but were all killed, including Judas, while Roman casualties amounted to only twelve dead with a few wounded.[2]

Lucilius Bassus died, apparently in the winter of 72 or early 73, so the Romans did not recommence their mopping-up operations until 74. When spring came that year and the campaigning season opened, Bassus's newly appointed successor, Lucius Flavius Silva, assembled all units available in Judea, about 10,000 men, and marched to Masada in the extreme south of the province, west of the Dead Sea. A fortress thought to be no less "impregnable" than Machaerus had been—Josephus considered it even stronger—this was garrisoned by 600 Zealots, whom, as so often, *The Jewish War* pejoratively calls *sicarii*, knifemen. Unlike the fainthearted defenders of Machaerus, they possessed an unusually gallant and charismatic commander in Eleazar ben Yair, who was a descendant and possibly a grandson of Judas the Galilean, founder of the Zealots.

Like Machaerus, Masada was another natural citadel that had been a favorite stronghold of the paranoiac King Herod. He had regarded it as the most secure of all his refuges, in case his subjects revolted or he should be attacked by Cleopatra, who coveted Judea and urged Mark Antony to destroy him. The king had lavished time and money on improving its fortifications, equipping it with an unusually large arsenal.

Like Machaerus, too, its greatest strength lay in its natural defenses. It was built on top of a great honey-colored rock whose sides seemed almost vertical. "Surrounded by ravines so deep that the eye cannot see down to the bottom of them, so steep as to be unclimbable by any living creature, there are only two paths by which it can be reached and then only with difficulty," says Josephus. "You have to go up to the fortress step by step, taking care where you put your feet. Death is always very near, since the chasms on each side are so vast that they terrify the toughest spirits. After climbing more than three miles, you finally reach the top and find not a summit but an open plain."[3] Herod had fortified the entire summit, which measured three-quarters of a mile in circumference, with a white limestone wall that was eighteen feet tall and twelve feet broad. This was buttressed by thirty-seven stone towers that were each seventy-five feet high. As at Machaerus, there were not only a beautiful palace and a synagogue inside the wall but fields where food could be grown and pasture for cattle and sheep.

When Eleazar had seized the fortress, he had discovered that its cellars held huge quantities of grain, pulses, dried fruit, wine, and oil that were in good condition, despite having been stored for a century, and which provided enough food to feed his men for many years. Enormous cisterns cut into the rock supplied water. The arsenal was packed with weapons of every type, and they had remained free from rust and were still usable.

(Josephus attributes the surprising preservation of the foodstuffs and weapons to the mountain air near the Dead Sea.)

Arriving early in March 73, Silva ordered the legionaries to build his headquarters camp on the inhospitable rocks to the northwest that joined the hill on which Masada stood to the nearby mountains. There was no convenient spring in so bleak and stony a landscape, so he had water and food brought from miles away by teams of Jewish prisoners. His next step was to order the building of a wall around the hill so that none of the defenders could escape. Stretching for two miles, it was the usual *circumvallatio*, complete with towers. The main bastion was a large camp to the southeast, supported by six small camps. There were also four small forts that blocked a pass through mountains to the north. Then he quickly identified the single natural feature that provided a chance of getting at his enemy.

The obvious approach was the only road up, the well-named "snake path" on the east side, a narrow track that, besides being alarmingly steep, twisted and turned every few yards. Not only was it guarded by a tower, but boulders had been heaped at each bend of the path to roll down onto enemies. Instead, Silva selected the "Leuce" or "White Cliff" on the west side, a large flat rock or ledge that jutted straight out from the hillside to within 450 feet of the summit, and sent troops to seize it.

The Romans then embarked on the Herculean task of building a ramp of packed earth on the White Cliff that would reach all the way up to the level of the fortress. With their usual amazing teamwork, the legionaries raised, in a short space of time, a mound well over 300 feet high, on top of which they erected a platform of timber and stones packed with earth that was 75 feet tall and as broad across. From this platform, iron-plated wooden siege towers, the biggest of which was 90 feet tall, were able to operate. Scorpions and onagers fired at the enemy so effectively from them that the defenders could not man the ramparts or use the vast supplies of javelins in their arsenal. Meanwhile, a ram battered the wall ceaselessly. Although it took longer than expected, eventually the masonry collapsed and opened a large breach.

The Zealots were ready, having built another wall inside that consisted of a framework of large beams of timber packed with earth. The ram could make no impression on this ingenious structure, since every blow only packed the earth more tightly. However, the resourceful Silva solved the problem by ordering his men to throw lighted torches at it. Although there was a dangerous moment when a breeze blew the flames back into the besiegers' faces, the wind changed, and the wooden beams caught fire, destroying the new wall. The Romans prepared to launch their final assault on the following day.

Eleazar ben Yair had no illusions about the situation, realizing that there was no possible means of escape. Assembling his comrades, he told them his solution, although, for reasons that will become apparent, what he actually said has not survived. However, Josephus's reconstruction is extremely convincing, since it reflects all the ideals of the Zealots. The speech is too long to give in its entirety, but here is a summary.

"We made up our minds long ago that we would never serve the Romans or anyone else other than God," he told them. "We were the first [Jews] to revolt and we are the last still fighting them, which is a blessing since it means we can still die honorably." Perhaps they should have guessed long ago that God had doomed the Jewish nation to destruction, and perhaps they were being punished for mistreating their countrymen, he continued. But by killing themselves and their families they would die less cruelly than if the Romans killed them, and their wives would escape dishonor and their children would never know what it meant to be a slave. "First we must burn our property and the fortress as it will disappoint the Romans to lose our bodies and our goods. Leave the food, since it shows we did not kill ourselves from hunger, but, as we swore at the start, prefer death to slavery."[4]

To Eleazar's chagrin, the majority of the garrison were reluctant to end their lives so abruptly, and many broke down and wept. He then delivered a magnificent second speech. Josephus's reconstruction contains an eloquent expression of Zealot philosophy, and he explains how they had seen the war with Rome. It is also a belated tribute from the author of *The Jewish War*, since it contradicts all that he had previously written about them. The speech is worth quoting at greater length than the first, even if there is not sufficient space to provide it in full.

"I made a very bad mistake in thinking that I was helping brave men who fight for freedom, men determined to live with honor or die," Eleazar began contemptuously. "It looks as if you are no better than anybody else in your courage or fortitude. You're even frightened of a death that could save you from the most ghastly suffering, at a moment when there is no time left for delay or seeking advice." Then he launched into a panegyric in praise of suicide:

> Life, not death, is man's real misfortune. For death gives freedom to our souls and lets them return to their own pure and natural home, where they will be immune from every calamity. So long as they are imprisoned in a mortal body and have to suffer its miseries, then they are in fact dead, because the mortal has nothing in common with the divine. No doubt, the soul may achieve a good deal even when confined inside a body, since it can use it as an instrument, moving it invisibly and enabling it to do things beyond the capacity of any mortal nature. However, only when freed from the weight that pulls it down to earth and allowed to go back to its rightful setting can the soul regain all its divinely bestowed energy and unhampered powers, becoming no less invisible to human eyes than God himself. It cannot be detected when in the body, entering it unseen and leaving unseen, its nature incorruptible, though causing the body to change. For whatever the soul touches is going to live and flourish, and whatever it abandons will wither away and die, because of its overwhelmingly immortal energy.
>
> Sleep is surely the best proof of what I am saying to you, the deep sleep during which the soul is undistracted by the body and, unfettered, enjoys its sweetest rest, when, once again in contact with God because of its close kinship with him, it travels through the universe and foresees many of the things that will happen in future times. So why then should we be frightened of death, when we are so fond of sleep? And how can it be anything else than misguided for us to hope for freedom in our lives while we are denying ourselves the freedom of eternity?

"We die by the will of God," he told his men. "It seems that long ago God must have passed a decree against the entire Jewish race—that we would have to leave this life if we didn't live it properly," he explained. "So don't blame yourselves or give the Romans any credit." Something infinitely more powerful than any human agency was responsible for the

Zealots' defeat. Why had the Jews of Caesarea been slaughtered on the Sabbath when they had not even thought of rebelling against Rome? Why had 18,000 Jews been butchered at Scythopolis despite being ready to fight against the Zealots? Why had every city in Syria murdered its Jewish population, even though it consisted of Jews loyal to Rome? Why had over 60,000 Jews been tortured to death in Egypt?

> Our weapons and ramparts, our supposedly impregnable fortresses, and our love of freedom that could never be cowed by any threat, encouraged us to rise in revolt. But this helped us for only a short time, raising our hopes before turning into a total disaster. We have all been defeated and have all fallen into the hands of the enemy, as if we had been meant to do no more than adorn their victory instead of saving the lives of our people. We must think of those of us who fell in battle as the really lucky ones, since at least they died defending liberty and they did not betray it. But who can fail to pity all the others now under the Roman heel? Who would not prefer to die rather than share their fate? Some have been broken on the rack, some have been burned or scourged to death. Some have been half-eaten by wild beasts and then kept alive to be fed to them for a second time, amid the jeers and laughter of their gloating enemies. The most wretched, however, are those who are still alive and pray for death, but who are never granted it.

Eleazar went on to mourn for the destruction of Jerusalem, mother city of the Jewish nation. "What has become of that city of ours in which it was believed that God himself dwelt?" It would have been better had they all died before seeing her overthrown and witnessing the profanation and destruction of the Temple. He and his comrades at Masada had hoped to avenge her, but now that hope had gone, they should at least die with honor.

Finally, he warned what they could expect if they surrendered to the Romans. "Ghastly will be the fate of young men who fall into their hands, whose sturdy bodies can stay alive for hours under prolonged torture, no less ghastly will be that of old men whose weaker physique will break sooner," he ended. "A husband will see his wife dragged away to be raped and will hear his child screaming for a father whose hands are bound."

But our hands are still unbound and they still hold swords. While they remain like this, give them the chance of doing good service. Let us die unenslaved by our enemies and leave this life with our wives and children, free men to the last. This is what our Law commands, this is what our families deserve. God has ordained we should do it, while the Romans want the exact opposite and for none of us to die before being captured. Hurry, then, so that instead of having the pleasure of taking us prisoner they will be astonished at our deaths and awed by our courage.[5]

He was unable to finish his speech, as his listeners rushed into the palace that they seem to have used as a barracks (although it appears that some lived in turrets on the walls). After embracing their families, they killed them, before piling up and setting fire to their possessions. Then, having chosen, by lot, ten comrades to put the rest to death, they lay down with their arms around the bodies of their wives and children and held up their throats. When the ten had completed their work, they drew lots with each other until only a single Zealot remained. After inspecting all the bodies to make sure that no one else was left alive, he set light to the palace and then drove his sword through his heart, falling dead beside his family. Nine hundred and sixty people, including women and children, died in the defenders' suicide pact, which took place on 15 April.[6]

The garrison had died in the belief that there were no survivors. However, a woman who was a relation of Eleazar and "superior to most females in intelligence and education," managed to escape the bloodbath, together with an old crone and five children. They did so by hiding in a cistern.[7]

The next morning, the Romans finally stormed into Masada through the breach, over plank bridges that they pushed across from the siege ramps. Inside the fortress, there was no sight or sound of anybody, while they could see flames rising from the palace. The silence everywhere was uncanny. Eventually, the bewildered legionaries gave a great shout, the sort of joint war cry they yelled after discharging a particularly large missile. On hearing it, the two women crept out of the cistern and explained what had happened. At first, they did not believe them, but at last they managed to extinguish some of the flames and enter the palace. When they found the dead bodies lying in neat rows, instead of crowing at the sight of so many defeated enemies, the Romans were awestruck.[8]

Fiercely proud of his Jewishness, Josephus finally came down on the side of the Zealots. No doubt, Eleazar's noble speeches, as they appear in *The Jewish War*, can only be inspired guesswork and owe a good deal to Greek literature. Eleazar's cousin, who survived to tell the tale, could not possibly have given a word-for-word account. The legionaries would only have jotted down a summary of what she told them, and it is very unlikely that Josephus ever spoke to her. He may have obtained information from Flavius Silva's war diary or from other Roman officers who had been present at the siege, but most of his account is the product of his own fertile imagination. Yet the speeches he puts into Eleazar's mouth are remarkably convincing and probably very near the truth.

What is so strange about Josephus's description of what took place at Masada is that he starts off with an impassioned denunciation of Zealots and *sicarii*, using phrases such as "barbarous towards their allies," "no work of perdition untried," or "wild and brutish disposition," and then portrays them as heroes. Similarly, his glowing eulogy of their mass suicide is in odd contrast to the disapproval of an easy way out that he had so eloquently expressed in the cave at Jotapata. The only possible explanation for these contradictions must be that as he learned more about what had happened, his latent patriotism was aroused by the defenders' unshakable integrity.

The historical importance of Masada rests on more than defenders' heroism or the legionaries' spectacular engineering. Eleazar's speeches give us an insight into the spirit that inspired the Zealots. Fortunately, Josephus was so moved that he tries to tell us what went on in their minds instead of dismissing them as just another band of knifemen in his customary, biased fashion. What is surprising is that their "Fourth Philosophy" had an unmistakably Platonic tinge. At the same time, they seem to have had some sort of link with the Essenes; archaeologists have found on the site a fragmented copy of the Book of Ecclesiasticus, which also occurs among the Dead Sea Scrolls.

In addition, the second of Eleazar's speeches gives us a glimpse of Josephus's true feelings about the war with Rome, something that he normally conceals in his books. It reveals his anguish at his country's destruction and the suffering of his fellow Jews.

A handful of Zealots remained after the fall of Masada, although not in Judea. A group 600 strong escaped to Alexandria where they tried to persuade the Diaspora to take revenge on the Romans, murdering people who disagreed. But after the Alexandrian elders warned the Egyptian Jews that these men would bring disaster on them, they were handed over to the authorities. They astonished everyone by the way they endured branding irons and flames rather than call the emperor "lord." Despite describing their presence as a "contagion," Josephus again hints at his divided loyalties when he comments that their commitment came from "desperation or strength of mind, call it what you will."[9] What struck spectators most was the behavior of Zealot children under torture; despite their puny little bodies, they were no less resolute than their parents.

Lupus, in charge of the administration at Alexandria, reported to Rome that he was having trouble with Jewish fanatics. Apprehensive about a possible Zealot revival and determined to eliminate any conceivable rallying point, Vespasian ordered him to destroy the Temple of Onias at Leontopolis. In the delta, near Memphis, this had been built three hundred and fifty years earlier by the high priest Onias, an exile from Jerusalem, who had hoped to erect a rival to the Sanctuary in Jerusalem. Although according to the description given by *The Jewish War*, it was much less impressive, it was served by priests who daily offered the sacrifices. Lupus closed the temple down at once, and in August 73 his successor, Paulinus, removed the furnishings and forbade its priests to go near it.[10]

Further indignities were inflicted on the Jews who survived in Judea. A huge amount of land was confiscated, which became the emperor's personal property or was put up for sale. There were, of course, a few exceptions from the general misery. Some of the old ruling class who had fled from Jerusalem were resettled, so that Judea's eleven administrative districts were once again controlled by its members, as Vespasian had always planned. The Sanhedrin reemerged, although as a council of learned men rather than magnates. Yohanan ben Zakkai's school at Jamnia flourished anew, so much so that it took the first steps toward a written codification of Jewish law.

On the whole, however, it was a time of unrelieved humiliation. The office of high priest was abolished, while, still more hurtful, the Temple tribute became a tax on all Jews, the *fiscus judaeicus*, which went toward the upkeep of the pagan temple of Jupiter Capitolinus at Rome. For years there was no resistance. Too many of the population had been killed or reduced to slavery.

Throughout the empire, Jews were taxed unmercifully, a vicious, long lasting legacy of the war in Judea. There was a relaxation under Nerva in the late 90s, but the crippling taxes were soon reintroduced. Driven beyond endurance, Jews of the Diaspora in Egypt, Cyrene, and Cyprus rose in desperation in 115, killing large numbers of their oppressors, though we do not know their precise objective. Whatever it was, within two years they had been put down with merciless savagery. The revolt did not involve Judea.

Yet nothing could destroy the spirit of the Jews so long as they stayed in their God-given homeland. Like Josephus, they expected that the Temple would be rebuilt, and Rabban Yohanan ben Zakkai prophesied the coming of a "King Hezekiah." Regardless of Josephus's warning that God was no longer on their side, they again challenged fate. The conflict is said to have been caused by the Emperor Hadrian's decision in 130 to build a new, pagan city on the ruins of Jerusalem, with a temple of Jupiter on the site of the Sanctuary. It was to be called Aelia Capitolina, Aelia being the emperor's family name. This was an intolerable provocation for the Jews, since it meant that a Third Temple could not arise. However, a late Roman source (Spartianus) gives a different explanation for the revolt, citing an edict of Hadrian that banned circumcision.

The Jews' leader was Simeon bar Kosiba (called Kokhba, "Son of the Star," in rabbinic accounts), who may well have been a descendant of Judas the Galilean. He was supported by one of the greatest scholars of the day, Rabbi Akiva ben Joseph, which shows the depth of his appeal. In 132, after a carefully planned campaign, he and his followers drove the Romans out of southern Judea, occupying Jerusalem and establishing a new Israel. Instead of relying on strongholds such as Masada, they used a network of tunnels for surprise attacks and beat off several Roman armies. For three years Simeon ruled as *Nasi* (Prince), at first governing with his uncle, Eleazar the Priest, but then having him put to death on a mistaken suspicion of treachery. Like the Zealots, Bar Kokhba hoped for help from the Parthians, which this time really looked as if it would come—until Parthia was unexpectedly invaded by barbarians.

Inevitably, Simeon was defeated and killed in 135, when Hadrian's legionaries stormed his last fortress at Bether in the mountains between Jerusalem and the sea, massacring its defenders. His supporters were ruthlessly hunted down and butchered, including Rabbi Akiva. Those few Jews who had not been exterminated were expelled from Judea, and the pagan city of Aelia Capitolina was finally built upon the ruins of Jerusalem.

24

A Roman Citizen

"So anxious was the Emperor Titus that my volumes should be the sole authority from which the world should be made aware of the facts that he put his own signature on them and gave orders for their publication."

JOSEPHUS, VITA, 361

WE POSSESS VERY LITTLE information about Josephus's later life, apart from the sparse details that he gives about himself in the *Vita* and the occasional reference to a friend or a patron—he does not seem to have had many—and to his enemies. However, he tells us that he lived in Rome for several decades, in reasonable prosperity. He boasts of favors from all three Flavian emperors and never complains of poverty. Indeed, he was sufficiently well off to own an expensive, highly educated slave as a tutor for his son. Clearly, he spent much of his time reading history and writing it.

According to Eusebius, he was so much admired that a statue of him was erected in Rome, and his books were placed in all the public libraries. (If there was a statue of him in Eusebius's time, it must have been set up later, by Christians, who argued that his account of the destruction of Jerusalem confirmed the prophecies of Jesus of Nazareth.[1]) In *The Jewish War* he claims to be one of the best-known Jews in Rome, but there is no evidence to support this, although one modern historian calls him "an important person in Roman society."[2]

In contrast, it has been convincingly suggested that he led a lonely, isolated life while he was working on his books, with no friends among the ruling class, not even among the officers whom he had met on the Judean campaign. Because of the war, the Romans' former amused tolerance of Jews had been replaced by a deep dislike, of the sort so harshly expressed by Tacitus.[3] Nor can the Diaspora have felt much affection for a turncoat who chronicled their nation's tragedy with such apparent enthusiasm and blackened the reputation of the Zealots.[4]

It may be that Josephus devoted his entire time to literature and never left Rome, yet this is improbable, given his energetic, enterprising personality. A plausible case can be made for his traveling extensively, on some sort of political business.[5] In addition, it seems unlikely that he did not return to Judea to inspect his estates and see relatives, and he could well have taken the opportunity to visit the distinguished new rabbinical community at Jamna (Yavneh). It also looks as if he met his final wife while visiting Crete. Admittedly, all this is based on conjecture.

He was to write several other books, and his literary output appears to indicate that living in Rome gave him a sense of purpose. It can be argued that one of the principal reasons why he wrote his later works was to show his highly sophisticated Roman readership that he and his fellow Jewish landowners—those few who survived—were just as much patricians as any of the aristocrats from the other countries in the eastern Roman Empire. Even if his books praised Rome and earned him a respected place in Greek literature and a reputation as a faithful servant of Caesar, he never ceased to be a Jew, proud of his nation and his faith.

We do not know when he finished the seven books of *The Jewish War*, although it is clear that the bulk of the manuscript was ready before Vespasian's death. "So confident was I about what I had written that I was bold enough to cite as witnesses for its accuracy the two commanders-in-chief during the war, Vespasian and Titus," he tells us in the *Contra Apionem*. "They were the first people to whom I presented my volumes, copies being later given to Romans who had served on the campaign, while I sold others to some of my fellow countrymen who appreciated

Greek literature."[6] Among these Jewish readers were "the most admirable King Agrippa" and his brother-in-law Julius Archelaus, who had married Agrippa's sister Mariamne. But it looks as if he submitted the book for imperial approval shortly before Vespasian died, since it was authorized by his successor. "So eager was Emperor Titus that my volumes should be the source from which the world learned the facts, that he affixed his signature to them and gave orders for their publication," he states in the *Vita*, indicating a date of 79 or 80 CE.[7]

"King Agrippa wrote sixty-two letters confirming the truth of my account," he adds somewhat defensively, quoting from two of them. The first reads, "King Agrippa to dearest Josephus, greeting. I have read your book with great pleasure. You seem to me have written with more care and accuracy than anyone else who has dealt with the subject. Send me the other volumes." The second says, "From what you have written, you appear to be in no need of further information to explain how it all happened, and from the start. But when we next meet, I shall tell you a lot that is not generally known."[8]

For a time, relations with King Agrippa were soured by the favor the king showed to a bitter enemy from Josephus's days as governor of Galilee, whom Agrippa appointed as his private secretary. This was Justus of Tiberias, who during the Judean campaign had escaped execution as a rebel only because of Queen Berenice's mediation. He was an odd choice as secretary as he had been in trouble with the king for forgery, even being condemned to death and then pardoned for a second time at Berenice's request. However, soon after his appointment Agrippa again sacked him for forgery, this time for good.

During late 78 or early 79, Josephus was reminded that Rome could be very unsafe, when he heard how a plot against his patron, Titus, had been crushed just in time. The conspirators were Caecina Alienus and Eprius Marcellus, two highly influential senators who were close friends of the late Mucianus. Since by now Vespasian was growing old and showing signs of ill health, the pair—together with a group of senior officers—decided to ensure that Titus would never succeed him, although we do not know the name of their candidate for the throne.

An impressive-looking man in early middle age, Caecina seems have enjoyed wide popularity, despite a long history of embezzlement and treachery. Quietly, he armed his supporters in readiness for a coup. At the very last moment the plot was revealed by an informant who gave Titus a copy of a speech that Caecina was on the verge of delivering to the soldiers, written in his own hand. Titus reacted by inviting Caecina to dinner and then having him stabbed as he left the dining room. Marcellus was arrested shortly afterward, cutting his throat in despair when brought before the Senate for questioning.

A reference to Caecina in *The Jewish War* is so outspoken as to indicate that Caecina must have been dead by the time it was written, which helps in trying to date the book's completion. Describing Caecina's betrayal of Vitellius during the civil war, the author says, "the scandal of his treachery was obscured by the unmerited honors that he received from Vespasian."[9] Had Caecina still been alive, Josephus would never have dared to write about so powerful a senator in such a way. The passage was calculated to please Titus, who must have been fairly sensitive about the subject of Caecina. Despite Caecina's attempted coup, his brutal assassination had shocked all Rome, and in retrospect even Suetonius expressed disapproval.[10]

From Josephus's point of view, the failed plot had one reassuring consequence: Queen Berenice was forced to leave Rome. The patron of Justus had come back during the late seventies and was living with Titus in his palace as if she were his wife, although she was at least ten years older. A single source claims that this inexhaustible lady had been sleeping with Caecina as well and cites this as the true reason why she was forced to leave the city, although the claim is not supported by any other authority. But it really does look as if Titus sent her away after Caecina's plot, perhaps because his romance with her was adding to his unpopularity.[11]

On 24 June 79, Vespasian died at sixty-nine, apparently from malaria. On his deathbed, he made a last joke. Referring to his imminent deification, he muttered, "How depressing! I think I'm turning into a god."[12] Despite Titus's amiable manners and outstanding record as a soldier, the citizens of Rome were suspicious of him, and there was a certain amount of hostility toward his succession. Executing Caecina and driving Marcellus to suicide were seen as the behavior of a tyrant rather than as self-defense. Many Romans were convinced that he was both cruel and debauched, and they were particularly upset by his affair with Queen Berenice. "People not only thought privately but said openly that he was going to be a second Nero," records Suetonius.[13]

Yet the Romans received a pleasant surprise, as Titus turned out to be genuinely benevolent. Far from indulging a Neronian taste for debauchery, he dismissed his troop of catamites and sent Berenice home—in Suetonius's famous phrase, *invitus invitam* ("he reluctant, she reluctant")—after she had tried to return to Rome, hoping to marry him. As for Josephus, "The way I was treated by the Emperors remained unchanged," he tells us in the *Vita*. "When Vespasian died, Titus, who succeeded to the empire, showed me the same consideration that his father had done, never believing any of the accusations that were always being made against me." It sounds as if he had plenty of enemies in Rome.[14] Unfortunately, Titus died of a fever after a reign of only two years.

The new emperor was Titus's younger brother, Domitian, whose good looks and quiet, shortsighted appearance concealed a brutal arrogance. He was unpredictable and treacherous, a truly horrible man who delighted in cruelty. At first, his subjects did not know what to make of him, as he liked to spend several hours a day alone—spearing flies with a needle. Even if Josephus writes that Domitian "showed the same esteem for me as his father," he must have lived in terror of him like everybody else in Rome.[15] Instead of providing the tranquil setting for a serene retirement, the city grew increasingly dangerous as the emperor developed into a tyrant.

Josephus did his best to flatter him in the seventh book of *The Jewish War*, which was probably altered during the new reign. Seemingly breathless with admiration, Josephus tells of a campaign waged by Domitian against the Gauls and Germans in 70, when Vespasian was not yet installed at Rome. "Endowed by nature with his father's heroism, possessing experience beyond his years, he at once advanced on the barbarians whose courage failed when they heard that he was coming and surrendered in terror," writes Josephus. The young man had gone home "covered in glory and praised by all for an achievement that was extraordinary for his age and worthy of his father."[16]

Writing after Domitian was safely dead, Suetonius has a rather different story. "To put himself on a level with his father and brother, he went off on an entirely unnecessary campaign in Gaul and Germany, despite his father's friends having tried to stop him." According to Suetonius,

Vespasian rebuked his son, who was made to live at the palace to keep him out of mischief.[17]

In the same book of *The Jewish War*, Josephus describes how Domitian made "a glorious appearance" when he accompanied his father and brother during their triumph, "riding beside them sumptuously appareled." All too clearly, this is an attempt to imply that he was sharing in it and must therefore have made an important contribution to their victory, which we know to be nonsense.[18]

Although Josephus can be accused of sycophancy, it is only fair to remember that historians dared not take chances in Domitian's Rome. Even omissions could lead to ruin. The emperor "put to death . . . Hermogenes of Tarsus because of [unspecified] allusion in his History, and went so far as to crucify the slaves who wrote it down," Suetonius informs us.[19] Where Domitian was concerned, it was dangerous not only to tell the truth but to refrain from fulsome compliments. This was especially the case with Josephus, who had so many enemies and whose survival had depended on imperial protection. Although there was an attempted rebellion by Antonius Saturninus in 89, it was discovered and crushed. By the time he was assassinated in 96, Domitian had become "an object of terror and hatred," according to Suetonius.[20] Looking back from the next century, Tacitus expressed his relief at writing in a time when he could tell the truth without fear.

Yet it was during Domitian's reign that Josephus added his description of the siege of Masada, in the seventh book, which completed *The Jewish War*. Vespasian and Titus, who might have objected to so much praise of Zealot heroism, were dead, whereas Domitian had not been involved in the Judean war. We also know from Suetonius that on the whole Domitian took very little interest in history; some exceptionally ill-natured person must have brought the tactless works of poor Hermogenes to his attention.

According to Josephus, Domitian was surprisingly kind to him. "He punished my Jewish accusers, and for a similar offence gave orders for the chastisement of a slave [who was] a eunuch and my son's tutor. He also exempted my property in Judea from taxation, a mark of high honor."[21] Why Josephus regarded this as so flattering is explained by Suetonius, who says that normally the emperor took pains to ensure that taxes were levied on Jews or people who lived as Jews without acknowledging their faith; Suetonius saw a man of ninety stripped and examined in court for evidence of circumcision.

What makes the way that Josephus prospered during Domitian's reign so unexpected is the hostile climate toward Jews that sprang up in Flavian Rome. The war had confirmed the Romans' instinctive distrust of monotheism and strengthened their antagonism toward Hebrews as interlopers from the East. Most of the Diaspora had a miserable time, living in fear of persecution and pogroms. We know of no rich or influential Jews in the city at this date. Even "god-fearers" who had not converted to Judaism were in danger. The emperor put to death his cousin Flavius Clemens, the consul and father of his intended heirs, for "godlessness" and banished Clemens's wife, Flavia Domitilla, who was also a relative, on the same charge. (Dio Cassius explains that "godlessness" meant "drifting into Jewish ways."[22]) The war had never been forgotten, and as late as the year 85, coins were still being struck with the legend *Iudaea capta*. Could Josephus have done the emperor some special service, perhaps as a diplomat or a spy?

Josephus also tells us in the *Vita* that "Domitia, Caesar's wife, never stopped conferring favors on me."[23] One would like to know more about these "favors" from an empress who, if not quite such a byword as Poppaea, enjoyed an unsavory reputation. Once Titus's mistress, she started sleeping with him again when he became emperor, according to rumors, but she later insisted on oath that it was untrue—"although she would never have denied it had there been the slightest bit of truth in the story, and would certainly have boasted of it, as she always did about all her scandalous behavior," comments Suetonius.[24] Furthermore, Domitia seems to have been involved in the plot to murder her husband.

To receive so many favors, Josephus must have attended court fairly often, in however modest a capacity. Its atmosphere cannot have been much different from that of Nero's court, dominated by money and sex. (Domitian was particularly fond of what he termed "bed-wrestling.") The place was packed with millionaires and bankrupt adventurers, with office-hunters and swindlers, with actors and prostitutes—male and female. Over all loomed the baleful shadow of the emperor, increasingly unbalanced, proclaiming himself to be a god while still alive and turning into a bloodthirsty paranoiac.

His growing bloodlust expressed itself in the invention of new types of gladiatorial combat. Some of the imperial games were staged at night, with the arena lit by torches, while there were mass battles between dwarves on one side and women on the other, all of whom were made to kill each other. During the last three years of his reign, nobody of any importance in Rome felt safe, since he was ordering executions every day. Josephus must have needed strong nerves to dance attendance on such a man.

It was surely a relief to retreat from court politics into ancient history. He found a new patron, who seems to have been a friend for a long time. "Epaphroditus, a man who loves all kinds of knowledge, and enjoys learning about history because he himself was involved in great affairs of state and saw many changes of fortune," is how he describes him in the preface to the *Antiquities of the Jews*. "Throughout [his life] he has shown the rare strength that comes from a noble nature combined with rock-like courage and principle."[25]

Unfortunately, it is not possible to identify Epaphroditus with any certainty. It used to be thought that he was Nero's former private secretary, the freedman who had helped him cut his throat and whom Domitian put to death for the lèse-majesté of having connived at an emperor's suicide. The most likely candidate, however, is another elderly freedman of the same name, an Alexandrian who had settled in Rome during Nero's time. Described as "big and dark like an elephant," Marcus Mettius Epaphroditus was a bibliophile, with a library of 30,000 volumes, who liked to pose as an expert on Homer and other Greek poets. Given his name, he does not seem to have been a Jew, although clearly he was intrigued by Judaism. Perhaps he gave Josephus the run of his library.

Josephus informs us in the preface that Epaphroditus has persuaded him to write the *Jewish Antiquities* (more correctly called *The Jewish Archaeology*). This is the history of his nation, which starts with the creation and closes with the misdeeds of the Procurator Florus. In eleven out of its twenty books he retells and reinterprets the Bible, ingeniously discovering scriptural predictions that Rome will rule the world and that the Jews should submit to their government; whenever possible, he tries to find agreement between Roman and Jewish values. To strengthen his argument, he adds a good deal of new material, while he makes odd omissions, such as the story of the Golden Calf, perhaps because it does not reflect flatteringly on his nation. The book contains some weirdly arcane information; for example, that the fallen angels, who were expelled from heaven with Lucifer, married women and begot terrifyingly evil sons, half angelic and half human, who persecuted Noah but were destroyed by the Flood.[26] Building bridges with his Roman readership, in the second half he reassures them by drawing to some extent on Greek authors with whom they were familiar, such as Polybius or Strabo. His account of what pagans saw as a mysterious people with an uncanny religion must have fascinated many who had never encountered the Jewish scriptures.

Interestingly, in the *Jewish Antiquities* he speaks of the Pharisees much more favorably than he does in *The Jewish War*. "They live according to what reason dictates," he tells us. "Believing everything is due to fate, they do not take away men's freedom from acting as they choose, since according to their view God prefers to create temperament as an instrument of fate, leaving a man free to act virtuously or viciously."[27] He also says that "Sadducees are listened to only by the rich and the people do not respect them, while the Pharisees have the ear of the multitude."[28] By now he writes as someone who is following the Pharisee way.

He knew that he had written a wonderful book, and he displays the same sort of vanity that is so evident in *The Jewish War*. "Nobody else, Jew or Gentile, would have been capable, however much they might have wanted, of producing quite so accurate an account as mine," he boasts at the end of the *Jewish Antiquities*. "My fellow countrymen freely admit that I excel them all in Jewish learning."

Then, out of the blue, he was attacked by Justus of Tiberias in a "chronicle" that has not survived. It described *The Jewish War* as a tissue of lies, making grave charges about the author's behavior during the campaign. He was accused of being one of the architects of the Jewish war, of forcing Galilean cities to rise against Rome, of looting on a massive scale and even of rape. Justus wrote so eloquently that Josephus found himself in serious danger. He was saved only by Domitian's protection. But while the emperor defused the authorities' suspicions, the accusations continued to fuel hostility toward him among the Jewish community, who may never have forgiven him for caricaturing the Zealots.

What made Justus so dangerous was that he was a Galilean who, like Josephus, had at first supported the war for independence but had then gone over to Rome. Since he had been personally involved, he was exceptionally well informed about what had happened in his native province in 66–67 and was able to demonstrate that, to some extent at least, the account given in *The Jewish War* was a distortion. He also wrote Greek fluently. His attack was the reason why Josephus wrote the *Vita*, most of which is an angry polemic against Justus, whom he charges with being a rabble-rouser during the war, of attempting to take over all Galilee, and of persuading Tiberias to rise against King Agrippa. He tries to convince readers that Justus was a criminal liar, who would never have dared to publish his book were Vespasian or Titus still alive because they knew what really took place. It is clear from Josephus's shrill tone that Justus thoroughly frightened him.

Accusations like this were to dog him for the rest of his career, as opponents attempted to demolish the account in *The Jewish War*. In his last book (the *Contra Apionem*, written toward the end of his life), he indignantly returns to the topic, claiming that his patrons "testify to my scrupulous concern for the truth, and they are scarcely persons who would conceal what they really thought or stay silent if I distorted anything or left out any of the facts from ignorance or prejudice. Yet contemptible people try to belittle my history, pretending that it reads like a prize essay for school boys."[29]

Josephus added the *Vita* to the *Jewish Antiquities* as an appendix. He may have meant to write a proper autobiography but was distracted by the urgent need to defend himself against Justus and expected that the *Antiquities* would have a wider circulation than the short *Vita* on its own. As a result, he unbalanced what could have been another superb book. Even so, he produced the only non-Christian autobiography to survive from the ancient world.[30] Although the *Vita* is more of a defense of a short period in his career than the story of his life, it supplies us with some fascinating details. Interestingly, he gives a different account of the war's origins from that in *The Jewish War*. There he had claimed that the Jews had always opposed the war against Rome, but that they were forced into it by a small group of fanatics. In the *Vita*, however, he admits that most Jews supported the war from the start. Yet he never quite explains his own position.

The *Jewish Antiquities* had taken him nearly two decades to write. At the end, he tells us he finished it during the thirteenth year of the reign of the Emperor Domitian and in the fifty-sixth year of his age, which means some date between September 93 and September the following year. Even in the *Jewish Antiquities* he was conscious of Domitian's shadow, portraying the appalling Emperor Tiberius in a flattering light and commending his skill at divining the future. Everybody knew that Domitian admired Tiberius; Suetonius says that the only books he ever read were his predecessor's memoirs and correspondence.

Josephus's *Contra Apionem*, written after the *Jewish Antiquities* and also dedicated to Epaphroditus, was an eloquent, neatly constructed treatise against the anti-Semitism of the period. Apion had been an Egyptian grammarian who, sixty years earlier, had led a deputation of carefully chosen scholars from Alexandria to Rome in order to launch a spiteful attack the Jewish religion in a debate with the redoubtable Philo. In his book, Josephus uses Apion as a stalking horse so that he can refute ignorant criticisms of the Jewish nation and faith and demonstrate that Jewish civilization—its religion, laws, and customs—is not only much older than Greek civilization but superior.

"In the first volume of this work, my most esteemed Epaphroditus, I demonstrated the antiquity of our race, corroborating my statements by the writings of Phoenicians, Chaldeans, and Egyptians, besides citing numerous Greek historians," is his summary of the first volume.[31] In the second he demolishes authors who have attacked Judaism, starting with a rebuttal of Apion that readers may think is occasionally a little callous. "An ulcer on his person rendered circumcision essential," he records joyfully of the long dead Apion's end. "The operation brought no relief, gangrene setting in, so that he died in terrible agonies."[32] Other opponents, such as Appolonius Molon, are accused of being "reprobates, sophists and deceivers of youth." In a more positive mood, he contrasts his people's concept of God with the paganism of Greece, while he reminds his readers that Jews have a far longer history than Greeks. It is generally agreed that *Contra Apionem* is his best-written book. He is still at the height of his intellectual powers.[33]

We do not know when Josephus died, only that the *Contra Apionem* was his last book and may have been published posthumously. It contains no compliments to Nerva, who succeeded Domitian in 96, so perhaps it was written before his accession, although there was no reason why Nerva should want to bestow any further favors on Josephus. On the other hand, he had good cause to thank the new emperor, who forbade Romans to accuse people of adopting Jewish ways and lifted the tax burden on the Jews, even issuing coins that proclaimed this act of clemency.[34]

Nothing more is known of Josephus. The *Vita* speaks of King Agrippa as being dead, and as it was believed for many years that the king had died about 100 CE, it used to be thought that Josephus, too, must have lived into the second century. However, recent scholarship shows that Agrippa's death took place earlier, and today the general opinion is that Josephus died in or about 95 CE. Nor is anything recorded of his children, although it is not impossible that he has descendants in the twenty-first century, unaware of their ancestry, among the many inheritors of the name by which he would call himself today—Cohen, the world's oldest surname. After the publication of *Contra Apionem* in the late nineties, Flavius Josephus, once Yossef ben Mattityahu ha-Kohen, passes into obscurity, if scarcely into oblivion.

25

History's Verdict

WHAT SORT OF A PERSON was Josephus in reality? Nothing written about him by contemporaries has survived, so we have to fall back on what he reveals in his books. Unfortunately, he was the sort of man who says a lot but who gives away very little indeed. Just like an actor playing to his audience, he was always too prone to write what he wanted readers to believe, and this depended on his mood. In *The Jewish War* he is Josephus the brave general and prophet sent by God, whereas in the *Vita* he is Josephus the shrewd statesman and benevolent governor of Galilee who never wanted war with Rome. It is all too easy for careful readers to find discrepancies and contradictions, boasting and exaggeration, even lies and untruths, in much of what he put on paper.

The title of this book is *Jerusalem's Traitor,* and that, no doubt, was how the Zealots on the city walls saw that accursed Yossef who had gone over to the enemy. Yet from the start of the war, he had questioned the Jews' ability to win it, and after experiencing firsthand the full, terrifying might of the Roman military machine at Jotapata, he realized that the conflict could only end in disaster for his religion, his country, and his people. If he helped the Romans with intelligence work, at least he never fought at their side. It can be argued that, far from being a quisling, he was a patriot who did his best to save Judea from the inevitable catastrophe.

The historians who know Josephus best—in the sense of having thought about him most—are baffled and arrive at very different conclusions. While William Whiston, the eighteenth-century Cambridge mathematician who is still his best-known translator, considered him to be more truthful than any other ancient writer, he regarded his personal character as "an historical enigma." (Admittedly, Whiston had some odd ideas about Josephus, being under the delusion that he was an Ebionite Christian.) In the nineteenth century, Emil Schürer passed a harsher verdict. "No one would wish to defend his character," he comments. "The basic features of his personality were vanity and complacency. And even if he was not the dishonourable traitor that his *Life* would seem to imply, nevertheless his going over to the Romans and his intimate alliance with the Flavian imperial house was performed with more ingenuity and indifference than was seemly in a person mourning the downfall of his nation."[1] Similarly, a century later, G. A. Williamson thought that Josephus's behavior at Jotapata was a horrifying story of cowardice and treason.[2] More than a few writers have been shocked by the "sinister" episode of the suicide pact in the cave.

Yet for Stewart Perowne, writing at the same time as Williamson, Josephus was sensitive and gregarious, an attractive figure whose main concern was to win the approval of his fellow men.[3] Even Schürer accepts that he wrote "with the intention of praising his people."[4] Robert Traill, who produced an English version of *The Jewish War* during the 1840s, thought that his books were those of a man whose principles were far from sordid—"ready to take in hand whatever might safely be attempted, with the hope of serving and saving his country, and of recommending its institutions to the good opinion of mankind."[5]

Perhaps the most eloquent of Josephus's latter-day critics is Richard Laqueur, writing in 1920. Laqueur believed that Josephus had been paid by Rome to persuade the Jews not to revolt but that, after setting himself up as ruler of Galilee, he was forced into leading a rebellion—and, as one of its instigators, was largely responsible for the ruin of Judea. For Laqueur, *The Jewish War* is essentially Roman propaganda.[6]

While conceding that there was an unpleasant side to Josephus, H. St J. Thackeray (the principal author of the Loeb translation of his books) has no time for Laqueur's "black portrait." In his view, Josephus realized from the start that it was hopeless to fight Rome but, having failed to make the Jews compromise, did his best to defend Galilee. During the siege of Jerusalem he tried to avert disaster by urging surrender, and after the catastrophe—when he might have been tempted to abandon Judaism—he spent the rest of his life writing in defense of it. "He has surely earned the name of patriot."[7]

Probably a majority would opt for Whiston's verdict, that Josephus is an enigma. As has been said, we only know about the most questionable episode in his career, the suicide pact at Jotapata, because he chose to tell us—he saw nothing sinister in it. If he was an opportunist, he was loyal in his own way to what he considered the best interests of his nation, although it is a simplification to say, as have some historians, that he began his literary career as a Roman apologist and ended as a Jewish nationalist.[8] When writing as a propagandist for his Flavian patrons, Josephus retained his integrity. Above all, he remained faithful to the religion of his ancestors.

One can guess with some certainty that the Zealots on the walls of Jerusalem had no doubt about the perfidy of that accursed Yossef who had gone over to the enemy and was doing his best to kill his former comrades. Yet from the start he had questioned the Jews' ability to win the war, and after encountering the Roman legions at Jotapata, he realized it could only end in disaster. At the same time, he was horrified by the Zealot takeover and the massacre of his own class. Had he escaped from Jotapata and returned to Jerusalem, he would almost certainly have been murdered. For all his opportunism, he, in his own way, did his best to save Judea.

Most unfairly, he is criticized for trying to stay Jewish while becoming Roman. Yet a need to reconcile two loyalties had been a problem for Jews of the Diaspora ever since the Babylonian captivity. Some think he succeeded brilliantly in showing people of his faith how to adapt to life outside their homeland. This was the view of the early twentieth-century German Jewish novelist Lion Feuchtwanger, for whom Josephus became an inspiration. However, Feuchtwanger's uneasy attitude toward Zionism led him to the mistaken conclusion that Josephus had despaired of a revival of Judea.[9]

Whatever conclusion is reached, no one would question the grandeur of *The Jewish War* as a literary achievement. Although some commentators have derided the opinion expressed in the fourth century by St Jerome (of the Vulgate Bible) that Josephus was the Greek Livy, today there is a growing consensus that the comparison is not so far-fetched after all. In Tessa Rajak's view, modern scholarship has confirmed his place among Jewish historians, and future research will rank him among the greatest Greek historians of Rome.[10] Geza Vermes cites with approval the opinion of another distinguished modern historian of Rome, Fergus Millar, who goes even further in claiming that the *Jewish Antiquities* of Josephus were "the most significant single work written in the Roman Empire." Moreover, by developing the fusion of the Greek and Jewish approaches to history begun by the Maccabees, and by bringing God into the picture, he had provided a model not only for the Christian historians of the fourth century but for those of later times.[11]

Beyond question, Flavius Josephus was vain and unscrupulous. It is hard to forgive his denigration of the Zealots, however much he may have atoned by preserving and immortalizing the story of Masada. Nonetheless, there are moments when it is difficult not to feel a certain admiration for him. Such unwavering belief in the destiny of his faith and nation, a belief unshaken by disaster, deserves our respect. After all, this was a man who could tell the world, "We have lost our land and our dearest possessions, but our Law will live for ever."[12]

NOTES

INTRODUCTION: THE LAND WHERE JOSEPHUS WAS BORN

1. Tacitus, *The Histories and The Annals*, trans. C. H. Moore and J. Jackson (London: Loeb Classical Library, 1925–1931), V, 6.

2. Josephus, *Complete Works*, trans. H. St. J. Thackeray, R. Marcus, A. Wikgren, and L. H. Feldman (London: Loeb Classical Library, 1926–1965), 3, 41–43. See note in Bibliography.

3. S. Schwartz, "Josephus in Galilee: Rural Patronage and Social Breakdown," in F. Parente and J. Sievers (eds.), *Josephus and the History of the Greco-Roman Period: Essays in Memory of Morton Smith* (Leiden: E. J. Brill, 1994), pp. 290–306.

4. Josephus, *The Jewish War*, in *Complete Works*, 3, 47.

5. Josephus, *Jewish Antiquities*, in *Complete Works*, 11, 341.

6. R. J. Coggins, "The Samaritans in Josephus," in L. H. Feldman and G. Hata (eds.), *Josephus, Judaism and Christianity* (Detroit: E. J. Brill, 1987), pp. 257–273.

7. Josephus, *The Jewish War*, in *Complete Works*, 3, 51–54.

8. Ibid., 5, 241.

9. S. Perowne, *The Life and Times of Herod the Great* (London: Hodder & Stoughton, 1956), p. 131.

10. Josephus, *The Jewish War*, in *Complete Works*, 5, 222.

11. E. Renan, *Jésus* (Paris, 1864), p. 136.

12. Josephus, *The Jewish War*, in *Complete Works*, 5, 223.

1. A YOUNG NOBLEMAN

1. Josephus, *Vita*, in *Complete Works*, 1.

2. Ibid., 2.

3. N. Avigad, *Discovering Jerusalem* (Oxford: Blackwell, 1984), pp. 97–120.

4. "Baba Bathra," in *Babylonian Talmud*, translated by I. Epstein (London: Soncino Press, 1935–1952), 21, a.

5. Josephus, *Vita*, in *Complete Works*, 8.

6. M. Goodman, *Rome and Jerusalem: The Clash of Ancient Civilisations* (London: Allen Lane, 2007), p. 174.

7. Josephus, *Vita*, in *Complete Works*, 10.

8. Josephus, *Jewish Antiquities*, in *Complete Works*, 18, 20.

9. Josephus, *The Jewish War*, in *Complete Works*, 2, 159.

10. Josephus, *Jewish Antiquities*, in *Complete Works*, 13, 171.

11. Ibid., 8, 419.

12. T. Rajak, "Josephus and the Essenes," in Parente and Sievers (eds.), *Josephus and the History of the Greco-Roman Period*, p. 158.

13. Josephus, *Vita*, in *Complete Works*, 11.

14. Ibid., 12.

15. Josephus, *The Jewish War*, in *Complete Works*, 2, 162–163.

16. H. Daniel-Rops, *La vie quotidienne en Palestine au temps de Jésus Christ* (Paris, 1959), p. 386.

17. Josephus, *The Jewish War*, in *Complete Works*, 2, 163.

18. Ibid., 2, 164–165.

19. S. Mason, *Flavius Josephus on the Pharisees* (Leiden: E. J. Brill, 1991), p. 370: G. Jossa, "Jews, Romans and Christians," in J. Sievers and G. Lembi (eds.), *Josephus and Jewish History in Flavian Rome and Beyond* (Leiden: E. J. Brill, 2005), p. 339.

20. Josephus, *The Jewish War*, in *Complete Works*, 2, 433.

21. Josephus, *Jewish Antiquities*, in *Complete Works*, 18, 4–10: Josephus, *The Jewish War*, in *Complete Works*, 2, 118, 433: T. Rajak, *Josephus* (London: Duckworth, 2002), pp. 86–87.

22. Josephus, *Jewish Antiquities*, in *Complete Works*, 18, 9.

23. Renan, *Jésus*, p. 128.

2. AN OCCUPIED COUNTRY

1. Luke, III, 14.

2. Goodman, *Rome and Jerusalem*, pp. 376–378.

3. Josephus, *Jewish Antiquities*, in *Complete Works*, 18, 177.

4. Ibid., 18, 63–64.

5. H. Schreckenberg, "The Works of Josephus and the Early Christian Church," in Feldman and Hata (eds.), *Josephus, Judaism and Christianity*, pp. 315–321.

6. G. Jossa, "Jews, Romans and Christians," in Sievers and Lembi (eds.), *Josephus and Jewish History*, p. 340.

7. E. M. Smallwood, *The Jews under Roman Rule from Pompey to Diocletian* (Leiden: E. J. Brill, 1976), p. 257.

8. Josephus, *Jewish Antiquities*, in *Complete Works*, 20, 97–99.

9. Josephus, *The Jewish War*, in *Complete Works*, 2, 224.

10. Acts, XXIV, 24–27.

11. Tacitus, *Annals*, XII, 54.

12. Josephus, *Jewish Antiquities*, in *Complete Works*, 20, 162–164.

13. Josephus, *The Jewish War*, in *Complete Works*, 2, 257.

14. Josephus, *Jewish Antiquities*, 20, 165.

15. Acts, XXIII, 21.

16. Ibid., XXI, 38.

17. Tacitus, *The Histories*, V, 9.

18. Josephus, *The Jewish War*, in *Complete Works*, 2, 265.

19. Josephus, *Jewish Antiquities*, in *Complete Works*, 20, 200.

20. Z. Baras, "The Testimonium Flavianum and the Martyrdom of James," in Feldman and Hata (eds.), *Josephus, Judaism and Christianity*, pp. 338–348.

21. *The Cambridge History of Judaism*, ed. W. Horbury, W. D. Davies, and J. Sturdy (Cambridge: Cambridge University Press, 1999), 3, p.146.

22. Josephus, *The Jewish War*, in *Complete Works*, 2, 272–277.

23. Josephus, *Jewish Antiquities*, in *Complete Works*, 20, 214.

24. Talmud, Menahoth 13 and Pesahim 57.

25. Josephus, *The Jewish War*, in *Complete Works*, 2, 276.

26. Ibid., 7, 261.

3. ROME AND POPPAEA

1. Josephus, *Vita*, in *Complete Works*, 13–14.

2. Josephus, *Jewish Antiquities*, in *Complete Works*, 20, 189–196.

3. Josephus, *Vita*, in *Complete Works*, 14–16.

4. Josephus, *Contra Apionem*, in *Complete Works*, II, 282.

5. Cicero, *Pro Flacco*, 28. 69.

6. Smallwood, *The Jews under Roman Rule*, pp. 212–215.

7. Goodman, *Rome and Jerusalem*, p. 385.

8. Horace, *Satires*, 1.4, 140–143.

9. Augustine of Hippo, *St. Augustine's Confessions*, trans. W. Watts (London: Loeb Classical Library, 1912), VI, 8.

10. Josephus, *Vita*, in *Complete Works*, 16.

11. Tacitus, *Annals*, XIII, 45–46.

12. Josephus, *Jewish Antiquities*, in *Complete Works*, 20, 195.

13. Josephus, *Vita*, in *Complete Works*, 16.

14. Suetonius, *The Lives of the Caesars*, trans. J. C. Rolfe (London: Loeb Classical Library, 1914), VI, Nero, xxxv, 3.

15. Tacitus, *Annals*, XVI, 6.

16. Ibid., XV, 44.

17. Suetonius, *Lives of the Caesars*, VI, Nero, li.

18. See G. Hata, "Imagining Some Dark Periods in Josephus's Life," in Parente and Sievers (eds.), *Josephus and the History of the Greco-Roman Period.*

19. Josephus, *Jewish Antiquities*, in *Complete Works*, 20, 154–156.

20. Suetonius, *Lives of the Caesars*, VI, Nero, xxxi, 2.

21. Tacitus, *The Histories*, I, 49.

22. Josephus, *The Jewish War*, in *Complete Works*, 3, 73–87 and 94–97.

23. Ibid., 3,109.

24. E. Schürer, *The History of the Jewish People in the Age of Jesus Christ, 175 bc–ad 135*, rev. and ed. G. Vermes and F. Millar (Edinburgh: T. and T. Clark, 1973), 1, p. 363.

25. Tacitus, *Annals*, XIII, 35.

4. THE JEW BAITER

1. Josephus, *Jewish Antiquities*, in *Complete Works*, 20, 252.

2. Josephus, *The Jewish War*, in *Complete Works*, 2, 278–279.

3. Smallwood, *The Jews under Roman Rule*, p. 272.

4. Tacitus, *The Histories*, V, 10.

5. Josephus, *Jewish Antiquities*, in *Complete Works*, 20, 184.

6. Ibid., 20, 184.

7. Josephus, *The Jewish War*, in *Complete Works*, 2, 308.

8. Ibid., 2, 335–341.

9. Ibid., 2, 345–401.

5. WAR

1. Josephus, *The Jewish War*, in Complete Works, 2, 409.

2. Ibid., 2, 410.

3. Ibid., 2, 427.

4. Ibid., 2, 420.

5. Ibid., 2, 441.

6. Ibid., 2, 455–456.

7. Ibid., 2, 497–498.

8. Ibid., 2, 462–465.

9. Josephus, *Vita*, in *Complete Works*, 17–19.

10. Ibid., 20–23.

11. Josephus, *The Jewish War*, in *Complete Works*, 2, 531.

6. GOVERNOR OF GALILEE

1. Goodman, *Rome and Jerusalem*, p. 424.

2. Josephus, *The Jewish War*, in *Complete Works*, 2, 556.

3. Eusebius, *The Ecclesiastical History*, trans. K. Lake and J. E. Oulton (London: Loeb Classical Library, 1914–1927), I, 171–177.

4. Josephus, *Vita*, in *Complete Works*, 25.

5. Ibid., 27.

6. Rajak, *Josephus*, p. 154.

7. Josephus, *Vita*, in *Complete Works*, 28–29.

8. Josephus, *The Jewish War*, in *Complete Works*, 2, 569–571.

9. Josephus, *Vita*, in *Complete Works*, 79.

10. Ibid., 79.

11. Ibid., 30–31.

12. Ibid., 40–42.

13. Ibid., 66.

14. Ibid., 134.

15. Josephus, *The Jewish War*, in *Complete Works*, 2, 585–589.

16. M. Goodman, *The Ruling Class of Judea: The Origins of the Jewish Revolt against Rome* (Cambridge: Cambridge University Press, 1987), p. 201.

17. Josephus, *The Jewish War*, in *Complete Works*, 2, 585–590.

18. Ibid., 2, 599–609; Josephus, *Vita*, in *Complete Works*, 132–141.

19. Josephus, *The Jewish War*, in *Complete Works*, 2, 610–613; Josephus, *Vita*, in *Complete Works*, 145–148.

20. Josephus, *Vita*, in *Complete Works*, 101.

21. Josephus, *The Jewish War*, in *Complete Works*, 2, 624–625.

22. Josephus, *Vita*, in *Complete Works*, 174.

23. Ibid., 175–178.

24. Ibid., 191.

25. Ibid., 225.

26. Ibid., 80.

27. Ibid., 84.

28. Ibid., 82.

29. Smallwood, *The Jews under Roman Rule*, pp. 305–306.

30. Josephus, *The Jewish War*, in *Complete Works*, 2, 647.

7. THE RETURN OF THE LEGIONS

1. Josephus, *The Jewish War*, in *Complete Works*, 3, 1–12.
2. Tacitus, *The Histories*, II, 5.
3. Suetonius, *Lives of the Caesars*, VIII, Vespasian, iv, 1.
4. Ibid., VIII, 4.
5. Josephus, *The Jewish War*, in *Complete Works*, 3, 9.
6. Ibid., 3, 63.
7. Ibid., 3, 115–126.

8. THE SIEGE OF JOTAPATA

1. Josephus, *The Jewish War*, in *Complete Works*, 3, 144.
2. Ibid., 3, 143.
3. Ibid., 3, 193.
4. Ibid., 3, 195–196.
5. Ibid., 3, 197–201.
6. Ibid., 3, 204–205.
7. Ibid., 3, 221.
8. Ibid., 3, 229.
9. Ibid., 3, 261.

9. THE CAVE AND THE PROPHECY

1. Josephus, *The Jewish War*, in *Complete Works*, 3, 341–343.
2. Ibid., 3, 351–352.
3. Ibid., 3, 354.
4. Suetonius, *Lives of the Caesars*, VIII, Vespasian, iv, 5.
5. Josephus, *The Jewish War*, in *Complete Works*, 3, 355–360.
6. Ibid., 3, 362–382.
7. Ibid., 3, 384–386.
8. Ibid., 3, 388–391.
9. Ibid., 3, 391.
10. Rajak, *Josephus*, p. 171, who cites M. Gardner, *Aha! Insight* (New York: Freeman, 1978), pp. 84 ff.
11. Suetonius, *Lives of the Caesars*, VIII, Vespasian, iv, 5.
12. Josephus, *The Jewish War*, in *Complete Works*, 3, 340.
13. Suetonius, *Lives of the Caesars*, VIII, Vespasian, xx.
14. Josephus, *The Jewish War*, in *Complete Works*, 3, 400–403.
15. Ibid., 3, 405.

16. Ibid., 3, 406.

17. Rajak, *Josephus*, p. 188.

18. Tacitus, *The Histories*, II, 78.

19. Schürer, *The History of the Jewish People in the Age of Jesus Christ*, I, p. 57.

20. M. Smith, "The Occult in Josephus," in Feldman and Hata (eds.), *Josephus, Judaism and Christianity*, pp.236–256; S. Mason, "Josephus, Daniel and the Flavian House," in Parente and Sievers (eds.), *Josephus and the History of the Greco-Roman Period*, pp. 161–191.

10. JOSEPHUS THE PRISONER

1. Josephus, *Jewish Antiquities*, in *Complete Works*, 8, 46–49.

2. Josephus, *The Jewish War*, in *Complete Works*, 3, 408.

3. Josephus, *Vita*, in *Complete Works*, 414.

4. Ibid., 414–415.

5. Josephus, *The Jewish War*, in *Complete Works*, 3, 432–442.

6. Rajak, *Josephus*, p. 154.

7. Josephus, *Contra Apionem*, in *Complete Works*, I, 48.

8. Suetonius, *Lives of the Caesars*, VIII, Vespasian, xxi.

9. Josephus, *The Jewish War*, in *Complete Works*, 3, 419–427.

10. Ibid., 3, 484.

11. Ibid., 3, 495–496.

12. Ibid., 3, 536–537.

13. Ibid., 4, 20.

14. Ibid., 4, 37–38.

15. Ibid., 4, 41–48.

16. Ibid., 4, 50.

17. Ibid., 4, 72.

11. JOHN OF GISCHALA COMES TO JERUSALEM

1. Josephus, *The Jewish War*, in *Complete Works*, 4, 86.

2. Ibid., 4, 92–96.

3. Ibid., 4, 105.

4. Ibid., 4, 127.

5. M. Goodman, *The Ruling Class of Judea*, pp. 199–200.

6. Josephus, *The Jewish War*, in *Complete Works*, 4, 145.

7. Ibid., 4, 155.

8. Rajak, *Josephus*, p. 133.

9. Josephus, *The Jewish War*, in *Complete Works*, 4, 161.

10. Ibid., 4, 162–192.
11. Ibid., 4, 208.
12. Ibid., 4, 216–223.

12. THE ZEALOT REVOLUTION

1. Josephus, *The Jewish War*, in *Complete Works*, 4, 233.
2. Ibid., 4, 241–243.
3. Ibid., 4, 271–282.
4. Ibid., 4, 310.
5. Ibid., 4, 318.
6. Ibid., 4, 326.
7. Ibid., 4, 328.
8. Goodman, *The Ruling Class of Judea*, p. 201; J. J. Price, *Jerusalem under Siege* (Leiden: E. J. Brill, Leiden, 1992).
9. Josephus, *The Jewish War*, in *Complete Works*, 4, 335–344.
10. Ibid., 4, 357.
11. Rajak, *Josephus*, p. 134.
12. Josephus, *The Jewish War*, 4, 397.
13. Ibid., 4, 389–393.

13. THE RECONQUEST OF JUDEA

1. Josephus, *The Jewish War*, in *Complete Works*, 4, 366–367.
2. Ibid., 4, 368–373.
3. Ibid., 4, 425.
4. Ibid., 4, 441–442.
5. Ibid., 4, 477.
6. J. Neusner, *A Life of Rabban Yohanan ben Zakkai* (Leiden: E. J. Brill, 1962), pp. 113–121.
7. Rajak, *Josephus*, p. 188.
8. Suetonius, *Lives of the Caesars*, VI, Nero, xlix, 3.

14. SIMON BAR GIORA

1. Josephus, *The Jewish War*, in *Complete Works*, 4, 503.
2. Goodman, *The Ruling Class of Judea*, p. 203.
3. Josephus, *The Jewish War*, in *Complete Works*, 4, 510.
4. Ibid., 4, 536.
5. Ibid., 4, 540.

6. Ibid., 4, 561–564.

7. Ibid., 4, 573.

8. Ibid., 4, 577.

9. Numbers, xxv, 8–11.

10. Rajak, *Josephus*, pp. 86–87.

15. THE YEAR OF THE FOUR EMPERORS

1. Josephus, *The Jewish War*, in *Complete Works*, 4, 493.

2. Tacitus, *The Histories*, V, 10.

3. Ibid., II, 68.

4. Josephus, *The Jewish War*, in *Complete Works*, 4, 501.

5. Tacitus, *The Histories*, II, 74.

6. Ibid., II, 76.

7. Josephus, *The Jewish War*, in *Complete Works*, 4, 623–629.

8. Josephus, *Contra Apionem*, in *Complete Works*, II, 34.

9. Josephus, *The Jewish War*, in *Complete Works*, 1, 68–69.

10. Suetonius, *Lives of the Caesars*, VII, Vitellius, iii–iv and xiii.

11. Josephus, *The Jewish War*, in *Complete Works*, 4, 652.

12. Ibid., 4, 657.

13. Ibid., 4, 657.

14. Ibid., 1, 5.

15. M. Goodman, "Josephus as Roman Citizen," in Parente and Sievers (eds.), *Josephus and the History of the Greco-Roman Period*, p. 335.

16. TITUS TAKES COMMAND

1. Josephus, *Vita*, in *Complete Works*, 416.

2. Suetonius, *Lives of the Caesars*, VIII, Titus, i.

3. Tacitus, *The Histories*, V, 1.

4. Josephus, *The Jewish War*, in *Complete Works*, 5, 45–46.

5. Ibid., 2, 220.

6. Josephus, *Jewish Antiquities*, in *Complete Works*, XX, 100.

7. Josephus, *The Jewish War*, in *Complete Works*, 5, 6–7.

8. Smallwood, *The Jews under Roman Rule*, p. 316.

9. Josephus, *The Jewish War*, in *Complete Works*, 5, 47–49.

10. Ibid., 3, 79–84.

11. Ibid., 5, 85.

12. Ibid., 5, 97.

13. Ibid., 5, 121–127.

17. THE SIEGE BEGINS

1. Tacitus, *The Histories*, V. 12.
2. Josephus, *The Jewish War*, in *Complete Works*, 5, 250.
3. Ibid., 5, 261.
4. Ibid., 5, 265.
5. Ibid., 5, 274.
6. Ibid., 5, 302.
7. Ibid., 5, 306.
8. Ibid., 5, 308.
9. Ibid., 5, 317–330.
10. Ibid., 5, 332–334.
11. Ibid., 5, 342–346.
12. G. Webster, *The Roman Imperial Army of the First and Second Centuries ad* (London: Adam Charles Black, 1969), pp. 132–135.
13. First Book of the Maccabees, vi, 39.
14. Ibid., iv, 8.
15. Josephus, *The Jewish War*, in *Complete Works*, 5, 355.
16. Dio Cassius, *Dio's Roman History with an English Translation*, trans. E. Cary (London: Loeb Classical Library, 1914–1927), vol. 8, lxv, 5.
17. Josephus, *The Jewish War*, in *Complete Works*, 5, 363–374.
18. Ibid., 5, 376–419.
19. Josephus, *Jewish Antiquities*, in *Complete Works*, 8, 418.
20. Mason, "Josephus, Daniel and the Flavian House," in Parente and Sievers (eds.), *Josephus and the History of the Greco-Roman Period*, p. 168.
21. Josephus, *The Jewish War*, in *Complete Works*, 1, 69; C. Thoma, "John Hyrcanus I as Seen by Josephus and Other Early Jewish Sources," in Parente and Sievers (eds.), *Josephus and the History of the Greco-Roman Period*, p. 136.
22. Josephus, *The Jewish War*, in *Complete Works*, 5, 393.

18. INSIDE JERUSALEM

1. Josephus, *Contra Apionem*, in *Complete Works*, I, 49.
2. Rajak, *Josephus*, p. 196.
3. Josephus, *The Jewish War*, in *Complete Works*, 435–437.
4. Ibid., 5, 441.
5. Ibid., 5, 442–446.
6. Ibid., 7, 268–270.
7. Ibid., 5, 455–456.

8. Ibid., 5, 460–65.

9. Ibid., 5, 474–477.

10. Ibid., 5, 485.

11. Ibid., 5, 486.

12. S. Perowne, *The Later Herods* (London: Hodder & Stoughton, 1958), p. 174.

19. THE WOODEN WALL

1. Josephus, *The Jewish War*, in *Complete Works*, 5, 512–518.

2. Ibid., 5, 519.

3. Ibid., 5, 526.

4. Ibid., 5, 534–540.

5. Ibid., 5, 541–547.

6. Ibid., 5, 552.

7. Ibid., 5, 563–564.

8. Ibid., 5, 565.

9. Ibid., 5, 566.

10. Ibid., 6, 4.

11. Ibid., 6, 7.

12. Ibid., 6, 17.

13. Ibid., 6, 34–53.

14. Ibid., 6, 55.

15. Ibid., 6, 57–58.

16. Ibid., 6, 81.

17. Ibid., 6, 81–90.

20. THE DESTRUCTION OF THE TEMPLE

1. Josephus, *The Jewish War*, in *Complete Works*, 6, 93–95.

2. Ibid., 6, 98–110.

3. Ibid., 6, 124–128.

4. Ibid., 6, 144.

5. Ibid., 6, 132.

6. Ibid., 6, 148.

7. Ibid., 6, 167.

8. Ibid., 6, 169–176.

9. Ibid., 6, 188–189.

10. Ibid., 6, 196–198.

11. Ibid., 6, 201–213.

12. Ibid., 6, 229–231.

13. Ibid., 6, 252.

14. Tacitus, *The Histories*, V, 13.

15. Josephus, *The Jewish War*, in *Complete Works*, 6, 250.

16. Ibid., 6, 267.

17. Ibid., 6, 270.

18. B. Levick, *Vespasian* (London: Routledge, 1999), p. 118.

19. F. Parente, "The Impotence of Titus," in Sievers and Lembi (eds.), *Josephus and Jewish History in Flavian Rome and Beyond*, p. 66.

20. Rajak, *Josephus*, p. 211.

21. F. M. Abel, *Histoire de Palestine depuis la conquête d'Alexandre jusqu'à l'invasion arabe* (Paris, 1952), I, p. 33. Tacitus, *The Histories*, II, 2.

22. Tacitus, *The Histories*, II, 2.

23. L. Feldman and G. Hata, "Editors' Preface," in L. Feldman and G. Hata (eds.), *Josephus, Judaism and Christianity*, p. 17.

21. A HOLOCAUST

1. Josephus, *The Jewish War*, in *Complete Works*, 6, 271–276.

2. Ibid., 6, 285.

3. Ibid., 6, 317.

4. Ibid., 6, 286.

5. Ibid., 6, 388.

6. Ibid., 6, 288.

7. Ibid., 6, 300–309.

8. Ibid., 6, 328–333.

9. Ibid., 6, 348–350.

10. Ibid., 6, 386.

11. Suetonius, *Lives of the Caesars*, VIII, Titus, v, 2.

12. Josephus, *The Jewish War*, in *Complete Works*, 6, 395–399.

13. Ibid., 6, 435.

14. Ibid., 6, 442.

15. Ibid., 7, 4.

16. Josephus, *The Jewish War*, in *Complete Works*, 6, 419.

17. Ibid., 6, 420.

18. Josephus, *Vita*, in *Complete Works*, 418.

19. Ibid., 419–421.

20. Josephus, *The Jewish War*, in *Complete Works*, 7, 38.

21. Ibid., 7, 119.

22. Josephus, *Vita*, in *Complete Works*, 422.

23. Suetonius, *Lives of the Caesars*, VIII, Titus, v, 3.

24. Ibid., VI, 1.

25. Josephus, *Vita*, in *Complete Works*, 423.

26. Josephus, *The Jewish War*, in *Complete Works*, 7, 132–157.

22. THE PROPAGANDIST

1. Josephus, *Vita*, in *Complete Works*, 422.

2. Z. Yavetz, "Reflections on Titus and Josephus," *Greek, Roman and Byzantine Studies* 16 (1975): 431–432.

3. Levick, *Vespasian*, pp. 79–74.

4. B. W. Jones, *The Emperor Titus* (London: Croom Helm, 1984), p. 87.

5. Josephus, *Vita*, in *Complete Works*, 425.

6. Josephus, *The Jewish War*, in *Complete Works*, 7, 453.

7. Josephus, *Vita*, in *Complete Works*, 424.

8. Ibid., 427.

9. Josephus, *The Jewish War*, in *Complete Works*, 1, 6.

10. F. Parente, "The Impotence of Titus," in Sievers and Lembi, *Josephus and Jewish History in Flavian Rome and Beyond*, p. 66.

11. Josephus, *Jewish Antiquities*, in *Complete Works*, 1, 1–3.

12. Ibid., 1, 4.

13. Ibid., 20, 263.

14. Josephus, *Contra Apionem*, in *Complete Works*, I, 50.

15. Rajak, *Josephus*, pp. 234–236.

23. MASADA AND THE LAST ZEALOTS

1. Josephus, *The Jewish War*, in *Complete Works*, 7, 163.

2. Ibid., 7, 190–215.

3. Ibid., 7, 284.

4. Ibid., 7, 323–336.

5. Ibid., 7, 341–388.

6. Ibid., 7, 401.

7. Ibid., 7, 399–401.

8. Ibid., 7, 406.

9. Ibid., 7, 419.

10. Ibid., 7, 433–436.

24. A ROMAN CITIZEN

1. Eusebius, *The Ecclesiastical History*, I, p. 227.

2. Goodman, "Josephus as Roman Citizen," in Parente and Sievers (eds.), *Josephus and the History of the Greco-Roman Period*, p. 332.

3. H. M. Cotton and W. Eck, "Josephus's Roman Audience: Josephus and the Roman Elite," in E. Edmondson, S. Mason, and J. Rives (eds.), *Flavius Josephus and Flavian Rome* (Oxford: Oxford University Press, 2005), p. 52.

4. P. Spilsbury, "Reading the Bible in Rome: Josephus and the Constraints of Empire," in Sievers and Lembi (eds.), *Josephus and Jewish History in Flavian Rome and Beyond*, p. 240.

5. Rajak, "Josephus and the Diaspora," in Edmondson, Mason, and Rives (eds.), *Flavius Josephus and Flavian Rome*, pp. 85–90.

6. Josephus, *Contra Apionem*, in *Complete Works*, 1, 51–52.

7. Josephus, *Vita*, in *Complete Works*, 363.

8. Ibid., 366.

9. Josephus, *The Jewish War*, in *Complete Works*, 4, 643.

10. Rajak, *Josephus*, p.195 n. 23.

11. Jones, *The Emperor Titus*, p. 93.

12. Suetonius, *Lives of the Caesars*, VIII, Vespasian, xxiii.

13. Ibid., VIII, Titus, vii.

14. Josephus, *Vita*, in *Complete Works*, 428.

15. Ibid., 429.

16. Josephus, *The Jewish War*, in *Complete Works*, 7, 85–88.

17. Suetonius, *Lives of the Caesars*, VIII, Domitian, ii, 1.

18. Josephus, *The Jewish War*, in *Complete Works*, 7, 152; S. Mason, "Reading Josephus's *Bellum Judaicum* in the Context of a Flavian Audience," in Sievers and Lembi (eds.), *Josephus and Jewish History in Flavian Rome and Beyond*, p. 100.

19. Suetonius, *Lives of the Caesars*, VIII, Domitian, x, 1.

20. Ibid., VIII, Domitian, xiv, 1.

21. Josephus, *Vita*, in *Complete Works*, 429.

22. Dio Cassius, *Roman History*, LXVII, 14, 3.

23. Josephus, *Vita*, in *Complete Works*, 429.

24. Suetonius, *Lives of the Caesars*, VIII, Titus, x.

25. Josephus, *Jewish Antiquities*, in *Complete Works*, 1, 8.

26. Spilsbury, "Reading the Bible in Rome," p. 213.

27. Josephus, *Jewish Antiquities*, in *Complete Works*, 18, 13.

28. Ibid., 13, 298.

29. Josephus, *Contra Apionem*, in *Complete Works*, I, 53.

30. S.J.D. Cohen, *Josephus in Galilee and Rome: His Vita and Development as a Historian* (Leiden: E. J. Brill, 1979), p. 101.

31. Josephus, *Contra Apionem*, in *Complete Works*, II, 1.

32. Ibid., II, 143.

33. J.M.G. Barclay, "Judean Historiography in Rome: Josephus and History in *Contra Apionem*, Book I," in Sievers and Lembi (eds.), *Josephus and Jewish History in Flavian Rome and Beyond*, p. 36.

34. M. Goodman, "The Fiscus Iudaicus and Attitudes to Judaism," in Edmondson, Mason, and Rives (eds.), *Flavius Josephus and Flavian Rome*, p. 25.

25. HISTORY'S VERDICT

1. Schürer, *The History of the Jewish People in the Age of Jesus Christ*, I, p. 57.

2. Josephus, *The Jewish War*, trans. G. A. Williamson (New York: Penguin, 1959), p. 11.

3. Perowne, *The Later Herods*, p. 109.

4. Schürer, *The History of the Jewish People*, I, p. 57.

5. Josephus, *The Works of Josephus*, trans. R. Traill (London, 1847), p. 12.

6. R. Laqueur, *Der jüdischer Histotiker Flavius Josephus* (Giesen, 1920).

7. H. St. J. Thackeray, *Josephus, the Man and the Historian* (New York: Jewish Institute of Religion Press, 1929), pp. 18–22.

8. S.J.D. Cohen, *Josephus in Galilee and Rome*, p. 240.

9. A. Bunzel, *La Trilogie de Josèphe de Lion Feuchtwanger*, Bibliothèque d'études germanique et centre-européennes, vol. 8, University of Montpellier, 2006, pp. 31–32.

10. Rajak, *Josephus*, p. xiv.

11. F. Millar, "Empire, Community, and Culture in the Roman Near East: Greeks, Syrians, Jews, and Arabs," *Journal of Jewish Studies* 38 (1987): 147.

12. Josephus, *Contra Apionem*, in *Complete Works*, II, 277.

SELECT BIBLIOGRAPHY

References to the works of Josephus given in my source notes are to the text of the definitive Loeb edition (see below), but nearly all the quotations and excerpts from his writings are my own renderings, which to some extent have been inspired by the translations of Whiston and Traill, although they are very much modernized. The literature on Josephus is vast, and it continues to grow at a rapid pace because of increasing interest. The selection of books and articles listed here, in addition to primary sources, is a reasonably representative selection of the more recent and more important scholarship.

PRIMARY SOURCES

Augustine of Hippo. *St. Augustine's Confessions.* Translated by W. Watts. 2 vols. London: Loeb Classical Library, 1912.

Babylonian Talmud. Translated by I. Epstein. 35 vols. London: Soncino Press, 1935–1952.

Dio Cassius. *Dio's Roman History with an English Translation.* Translated by E. Cary. 9 vols. London: Loeb Classical Library, 1914–1927.

Eusebius. *The Ecclesiastical History.* Translated by K. Lake and J.E.L. Oulton. 2 vols. London: Loeb Classical Library, 1926, 1932.

Josephus. *Josephus: Complete Works.* Translated by H. St. J. Thackeray, R. Marcus, A. Wikgren, and L. H. Feldman. 9 vols. London: Loeb Classical Library, 1926–1965.

_____. *The Jewish War.* Translated by G. A. Williamson. New York: Penguin, 1959.

_____. *Oeuvres complètes de Flavius Josephus.* Translated by J. Weill. 5 vols. Paris, 1900.

_____. *The Works of Flavius Josephus, the Learned and Authentic Jewish Historian.* Translated by W. Whiston. London, 1736.

_____. *The Works of Josephus: A New Translation*. Translated by R. Traill. London, 1847, 1851.

The Mishna. Translated by H. Danby. Oxford: Oxford University Press, 1934.

Petronius. *Petronius with an English Translation*. Translated by M. Heseltine. London: Loeb Classical Library, 1913.

_____. *The Satyricon*. Translated by P. G. Walsh. Oxford: Clarendon Press, 1996.

Philo of Alexandria. *Philo with an English Translation*. Translated by F. H. Colson and G. H. Whitaker. 10 vols. London: Loeb Classical Library, 1962.

Pliny. *Letters*. Translated by W. Melmoth and W.M.L. Hutchinson. 2 vols. London: Loeb Classical Library, 1915.

Suetonius. *The Lives of the Caesars*. Vol. 2. Translated by J. C. Rolfe. London: Loeb Classical Library, 1914.

Tacitus. *The Histories and The Annals*. Translated by C. H. Moore and J. Jackson. 4 vols. London: Loeb Classical Library, 1925–1931.

MODERN SOURCES

Abel, F. M. *Géographie de la Palestine*. Paris, 1967.

_____. *Histoire de la Palestine depuis la conquête d'Alexandre jusqu'à l'invasion arabe*. Paris, 1952.

_____. "Topographie du siège de Jerusalem en 70," *Révue Biblique* (Paris), 1949.

Alon, E. T. *Jews, Judaism and the Classical World*. Translated by I. Abrahams. Jerusalem, 1977.

Appelbaum, S. "The Zealots: The Case for Re-evaluation." *Journal for Roman Studies* 61:155–170.

Avigad, N. *Discovering Jerusalem*. Oxford: Blackwell, 1984.

Baras, Z. "The Testimonium Flavianum and the Martyrdom of James." In Feldman and Hata (eds.), *Josephus, Judaism and Christianity*.

Barclay, J.M.G. *Jews in the Mediterranean Diaspora from Alexander to Trajan*. Edinburgh: T. and T. Clarke, 1996.

_____. "Judean Historiography in Rome: Josephus and History in Contra Apionem, Book I." In Sievers and Lembi (eds.), *Josephus and Jewish History in Flavian Rome and Beyond*.

Barnes, T. D. "The Sack of the Temple in Josephus and Tacitus." In Edmondson, Mason, and Rives (eds.), *Flavius Josephus and Flavian Rome*.

Baron, S. W. *A Social and Religious History of the Jews*. Vols. 1 & 2. New York: Columbia University Press, 1962.

Betz, O. "Miracles in the Writings of Flavius Josephus." In Feldman and Hata (eds.), *Josephus, Judaism and Christianity*.

Bilde, P. "Flavius Josephus between Jerusalem and Rome: His Life, His Works and Their Importance." *Journal for the Study of the Pseudoepigraph* (Sheffield), 1988.

Bonsirven, J. *Le Judaisme Palestinien*. 2 vols. Paris, 1934–1935.

_____. *Textes rabbiniques des deux premiers siècles chrétiens*. Rome, 1955.

Brinton, C. *The Anatomy of a Revolution*. New York: W. W. Norton, 1938.

Bunzel, A. *La Trilogie de Josèphe de Lion Feuchtwanger*. Bibliothèque germanique et centre-européennes. Vol. 8. University of Montpellier, 2006.

Cambridge History of Judaeism. Vol. 3. Edited by W. Horbury, W. D. Davies, and J. Sturdy. Cambridge: Cambridge University Press, 1999.

Coggins, R. J. "The Samaritans in Josephus." In Feldman and Hata (eds.), *Josephus, Judaism and Christianity*.

Cohen, A. *Everyman's Talmud*. London: J. M. Dent, 1949.

Cohen, S.J.D. *Josephus in Galilee and Rome: His Vita and Development as a Historian*. Leiden: E. J. Brill, 1979.

_____. *From the Maccabees to the Mishnah*. Louisville, Ky.: Westminster John Knox Press, 2006.

Comay, J. *The Temple of Jerusalem with the History of the Temple Mount*. New York: Holt, Reinhart & Winston, 1975.

Cotton, H. M., and W. Eck. "Josephus's Roman Audience: Josephus and the Roman Elites." In Edmondson, Mason, and Rives (eds.), *Flavius Josephus and Flavian Rome*.

Crook, J. "Titus and Berenice." *American Journal of Philology* 72 (1951):162–175.

Daniel-Rops, H. *Jésus en son temps*. Paris, 1945.

_____. *La vie quotidienne en Palestine au temps de Jésus Christ*. Paris, 1959.

Edersheim, A. *The Temple: Its Ministry and Services*. Rev. ed. Peabody, Mass.: Hendrickson, 1994.

Edmondson, E., S. Mason, and J. Rives (eds.). *Flavius Josephus and Flavian Rome*. Oxford: Oxford University Press, 2005.

Farmer, W. R. *Maccabees, Zealots, and Josephus*. New York: Columbia University Press, 1956.

Feldman, L. H. "Flavius Josephus Revisited: The Man, His Writings, and His Significance." In *Aufstieg und Niedergang der romischen Welt*. Part 2. Edited by Wolfgang Haase. Berlin: Walter de Gruyter, 1984.

Feldman, L. H., and G. Hata (eds.). *Josephus, Judaism and Christianity*. Detroit: E. J. Brill, 1987.

_____ (eds.). *Josephus, the Bible, and History*. Detroit: Wayne State University Press, 1989.

Feldman, W. M. *The Jewish Child*. London: Bailliere, Tindall, and Cox, 1917.

Ferrar, W. J. *The Uncanonical Jewish Books: Short Introduction to the Apocrypha and Other Jewish Writings, 200 bc–100 ad*. London, 1918.

Feuchtwanger, L. *Der Jüdische Krieg.* Berlin, 1932.

Freyne, S. *Galilee from Alexander the Great to Hadrian, 323 bce to 135 ce.* Wilmington, Del.: Michael Glazier / Notre Dame, Ind.: Notre Dame University Press, 1980.

Goodman, M. "The Fiscus Iudaicus and Gentile Attitudes to Judaism in Flavian Rome." In Edmondson, Mason, and Rives (eds.), *Flavius Josephus and Flavian Rome.*

_____ (ed.). *Jews in the Graeco-Roman World.* Oxford: Oxford University Press, 1998.

_____. "Josephus as Roman Citizen." In Parente and Sievers (eds.), *Josephus and the History of the Greco-Roman Period.*

_____ (ed.). *Oxford Handbook of Jewish Studies.* Oxford: Oxford University Press, 2002.

_____. *The Roman World, 44 bc–ad 140.* London: Routledge, 1997.

_____. *Rome and Jerusalem: The Clash of Ancient Civilisations.* London: Allen Lane, 2007.

_____. *The Ruling Class of Judea: The Origins of the Jewish Revolt against Rome.* Cambridge: Cambridge University Press, 1987.

Grabbe, L. L. *Judaism from Cyrus to Hadrian.* London: SCM Press, 1994.

Gray, R. *Prophetic Figures in Late Second Temple Jewish Palestine: The Evidence from Josephus.* Oxford: Oxford University Press, 1993.

Greenhalgh, P.A.L. *The Year of the Four Emperors.* London: Weidenfeld & Nicolson, 1975.

Hadas-Lebel, M. *Flavius Josephus: Eyewitness to Rome's First Century Conquest of Judea.* Translated by R. Miller. New York: Macmillan, 1993.

_____. "Flavius Josephus, Historian of Rome." In Parente and Sievers (eds.), *Josephus and the History of the Greco-Roman Period.*

Hata, G. "Imagining Some Dark Periods in Josephus's Life." In Parente and Sievers (eds.), *Josephus and the History of the Greco-Roman Period.*

Hazel, J. *Who's Who in the Roman World.* London: Routledge, 2002.

Hengel, M. *The Zealots.* Edinburgh: T. and T. Clarke, 1989.

Hornblower, S., and A. Spawforth (eds.). *The Oxford Classical Dictionary.* Oxford: Oxford University Press, 2003.

Horsley, R. A. *Jesus and the Spiral of Violence: Popular Jewish Resistance in Roman Palestine.* San Francisco: Harper & Row, 1987.

Horsley, R. A., and J. S. Hanson. *Bandits, Prophets, and Messiahs: Popular Movements at the Time of Jesus.* San Francisco: Harper & Row, 1988.

Jeremias, J. *Jerusalem in the Time of Jesus.* London: SCM Press, 1969.

Johnson, P. *A History of the Jews.* London: Weidenfeld & Nicolson, 1987.

Jones, B. W. *The Emperor Titus.* London: Croom Helm / New York: St. Martin's Press, 1984.

_____. *The Emperor Domitian*. London: Routledge, 1992.

Jordan, R. *Berenice*. London: Constable, 1974.

Jossa, G. "Jews, Romans and Christians from the Bellum Judaicum to the Antiquitates." In Sievers and Lembi (eds.), *Josephus and Jewish History in Flavian Rome and Beyond*.

_____. "Josephus's Action in Galilee during the Jewish War." In Parente and Sievers (eds.), *Josephus and the History of the Greco-Roman Period*.

Kadman, L. *The Coins of the Jewish War of 66–73 ce*. Vol. 3 of *Corpus Nummorum Palaestinensium*. Tel Aviv: Schocken, 1960.

Ladouceur, D. J. "Josephus and Masada." In Feldman and Hata (eds.), *Josephus, Judaism and Christianity*.

Laqueur, R. *Der jüdischer Historiker Flavius Josephus*. Giessen, 1920.

Leon, H. J. *The Jews of Ancient Rome*. Philadelphia: Jewish Publications in America, 1960.

Levick, B. *Vespasian*. London: Routledge, 1999.

Levine, I. L. "Josephus's Description of the Jerusalem Temple: War, Antiquities and Other Sources." In Parente and Sievers (eds.), *Josephus and the History of the Greco-Roman Period*.

Madden, F. W. *The Coins of the Jews*, London, 1881.

_____. *History of Jewish Coinage*. London, 1864.

Masada: The Yigael Yadin Excavations, 1963–1965. Final Report, 6 vols. Jerusalem, 1989.

Mason, S. *Flavius Josephus on the Pharisees*. Leiden: E. J. Brill, 1991.

_____. *Josephus and the New Testament*. Peabody, Mass.: Hendrickson, 1992.

_____. "Josephus, Daniel and the Flavian House." In Parente and Sievers (eds.), *Josephus and the History of the Greco-Roman Period*.

_____. "Of Audience and Meaning: Reading Josephus's Bellum Judaicum in the Context of a Flavian Audience." In Sievers and Lembi (eds.), *Josephus and Jewish History in Flavian Rome and Beyond*.

_____. *Understanding Josephus: Seven Perspectives*. Sheffield: Sheffield Academic Press, 1988.

Mattingly, H., and R.A.G. Carson. *Coins of the Roman Empire in the British Museum*. 9 vols. London, 1932–1975.

McLaren, J. S. "Josephus on Titus: The Vanquished Writing about the Victor." In Sievers and Lembi (eds.), *Josephus and Jewish History in Flavian Rome and Beyond*.

_____. *Turbulent Times? Josephus and Scholarship on Judea in the First Century ce*. Sheffield: Sheffield University Press, 1998.

Mendels, D. *The Rise and Fall of Jewish Nationalism*. New York: Doubleday, 1992.

Meshorer, Y. *Jewish Coins of the Second Temple Period*. Translated by I. H. Levine. 2 vols. New York, 1982.

Millar, F.G.B. "Last Year in Jerusalem: Monuments of the Jewish War in Rome." In Edmondson, Mason, and Rives (eds.), *Flavius Josephus and Flavian Rome*.

_____. *The Roman Near East, 31 bc–ad 337*. London and Cambridge, Mass.: Harvard University Press, 1993.

_____. "Empire, Community, and Culture in the Roman Near East: Greeks, Syrians, Jews, and Arabs." *Journal of Jewish Studies* 38 (1987).

Mireaux, E. *La Reine Bérénice*. Paris: Albin Michel, 1951.

Mommsen, T. *The Provinces of the Roman Empire*. Translated by W. P. Dickson. 2 vols. London, 1909.

Morgan, G. *69 ad: The Year of Four Emperors*. Oxford: Oxford University Press, 2006.

Neusner, J. *A Life of Rabban Yohanan ben Zakkai*. Leiden: E. J. Brill, 1962.

_____. "Josephus's Pharisees: A Complete Repertoire." In Feldman and Hata (eds.), *Josephus, Judaism and Christianity*.

Noy, D. *Foreigners at Rome: Citizens and Strangers*. London: Duckworth, 2000.

Parente, F., and J. Sievers (eds.). *Josephus and the History of the Greco-Roman Period: Essays in Memory of Morton Smith*. Leiden: E. J. Brill, 1994.

Perowne, S. *The Later Herods*. London: Hodder & Stoughton, 1958.

_____. *The Life and Times of Herod the Great*. London: Hodder & Stoughton, 1956.

Price, J. J. *Jerusalem under Siege*. Leiden: E. J. Brill, 1992.

_____. "The Provincial Historian in Rome." In Sievers and Lembi (eds.), *Josephus and Jewish History in Flavian Rome and Beyond*.

Rajak, T. *The Jewish Dialogue with Greece and Rome*. Leiden: E. J. Brill, 2001.

_____. "Josephus and Justus of Tiberias." In Feldman and Hata (eds.), *Josephus, Judaism and Christianity*.

_____. "Josephus and the Essenes." In Parente and Sievers (eds.), *Josephus and the History of the Greco-Roman Period*.

_____. "Josephus and the Diaspora." In Edmondson, Mason, and Rives (eds.), *Flavius Josephus and Flavian Rome*.

_____. *Josephus: The Historian and His Society*. London: Duckworth, 2002.

Rappaport, U. "Flavian Religious Policy and the Destruction of the Jerusalem Temple." In Edmondson, Mason, and Rives (eds.), *Flavius Josephus and Flavian Rome*.

_____. "Where Was Josephus Lying—In His Life or in the War?" In Parente and Sievers (eds.), *Josephus and the History of the Greco-Roman Period*.

Renan, J. *Jésus*. Paris, 1864.

Roth, C. *A Short History of the Jewish People*. London: East and West Library, Horovitz Publishing, 1969.

_____ (ed.). *Encyclopedia Judaica*. 16 vols. Jerusalem, 1972.

Saddington, D. B. *The Development of the Roman Auxiliary Forces from Caesar to Vespasian (49 bc–ad 79)*. Harare: University of Zimbabwe Press, 1982.

Saulnier, C. "Flavius Josèphe et la propaganda Flavienne." *Révue Biblique* 96 (1989): 545–562.

Schäfer, P. *The History of the Jews in the Greco-Roman World*. London: Routledge, 2003.

Schreckenberg, H. "The Works of Josephus and the Early Christian Church." In Feldman and Hata (eds.), *Josephus, Judaism and Christianity*.

Schürer, E. *The History of the Jewish People in the Age of Jesus Christ, 175 bc–ad 135*. Revised and edited by G. Vermes and F. Millar. 3 vols. Edinburgh: T. and T. Clarke, 1973.

Schwartz, D. "Herodians and Ioudaioi in Flavian Rome." In Edmondson, Mason, and Rives (eds.), *Flavius Josephus and Flavian Rome*.

Schwartz, S. "Josephus in Galilee: Rural Patronage and Social Breakdown." In Parente and Sievers (eds.), *Josephus and the History of the Greco-Roman Period*.

Shuttleworth Kraus, C. "From Exempla to Exemplar? Writing History around the Emperor in Imperial Rome." In Edmondson, Mason, and Rives (eds.), *Flavius Josephus and Flavian Rome*.

Sievers, J., and G. Lembi (eds.). *Josephus and Jewish History in Flavian Rome and Beyond*. Leiden: E. J. Brill, 2005.

Simon, M. *Les sects juives au temps de Jésus*. Paris, 1960.

Smallwood, E. M. *The Jews under Roman Rule from Pompey to Diocletian*. Leiden: E. J. Brill, 1976.

Smith, M. "The Occult in Josephus." In Feldman and Hata (eds.), *Josephus, Judaism and Christianity*.

Sparks, S. (ed.). *The Apocryphal Old Testament*. Oxford: Clarendon Press, 1984.

Spilsbury, P. "Reading the Bible in Rome: Josephus and the Constraints of Empire." In Sievers and Lembi (eds.), *Josephus and Jewish History in Flavian Rome and Beyond*.

Stern, M. "Josephus and the Roman Empire as Reflected in the Jewish War." In Feldman and Hata (eds.), *Josephus, Judaism and Christianity*.

———. *Greek and Latin Authors on Jews and Jerusalem*. 3 vols. Jerusalem: Israel Academy of Sciences and Humanities, 1974–1984.

Thackeray, H. St. J. *Josephus, the Man and the Historian*. New York, 1929.

Thiersch, H. *Pharos: Antike, Islam und Occident*. Leipzig and Berlin: B. G. Teubner, 1909.

Thoma, C. "John Hyrcanus I as Seen by Josephus and Other Early Jewish Sources." In Parente and Sievers (eds.), *Josephus and the History of the Greco-Roman Period*.

Vermes, G. *The Complete Dead Sea Scrolls in English*. London: Penguin, 2004.

_____. *Jesus the Jew*. London: SCM Press, 2001.

_____. *Who's Who in the Age of Jesus*. London: Penguin, 2006.

Vogelstein, H. *History of the Jews in Rome*. Translated by M. Hadas. Philadelphia: Jewish Publication Society of America, 1940.

de Vogüé, J. *Le Temple de Jérusalem*. Paris, 1864.

Watson, G. R. *The Roman Soldier*. London: Thames & Hudson, 1969.

Webster, G. *The Roman Imperial Army of the First and Second Centuries ad*. London: Adam and Charles Black, 1969.

Williamson, G. A. *The World of Josephus*. London: Secker & Warburg, 1964.

Yadin, Y. *Bar-Kokhba*. London: Weidenfeld & Nicolson, 1971.

_____. *Masada: Herod's Fortress and the Zealots' Last Stand*. Translated by M. Pearlman. London: Weidenfeld & Nicolson, 1966.

Yavetz, Z. "Reflections on Titus and Josephus." *Greek, Roman and Byzantine Studies* 16 (1975):411–432.

INDEX